K

YOUTH: POSITIONS AND OPPOSITIONS

For my father, Tom Blackman

Youth: Positions and Oppositions

Style, sexuality and schooling

SHANE J. BLACKMAN
Department of Applied Social Science
Canterbury Christ Church College

Avebury

Aldershot • Brookfield USA • Hong Kong • Singapore • Sydney

Published by
Avebury
Ashgate Publishing Limited
Gower House
Croft Road
Aldershot
Hants GU11 3HR
England

Ashgate Publishing Company
Old Post Road
Brookfield
Vermont 05036
USA

A CIP catalogue record for this book is available from the British Library

ISBN 1 85628 637 1

Library of Congress Catalog Card Number: 95-76712

Printed and bound by Athenæum Press Ltd., Gateshead, Tyne & Wear.

Contents

Contents

Acknowledgments

This book is based on my Ph.D thesis completed at the Institute of Education, University of London. I doubt whether I would ever have been there but for the early encouragement and support of Michael O'Dell, Keith Arthurs and Kenneth Mackinnon.

In the early stages of the fieldwork I was very grateful to the staff at Rough Trade Records, London who allowed me access to their resources. For their contributions to my research experience at the Institute of Education, I should like to thank all staff and students from the department of the sociology of education, who gave me their valuable time. I am particularly grateful for tutorial support from Stephen Ball, Lesley Caldwell, Philip Cohen, Philip Corrigan, Tony Green, John Hayes, Roger Hewitt, Janet Holland, Diana Leonard, and Keith Swanwick. I would also like to express my thanks to Philip Brown, Clyde Chitty, Bernadette Cifuentes, Ann Lahiff, Norah Marks, and Robert MacDonald who offered advice and criticism. I am grateful too for the support and encouragement of the staff at Avebury, Jo Gooderham, Sarah Anthony, Suzanne Evins and Pat Marks. I also extend my gratitude to the publishers of Youth and Policy for allowing permission to make use of the paper 'Pro-School Pupils' first published in 1992.

I would like to offer very special thanks to my supervisor Professor Basil Bernstein, for all his encouragement, inspiration and practical support. In the production of this book I received much warm support and critical comment from Debbie Cox, for which thanks.

Finally, I owe a sincere debt to the Head Teacher of the school and his colleagues for assistance and encouragement. My greatest debt is to the boffin girls and boys, the criminal boys, the new wave girls and the mod boys who always made me welcome and research a pleasure.

Introduction

This book follows a well established tradition in qualitative sociology which examines the culture and behaviour of young people from the perspective of grounded theory (Glaser and Strauss 1967). In the UK the gradual movement towards an acceptance of qualitative methods of inquiry was a result of the anthropological studies undertaken at the Institute of Community Studies in East London during the 1950s, and the educational studies undertaken at the University of Manchester during the 1960s (Hargreaves 1967, Willmott 1985). During the 1970s and 1980s this qualitative tradition was developed further, initially by Marxist and then feminist case studies on young people. One major criticism of these ethnographic case studies throughout this period is that few generated a theoretical contribution; their preoccupation was with localised accounts within a micro-interactional perspective Hammersley (1985). This apparent lack of theory has led to further criticism of ethnography from certain of its previous advocates, who assert that ethnography is not an effective research method (Hammersley 1992).

This study on youth and pupil groups at Marshlands Comprehensive school seeks to advance the case for ethnography as a valuable approach to think about and understand meaning and also as a useful tool to conduct social research. Therefore, this book is about the close relationship between method and theory and the consequent problems of bringing the two together. The research is concerned further to explore the relationships between social class, sexuality and patriarchy for young people. The sample consists of over 120 girls and boys in a secondary school in the South of England. Four major groups are identified: Mod Boys, New Wave Girls, Boffin Boys and Boffin Girls. All the young people were studying for a number of GCE examinations. From this point of view the sample is unusual in British research, as it offers the possibility of studying forms of resistance and conformity among those whom the school considers as the pedagogic elite.

The method used was ethnographic and entailed sharing the experiences of the various groups which included male and female, working and middle class pupils, both inside and outside the school (leisure and family spaces), over a period of two years. The data is supported by extensive interviews with school staff. Tape recorded discussions took place in and out of school with groups and individuals. The research provides the basis for a theory of youth cultural forms which integrates structural, communicative and semiotic practices. The theory has arisen out of, and in part controlled the collection of the ethnographic data. This theoretical description was successfully applied to the youth cultural groups: new wave girls and mod boys, but was found to be not relevant to the two pupil groups: boffin girls and boffin boys, at every level of analysis. The development of other theoretical frameworks and descriptions became necessary in order to explain the boffin groups' different cultural practices and relationships. This limitation and the need to develop further theory added to an understanding of the differences within and between the youth and pupil groups both inside and outside the context of the school.

Youth subculture: a theoretical critique

The theoretical language of description developed in this study arose in part because of the weakness and conceptual inadequacy found when attempting to use the concept(s) of subculture to interpret the ethnographic data on working class and middle class, male and female students. Since the late 1950s sociological theories and empirical conceptual understandings of youth have been dominated by the theory of subculture.

The Chicago School in the early 1920s did not elaborate theoretically the concept of subculture. The original application within the sociology of deviance derives from Cohen's (1955) functionalist theory of male delinquent gangs defined as subcultures. Cohen adapted Merton's theory of anomie by applying the structural correspondence of differentiation within anomie to subculture. Cohen transferred the framework of Merton's theoretical arguments concerning cultural goals and institutional means to his development of the concept of subculture. Cohen redefined Merton's scale of 'individual adaptations' to mean a 'collective response' of aggression by working class adolescents. Cohen's concept of subculture results from a fusion of Merton's theory of anomie, with psychological theories of aggression (Dollard et al, 1939).

From this perspective the collective response of 'aggressive behaviour' associated with working class youth is seen primarily as a function of status frustration (Merton, 1938, 1957) arising out of contact with middle class values. The class position of working class youth generates structural strain which causes the problems of status frustration. The concept of subculture is essentially functionalist and the theory is constructed with reference only to secondary sources (from the Chicago School). Unlike functionalist theorists, the Chicago School did not perceive deviance as exceptional; in fact most Chicago School studies interpret deviance as a normal part of the community (Bulmer 1984).

Cohen's (1955) theory is based upon an interpretation of anomie, which supports his notion that the working class and the middle class are in opposition. This theory is derived from a reading of Whyte's (1943) *Street Corner Society* which posits a conflict of values between college and corner boys. Mannheim (1965) states, "Cohen uses certain fundamental notions as convenient assumptions and not as a description of processes that have been actually observed." (p.511). Cohen also assumes that the majority of working class youth automatically want to become middle class. Such a hypothesis may apply to American working class youth but in Britain Goldthorpe et al (1968) argued that the majority of working class youth wished to maintain their own values rather than adopt those of the middle class. A central criticism of Cohen's concept of subculture relates to the interpretation of gangs as suffering from normlessness, which is inconsistent with previous findings by the Chicago School which demonstrate empirically the complex divisions of labour, relations and values in working class groups (Thrasher 1927, Shaw and Mckay 1927).

The British concept of subculture in the 1950s and 1960s was, however, quite differently defined as a sub set of values existing within the working class. Even so, the British concept of

3

subculture is similar to the American in agreeing that working class youth who form collective responses, such as subcultures (or groups) are psychologically disturbed or inadequately socialised. In British sociology of the period a major influence was psychoanalysis, with particular reference to explanations of juvenile delinquency (Bowlby 1946, Friedlander 1947, Bowlby 1953, Mays 1954). The concept of subculture was embedded in the thesis of the so called deviant working class 'affectionless personality'.

Downes (1966) and Taylor (1968) suggested the psychological underpining of the concept of subculture and acutely questioned the application of American subcultural theory to Britain; preparing the way for the development of a more indigenous and sophisticated British form of labelling theory. The development of the concept of subculture by the Centre for Contemporary Cultural Studies (CCCS) within 'Stencilled Occasional papers' and *Resistance Through Ritual* in 1975 is essentially taken from Phil Cohen's (1972) interpretation of subcultural conflict at a community level. The concept of subculture is applied theoretically as a device within the complex Marxist base and superstructure problematic. Major Marxist theorists such as Althusser and Gramsci, and major structuralist theorists such as Levi-Strauss and Barthes are employed to re-define the concept of subculture as a potential space for youth as a creative agency to occupy. The CCCS in their elaboration of the Marxist base and superstructure metaphor created a macro theoretical model for the general reading of micro youth groups' styles (Hall and Jefferson 1975). However, 'literary ethnography' on the three subcultures analysed, is substituted for direct empirical observation as a means of obtaining evidence for their theory.

The concept of subculture here refers to a location containing the possibility to create, re-create and win space offering a relative autonomy at an ideological level. The concept of subculture is not at an economic or political level because subcultures are defined as possessing only imaginary solutions arising out of their location within leisure rather than within labour processes. The subcultural response of youth is related to structural features of hegemony at the level of class, culture and generation, but not to gender and race. Hebdige (1979) redresses the neglect of race and black youth cultures and introduces an analysis of the race-specific nature of most youth subcultures. Unfortunately, Hebdige does not address either the position of women in subcultures or the double invisibility of black women. The interpretation and application of the concept of

4

subculture is predominantly masculine (McRobbie and Garber 1975, Davies 1984). Girls and young women may be referred to or partially included as members of a subculture but no priority or significance is given to women at either the empirical or theoretical level, or only on the basis of 'a gang of lads' model' (Griffin 1993).

The work of Hebdige (1979) further elaborates the literary studies understanding of the concept of subculture in relation to youth style suggesting that "The challenge to hegemony which subcultures represent is not issued directly by them. Rather it is expressed obliquely, in style." (p.17). His concern is to establish a popular aesthetic and to show working class cultural practices within a framework of 'high culture'. One central problem in Hebdige's understanding of youth subcultural style is that as a theorist he over-emphasizes the political significance of style.

The priority given to subcultural style as creative resistance aiming to define a social space is a legacy of the Leavisite tradition of literary interpretation. It insists that creativity can only occur through small groups (youth subcultures) for reasons of creativity itself. However, as only a minority of working class youth enter subcultures, the Leavisite interpretation of working class culture is elitist; only those youths in subcultures are seen as the select groups who possess the real working class creative potential to challenge bourgeois order (Filmer 1977). The Leavisite subcultural interpretation rests fundamentally upon a false dichotomy between youth who are 'stylists' and 'style-less'. The literary studies approach places emphasis upon the potential resistance of those few working class youth involved in subcultural styles, while ignoring the remaining working class youth who are seen as straight or ordinary (Hebdige 1988).

The ground breaking work at the CCCS on young people redefined and transformed the field of youth studies, although ironically it led to a debate about the 'end of youth culture' (Frith 1984). This decline was attributed to the 'Thatcher Generation' of young people who were identified as no longer rebellious (Milne 1988, Mintel 1988). However, it may be more accurate to assert that sociologists were no longer interested in looking at youth. Universities under the heavy weight of the burgeoning new right ideology, moved away from a focus on youth culture towards a critical examination of the social policies and political contexts that were defining opportunities for young people. Thus under the material limitations of the 1980s youth studies moved in two directions: towards new vocationalism and post modern cultural ethnographies. The former was preoccupied with critically exposing the new inequalities of education and training and the latter was concerned to tell post-structuralist tales about levels of style, commodities and consumption without speaking to any young person (McRobbie 1994).

General organisation of the chapters

This book sets out to apply an ethnographic method to the study of youth and pupil groups inside and outside the context of a secondary school. I shall focus on two middle class pupils groups, the boffin girls and the boffin boys, and two working/lower middle class youth cultural groups, the new wave girls and the mod boys.

Part 1 is concerned with theory and method. *Chapter 1* provides an account of the methods used in the study and a description of the school, its structure and organisation, together with a brief introduction to the youth and pupil groups. *Chapter 2* presents a new theoretical language of description, which I termed a theory of youth cultural forms. The description creates sets of hypotheses which are explored in turn in an attempt to make sense of the ethnographic data. The theory is concerned with a number of features: the internal relations and structure within groups, the social relations between groups, their specialised practices and also each youth group's position within the wider youth cultural field.

Part 2 is concerned with youth style, gender and conflict. Here the style groups will be introduced and I take up issues essentially arising out of the relations between style and gender, mediated through the internal organisation of the groups. *Chapter 3* consists of a comparative analysis of the new wave girls and the mod boys, which deals with their different forms of private and public communication, in the areas of gender conflict, sexuality and discrimination. This is in preparation for *Chapter 4* which deals with rituals of violence and masculine potency at the real and symbolic levels and *Chapter 5* which explores intimacy and ritual communications within a female youth cultural style group, applying feminist concepts to the data.

Part 3 is concerned with issues of social class, careers and conformity. *Chapter 6* theoretically explores a model of middle class conformist relations from the perspective of the pro-school girl group, the 'boffin girls', in terms of their examination successes and their sexual vulnerabilities. *Chapters 7* is an account of the pro-school boys' middle class identity and their relationship to school via an examination of their social class aspirations and sexual vulnerabilities. *Part 4* presents a comparative analysis of the oppositions and resistance within pupils' gender relations and schooling experience. *Chapter 8* focuses upon pupil deviance and transitions, and explores male sexuality via the boys' view of parental surveillance of their sexual behaviour, use of the condom and male virginity. *Chapter 9* examines the girl groups' relationships with their parents. It then goes on to critically examine the concept of resistance as applied to the different forms of female deviance inside and outside school, and also assess the difficulties encountered by the new wave girls' proto-feminist stance. *Chapter 10* explores how each girl group deals with different forms of sexist male aggression, and examines the extent to which girls can develop challenges to male authority. This chapter concludes with an ethnographic account of two adolescent girl parties.

In the final chapter I shall draw together the most important findings such as the significance of gender relations in terms of explaining and understanding the identity of and social relations between young people at school and in their own spaces. One of the conclusions of this book is that existing concepts such as gang, peer group, differentiation/polarisation and subculture are unable to explain or account for the different types of responses by working class and middle class girls and boys to schooling, sexuality and society. This qualitative study seeks to question the previous theoretical explanations concerning what is understood as the generation of different forms of identity defined as either resistant, or conformist.

This book is written for those people who work with or study young people. The study sets out to apply an ethnographic method to the study of youth and pupil groups, via an examination of their social and sexual identities in both private and public spheres. Ethnography produces are very personal story and this study reveals the loves and lives of a number of young adults as they struggle with and forge their identity. It is an account from inside four different young people's groups which shows how they experience the contradictory pressures of contemporary capitalist culture.

1   Methods and an introduction to the key protagonists

Marshlands school: the research context

The school is a large comprehensive with over one thousand five hundred pupils. The area around Marshlands is heavily dependent on the seasonal tourist industry, agriculture and distant large towns to offer employment. The region has a high level of unemployment, especially amongst the youth labour force, a reflection of the economic crisis of the 1980s when this study was undertaken (Gleeson 1989). The pupil intake of Marshlands is overwhelmingly white, equally divided between working class and middle class pupils. An important characteristic of the social class structure of the rural area is that people have been established in the vicinity for a long time; teachers stated that they had taught some of the pupils' mothers, fathers, aunts and uncles.

Marshlands Comprehensive has a large teaching staff numbering ninety two teachers. The school is organised on two sites consisting of a lower and an upper school. At the outset of the field relations in school I decided to help the teaching staff in any way possible providing this did not compromise future communications with pupils. During the whole period of school based fieldwork I observed over twenty five different teachers in classroom situations.

The youth groups

Each name or term which refers to the groups in this case study derives from the various youth groups. The labels are not my invention.

The four major groups were able not only to define their own relations and positions in the school but could define other groups and individuals. A group's ability to define other groups in the context of the school reveals who controls the status and meaning of social, academic and territorial practices. Certain groups would not accept the label and status location assigned to them by others. The capacity of a group to determine their status (outside their own group) is in part dependent on the strength of the group's internal division of labour and collective solidarity. The four major groups in the study fall into two categories:-

a. Youth cultural groups: mod boys and new wave girls
b. Pupil groups: boffin girls and boffin boys

The other smaller fifth year groups at Marshlands Comprehensive included:
a) Youth cultural groups: punk boys, rock-a-billy rebels (girls and boys), rockers (including headbangers and heavy metal girls and boys), soul girls and rude boys.
b) Pupil groups: square boffin girls, square boffin boys, straight boys, straight girls, remedial girls, remedial boys.
c) Delinquent group: criminal boys (individuals from this group were removed from the area during the study) .

I shall now describe briefly the membership, culture and relations of the groups found for the basis of this study.

Mod boys

Membership: the mod boys group contained nine individuals: Paul, Rich, Keef, Hat, Tosh, Gangster, Hendrix, Rod and Header. The mod boys' girlfriends were Annette (Paul), Clare (Rich), Tracey (Keef) and Janet (Hat). There were two different types of marginal members of the mod group. Firstly, there were five older boys who had already left school, Joey, Craig, John, Tony and Baz. Secondly, there were four younger boys in the fourth year, Dave, Roger, Carrot and Stu.

Description: mod is a youth cultural style developed in the late 1950s. The youth style was not a response to the 'rockers' but a development and gradual stylistic change from the 'teddy boy'. Three influences on the mod emergence in the late fifties were the appearance of Italian and French clothes in London, the growth of black culture in such forms as modern jazz, 'new clubs', soul and ska music; and the increasing use of drugs within the context of the 'subcultural underworld' (Melly, 1972).

For the mod boys the 'mod revival' of the 1980s had much to do with punk and in particular the position of Paul Weller within the bands The Jam and the Style Council. The mod boys' youth cultural style had three features:

(a) *Music*: The mod boys played and were influenced by a range of musical styles associated with the mod style in the 1960s - R and B, soul music, northern soul, blue beat, ska, Tamla Motown, and English bands in 1960s such as The Small Faces and The Who, and contemporary bands associated as mod.

(b) *Style*: Originally business style neatness and colour co-ordination fused with 'cool blackness' and 'hard indigenous gangsterism' provided the mod style with immense variation (Barnes, 1979). The mod revival reduced the style to a restricted number of items such as short hair, suit, collar and tie, Fred Perrys or loafers, underneath a parka or a crombie. Because of the substantial documentation of the 1960s mod style, the mod boys could experiment with original ideas from the 1960s within the limitations imposed by the contemporary revival.

(c) *Objects and life-style*: The mod boys possessed the obligatory scooters. They went to scooter rallies around the country to celebrate features of mod and scooter activities and club relations and to collect specialist items. Their life-style included intense shopping adventures, discos, parties, gigs, clubs and pubs, drug taking experiments and visits to the seafront for ritual promenades. The mod boys were historically informed; they regarded themselves as not only taking from the past but also redeveloping, strengthening and articulating mod style to make it relevant to the present.

Social relations: the mod boys' control of territory was both symbolic and social; symbolically the boys' coherent youth cultural style supported and emphasised their solidarity, whilst socially the number of mod boys and their physical strength combined to make the boys a substantial territorial force. The boys' physical strength was important in situations where they might be challenged by an oppositional group. The mod boys established their own scooter club called 'The Undecideds', with a bank account, journal, newsletters, badges and so on. Through the scooter club the mod boys' group became an official organisation, with national contacts and a reputation, resulting from their attendance at scooter rallies conventions and parties.

Most of the mod boys and in particular Paul, Rich, Hat and Keef had girlfriends. The mod boys enjoyed talking about sexual experiences both privately and publicly, especially in the presence of the boffin boys. All except one of the mod boys girlfriends were younger and in the lower forms in the school.

The mod boys had experience of work in the local labour market. This usually took the form of working on Saturdays, Sundays, in the evenings or during the holidays. The jobs involved working in a garage, on a farm, on a building site, with photographers, in an amusement park and restaurants. Thus, before leaving school the boys had acquired considerable experience of the local labour market (Brown and Ashton 1987). The boys' parents were largely working class but some had bought their own houses. The mod boys would occasionally receive some financial assistance but all parents expected the boys to work hard whether for them or for their employers.

At school the mod boys were taking O' levels and some vocational examinations. All the boys were in the upper or middle band of the streaming system. The mod boys walked a fine line in school between deviant and appropriate school behaviour. However, the boys could use their academic position as a resource to negotiate with teachers when caught breaking school rules.

New wave girls

Membership: the new wave girls group contained ten individuals: Clare, Debbie, Sioux, Cathy, Sally, Lynne, Cat, Collen, Steff and Denise. The new wave girls' boyfriends were Rich (Clare), Peter (Sally), Slim (Sioux), Bloc (Cathy), Stephen (Collen), Gaz (Steff), Mick (Debbie) and Julian (Lynne). There were an additional nine marginal members to the new wave girls group: Christina, Katy, Dianne, Pat, Rachel, Jane, Jan, Paulette and Phil.

11

Description: new wave is a term borrowed from the cinema. The label allows for a broad definition and description. The musical meaning originally referred to the alternative and different American new bands during the period 1975/1977. In Britain new wave was different from punk, although both shared common values and causes like independence, creativity and diversity (Savage, 1991). The influence of punk and new wave went further than challenging musical structure/style, it challenged the conventional and taken-for-granted aspects of cultural practice. Issues of discrimination were explicitly brought out into the open and made central. Punk demanded that people question assumptions and look at their own lives and social relations (Frith 1988).

Thus the idea of punk was not only confrontation or refusal to accept what was traditionally thought appropriate. Punk was also about 'doing it yourself'. For many of its adherents (though not all) punk was both explicitly and implicitly feminist, in that on various levels it challenged male domination, romance, sexual embarrassment and violence. Punk was concerned not only to expose but crucially to ridicule forms of social injustice. The political growth of formal organisations such as Rock Against Racism and the Anti Nazi League were clear expressions of punk at its most politically powerful (Widgery 1986).

For the new wave girls punk and new wave provided a means to disturb, disrupt and undervalue the commonly accepted values concerning appropriate female behaviour. Hebdige (1979) states, "Behind punk's favoured 'cut ups' lay hints of disorder, of breakdown and category confusion: a desire ... to erode racial and gender boundaries" (p.123). The new wave girls seized the independence and diversity within the meaning of punk and new wave to challenge female 'passivity' and to reinforce their own female solidarity.

The new wave girls' style had three features,

(a) *Music*: The girls were into new wave, punk, reggae and dub. For example, they played The Cure, Joy Division, New Order, Siouxsie and the Banshees, Talking Heads, The Clash, Sex Pistols, The Damned, Crass, The Buzzcocks, UB40, Steel Pulse, Basement Five, Joan Armatrading, Teardrop Explodes, Devo, and Joe Jackson.

(b) *Style*: In a number of ways the new wave girls held to the idea of punk clothes, for example 'confrontational' dressing through oppositions such as wearing a skirt and Doctor Martens boots under a 'dirty mac'. The new wave girls would attempt experimental combinations. The girls predominantly wore trousers which were usually black, with t-shirts of various types, monkey boots and large jumpers.

(c) *Objects and life style*: The new wave girls' general appearance was in non-traditional female clothes. The girls sometimes made and adapted their own clothes and shoes. A significant feature of the girls' style was omission of the iconography of sexual fetishism associated with punk. The girls questioned the dominance of sexual fetishism and inverted the meaning of its expression. Thus, the safety pin or 'DM's' were used to establish an alternative mode to the dominant forms for teenager girls.

Their appearance was a combination of challenge and alternative practice. The girls were differently disposed to the use of make-up. Most of the girls would wear little; others would use make-up in a non conventional manner and others banned it because of its link with animals. The new wave girls did not conform to traditional markers of female beauty.

Social relations: The new wave girls' youth cultural style and inappropriate school uniform made them a highly visible group. The girls' stylistic solidarity and very close physical contact emphasised their confidence and strength. The fifth year boys of Marshlands Comprehensive were wary of the new wave girls, in fact, most boys kept their distance. One of the criminal boys said "Coming home one evening, I saw this group by the 'Chippy' about hundred yards away. I thought fuck it, I might get a beating here. So I crossed the road, right. When I got closer it was the girls - really put the shit up me for a bit - was about ten of them."

The majority of the new wave girls had boyfriends who were either in the upper sixth form, college or in employment.

The new wave girls had experience of working in the local labour market, on Saturdays, Sundays or midweek and during the school holidays. Their employment ranged from hotel work, to working in restaurants, public houses, farms and running a shop. When the girls were younger they baby sat. The new wave girls did their share of domestic labour in the home (unlike the mod boys), although the extent of this work was limited by the girls' ability to gain economic independence and by the nature of their familial relations. The new wave girls' parents were lower middle class and working class. The girls received more financial support than the mod boys but the girls had to work to gain a disposable income.

The girls were taking O' levels and some vocational examinations. All the new wave girls were in the upper or middle band of the streaming system. Somewhat like the mod boys, the new wave girls kept a fine balance between school deviance and appropriate behaviour. However, the girls completed more school homework and were more selective in their 'skiving' and school deviance. The new wave girls were liked by many of the teachers because they were assertive in the classroom and would not tolerate sexism from the boys.

Boffin girls and boffin boys

Membership: The boffin girls' group contained thirteen individuals who could be divided into three smaller groupings.
Core group: Kerry, Rose, Mary, Monica, Ellen.
Group A: Rosemary, Sarah, Alison and Wendy.
Group B: Valerie, Lousie, Donna and Madeleine.
There were an additional eight close marginal members to the boffin girls' group: Michelle, Claire, Sharon, Caroline, April, Angela, Jennifer and Elizabeth.
  The boffin boys' group contained three central members: Howard, Gary and James. There were an additional eight close marginal members to the boffin boys group: Davey, Will, Russ, Nick, Paul, Christopher, Benjamin and Cyril.

Description: boffin is R.A.F. slang for a scientist employed by the armed services. In the context of Marshlands Comprehensive boffins were those pupils who specialised in academic superiority; for such pupils this was the major prestige marker. Depending upon who was using the term and for what reason, the term boffin had a dual function, it could be a label of status or of abuse. The boffins themselves would accept the name in the presence of an all boffin gathering but where other groups or individuals were present the boffins were reluctant to regard themselves in this way. This shows that the definition of boffin, in the wider school sense, not only referred to academic skill but also signified inferior social and sexual attitudes.
  The boffin groups were pupil groups shaped through the process of streaming and significantly sustained by individual competition to succeed in formal examinations. From the boffins' perspective it was important that they were understood by all non-group members as supportive of the school system and values. The

14

boffins were not entirely like Jackson and Marsden's (1962) 'respectables', Lacey's (1970) pro-school pupils, Willis' (1977) 'ear'oles', or Turner's (1983) and Brown's (1987) 'swots'. The purpose of the boffin identity was to mobilise and incorporate the school examination system into their own school image. The boffin groups would respect and obey school regulation and authority, especially when visible to other pupils. They were reluctant to initiate collective actions unless these were in support of the formal school process.

The boffin girls featured a range of youth cultural styles for example, mod, soul and rockabilly rebel. Similarly among the boffin boys were certain members who followed specific youth cultural styles such as hip hop, soul, funk and rude boy. Some of the boffin boys were involved in a youth cultural style at the level of 'singleton' that is they possessed the style but did not engage in its social relations of style; their social relations were only pedagogic. A difference between the two boffin groups was that within the boffin girl group there was an internal hippie group who were interested in the ideas of C.N.D. and Greenpeace.

Boffin girls' social relations: a strength of the boffin girls was that they were a large group. The size of the girls' group acted as a positive resource for some of the girls who appeared shy, such girls could have been easy targets for humiliation in small groups, pairs or on their own. The boffin girls did not define the other boffin groups, unlike the boffin boys, who insisted upon a boffin hierarchy with themselves at the top.

The boffin girls spent most of their time, both inside or outside school within their own group(s) or with the boffin boys. The girls did not have contact with any other grouping except other 'low status' boffin groups. The girls did not speak to the criminal boys and kept out of reach of the mod boys because contact with such boys would nearly always result in the girls' embarrassment. The boffin girls had occasional contacts with the new wave girls; however, these relations were brief and concerned only issues of schooling. The two girls groups did not share any space inside the school and they never came into contact outside the school.

The boffin girls did not have any regular boyfriends (one of the boffin girls had been out with one of the boffin boys). The boffin girls were closely restricted by their parents in all of their out of school activities. The boffin girls spent a substantial amount of time in the home doing homework, and unlike the boffin boys, the girls did domestic labour chores. The parents of the boffin girls were mainly middle and lower middle class. The parents expected that their daughters would enter the sixth form and prepare to go to college or university and begin a career. The majority of the boffin girls did not have part time jobs, but some worked occasionally in shops. The only regular work the girls did was baby sitting. This was their only access to an independent income, to enable them to buy clothes and commodities without their parents' control.

The boffin girls were taking O' levels and a majority of them had passed from one to four O' levels a year early in the fourth year. The boffin girls were in the upper band of the streaming system. They were academically bright and were taking both arts and sciences. Overall, the boffin girls were more accepting of school rules and values than the boffin boys.

Boffin boys' social relations: the boffin boys' territorial powers in school derived from their status position within the school as the top fifth year examinees among the boys. The boffin boys could define the social positions of all pupils taking examinations, except the mod boys and the new wave girls. Other boffin groups in school were subject to the boffin boys' academic status relations. The boffin boys' capacity to control the social relations inside school for the 'conforming' groups did not apply to the boffin girls' group. The boffin girls refused to accept the boffin boys' territorial claims. The girls' rejection of the boffin boys was both pedagogic and social. Firstly, the girls asserted that they were 'brighter' and secondly, they stated "They're not worth going out with, anyway". Only one boffin boy had been out with a girl; in general the boffin boys did not have regular girlfriends.

The boffin boys, unlike the mod boys and the new wave girls, can be said to have two social identities, one of which was visible in the school and the other invisible. In the school the social identity was marked by conventional appropriate dress but outside school their dress changed. As a consequence it would be inappropriate to 'read' the boffin boys only in terms of their school presentations. There is then a visible academic identity and an invisible social identity.

The boffin boys did not have part time jobs although some would occasionally collect golf balls or caddie but most of their time was spent on homework and this excluded them from work in the local labour market and importantly, domestic labour in the home. The majority of the boffin boys' parents were middle and lower middle class although some were working class. All the boys received encouragement and sometimes practical help from their parents. The boffin boys were taking O' levels and two of them had passed some O' level examinations a year early in the fourth year. The boffin boys' primary public image was that of academic achievements.

Marginal group members

There were a substantial number of marginal members to the four major groups in the school. There were different degrees of marginality not only in terms of the distance relation to the main groups but also in terms of numbers and variations between different types of marginal members. The marginal relations could be based upon:

a. An individual living near members of a major group.
b. Friendship of a girl or boy friend within a major group.
c. Academic contact , arising out of the sharing of subjects or of a form room.
d. Common interest, such as a particular sport, job, type of musical artist, hobby, or family relation.

The marginal members encapsulated a whole series of different relations. The only feature which united these marginals is the status of marginality. They did not share a common ground to establish their own group. The marginals operated a complex arrangement of relations both within and between the different major groups (Farrant 1965). At times, marginal members were of special importance to the members of a major group. Such a relation would not necessarily increase the marginals' opportunity to enter the major group but would demonstrate the marginals' status position. Thus, certain marginals were favoured for a period of time to 'hang around' with the individuals of the major group. Certain marginals preferred to remain on the margin rather than become centrally involved because too many pressures existed within the major groups. Some marginals appeared to want only a temporary contact with the major groups rather than a permanent relation. Marginals, then, used the major groups as well as being used. In addition to the marginal members there existed other non-group relations:-

Singletons were individuals who practised a youth cultural style but possessed no relation to a social group.

Trend followers were individuals who attempted to display a youth cultural style but lacked deep knowledge of its history, practice and relationship.

Loners were individuals in the school who appeared to have no close friends as they preferred a solitary existence.

Pairings of two individuals of the same sex who did not become greatly involved with other pupils , either inside or outside the school.

'Loving couples' were heterosexual couples who had only limited contact with others because they spent the majority of their time with each other.

'Freaks'; a term used by pupils to describe an individual who remained set apart owing to a physical , social or psychological abnormality.

Ethnography

The aim of the fieldwork became the collection of a thick description through learning and observing the relations, practices, positions and rituals of each different youth group (Geertz 1973). The biography of a researcher who undertakes a qualitative study is an important facet in understanding firstly, the focus of the research, secondly, the methods used to gain information, and finally the type of study produced. My own biographical features which were important in the development of the field relations with the different youth groups were on the one hand a recent experience of the processes of secondary schooling and on the other hand a number of shared interests and experiences. My relevant experiences were as follows:-

Direct interest in youth cultural style and music.
Close knowledge of the local area and community.
Successful progression through the education system from sixth form to university.
Experience of beginning a music-related managerial career.
Experience of labouring and unemployment
Contact with some deviant and low-life activities.

These different facets of experience were useful in communicating with the two groups of pupils, the youth cultural groups and the academic groups. Such relevant biographical experiences were resources to establish rapport with the different groups (Hammersley and Atkinson 1983).

To gain rapport with the different groups and the individual members within each group I had to develop different modes of interaction, negotiation and exchange. This process could be called an apprenticeship. The consequence of the differences between the groups was that not only did each demand different relations but also different forms of apprenticeship. The purpose of taking an apprentice role is to learn from the groups themselves. The biographic experience provided only an initial stepping stone in establishing access to, and contact with, each group. The two groupings made contingent attempts to locate the researcher within their own experience. Here I could mobilise the biography to support the transition from the initial position of being an 'outsider' to being an 'insider', able to receive an apprenticeship in the learning and recording of each group in action.

An important element in the apprenticeship was to recognise that the youths were in a learning and growing situation both in terms of the school and the wider culture. I was sharing with members from the different groups their first experience of certain events. Through such opportunities, I was able to establish an intimate and sensitive body of shared experiences at the level of initiation, and to get 'in solid' with the youth groups.

As a male researcher the process of gaining access to the female groups of the boffin girls and new wave girls differed from that of gaining access to the male groups of the boffins boys and mods. I established a close relationship more quickly with the youth groups with whom I shared an interest in youth cultural style and music, than with the academic groups. But also it took a much longer period of time to attain the same level of trust among the girls' groups than among the boys groupings. Maintaining contact with the girls' groups was also subject to more complexities in terms of how my position was viewed by other groups and individuals. I enjoyed a close and friendship-based relation with all members of each group. However, within each group there were certain boys and girls to whom I had a closer personal relation simply because we got on very well.

A fundamental feature of the relationship of shared experience with the girls was that it was not based on sexual relations. In different contexts the girls would expect different relations; for example, support in their anti-sexist arguments against certain boys or in their own counter attack. On the one hand the girls would expect constructive advice, discussion or helpful guidance, while on the other hand, they would expect acknowledgement of their sexual attractiveness and desirability. The two roles may be contradictory but were fundamental features of the field relations within both groups of girls (Warren 1988).

Once I had gained the trust of the girls' groups I had a similar degree of participation in their activities as for the boys' groups. Thus during the fieldwork I gained access in the case of both boys and girls to the 'private world of bedroom culture' (McRobbie 1990) and was included in all-girl discussions, girls nights out, girls' parties and girls' outings. Interviews with youth groups were carried out on the basis of discussion or conversation. Locations of recorded discussions inside school included the careers room, a small classroom, the library, corridors, play ground and sports field. Outside school they included parents' houses, (sitting room, bedroom), walking along the street, inside shops, public houses, cafes, parties and bus stops.

I did not begin recording discussions until a sufficient body of common experience had been established with each youth group. After this initial period I conducted discussions throughout the fieldwork. The aim of the group discussions was to gain an understanding of the youth groups in action. Once rapport had been established and relations developed I did not face the problem of selecting pupils for group interview, because the members of the youth group would make their own selection according to who was available at the specific time.

The discussions represent the surface data built upon a carefully constructed ethnographic base. These discussions could not have occurred unless I had made close and personal contact with each of the different groups, on their own ground and in their own time. The foundation of these discussions was friendship, involving shared experience and common interests. There was no great necessity or urgency to ask formalised questions during interviews because the conversations were not 'one off' situations. The strategy of asking questions to gain information took second place to the gaining of an understanding of the youth groups' cultural practices in action. I could always ask specific questions away from the discussion situation at a later date. Ethnography is two things at the same time, a research method and an experience. The field relations create and sustain personal responsibility. In this study, the application of one fundamental rule of communication in the field relations was not to speak about personal issues of pupils to teachers and vice versa. The strategy was not to betray the trust of one pupil group to another nor betray the trust of pupils and teachers. No source of gossip was to be traded, even when it would be an advantage to exchange confidences. This was one ethical stand which I tried to maintain.

Conclusions

This short introduction was thought necessary in order to provide the reader with an initial understanding of the protagonists of the narrative , and also a context within which to interpret their actions and relations. Conducting a qualitative field study on female and male youth is an experience that is both intimate and intense. Ethnographic research requires relationships based upon exchange. The researcher engages in a special relationship with informants, yet the researcher should never forget that she or he is not one of the group. The price of increased freedom in the research method is that the ethnographic researcher becomes more vulnerable than the quantitative sociologist. Informants may push towards extreme situations from which the researcher cannot escape, and to which he/she must respond. At one level a complex game is set up, at another there is a serious exploration of intention.

In this case study the relation between theory and method is not so much an initial guiding perspective as a continuous attempt to understand as the groups studied unfold. If there is any hypothesis it is the testing and comprehending of the researcher's understanding of the group, and the group at some point indicate one's failures.

2   A theory of youth cultural forms

Introduction

In the first chapter the reasons for not applying the concept of subculture in this case study were put forward. The concept was considered not particularly useful to interpret youth cultural relations, paradigms, practices, positions, rituals or styles. The two theories of subculture, namely, the psychological/psycho-analytic and the more structural analysis, do not explain the relations within or between groups (Hargreaves 1967 and Cohen 1972). The reason for not applying the concept of subculture then, does not rest on the variations between different competing definitions, but on the capacity of the concept to explain youth cultural groups in action: both in their internal and external relations. The category of subculture not only homogenises the practices of youth but fails to allow for local variation. Furthermore, the lived practices of youth are rarely the object of qualitative empirical research.

Previous theories are on the one hand very dependent in the final instance upon psychoanalytic constructs to define youth socially, and their fundamental notions do not so much arise out of observed relations and practices as make assumptions about them. On the other hand these theories do connect the study of youth to macro levels of analysis, essentially through social class. However, studies of youth adopting an interactionist approach seem, necessarily to disconnect youth from the wider structures of class, gender and race.

In order to describe the internal relations *within* the youth cultural forms of the study, the relations *between* these social forms *and* their inter-relations with wider social structures it was necessary to create what I call here a language of description. That is, a set of concepts which generate relations capable of describing the styles, forms and practices, conflicts and tensions of the various groups. The language of description reduces the arbitrariness of the ethnographic account by making explicit the principles of interpretation. This language was initially developed whilst in the field and, in this sense, arose out of the ethnography. However, a more rigorous development of the language took place after the field work was completed. The language of description is itself produced by sets of hypotheses developed to make sense of the ethnographic data, and acts both as a grid for interpretation and as a grid to be tested, or rather explored, for its power of description. From this point of view the theoretical language is not an elaboration of pre-determined categories nor a naive development of the groups' 'naturalistic' practices but a complex data-informed and explored construction, to interpret the ethnographic data. In short, the language of description provides principles of analysis to interpret data. These principles of analysis are not so much used to distinguish between levels of analysis as to produce a selective focus upon aspects of an emergent totality whose identity, forms, practices, semiotic and external relationships create both order and conflict.

A minimum definition of a youth cultural form is that it is a grouping of youth on the basis of a specialisation of style which creates a particular solidarity, territoriality, history, set of practices and semiotic, played out in relations which are oppositional and complementary to other style specialisations. This minimum definition will be elaborated later in the chapter.

It was clear that the internal group relations of the style groups in the school were very different from friendship groups, cliques or gangs as these have been discussed in the literature. The analysis that follows is an attempt to describe the particular pattern of positions, division of labour and interaction which are considered to typify youth cultural groups. The description which follows although only based on the fieldwork is tentatively put forward as a model for describing youth cultural forms.

The theory of youth cultural forms will be divided into four major sections: specialised positions, social relations of the face, specialised semiotic and signature.

Group structure : specialised positions

The model of the specialised positions describes the positions, relations and communication within a youth cultural group. There are two forms which have two specialised positions:

Symbolic forms:	*Style leader*
	Cultural ransacker
Social forms:	*Peer group spokesperson*
	Peer group consolidator

Here I will briefly introduce the specialised positions. The symbolic forms regulate the specialised semiotic of the youth cultural group: i.e. the condition for stylistic solidarity. The style leader is predominantly concerned with the identity of the style. The cultural ransacker's priority is towards the structural relations of style, in particular the authenticity of style. The social forms operate control over the social relations of the youth cultural group: i.e. its collective solidarity. The peer group spokesperson is predominantly concerned with maintenance and assertion of collective solidarity. The peer group consolidator's priority is towards affirmation and reparation of group solidarity.

Style leader (SL)

The SL is dedicated to style initiation. He or she will be the first to adopt items of a new style or purchase the recognised elements of the legitimate style. The SL gives direction and regulates the dress and appearance of the youth cultural group.

The SL controls the promenading rituals and their initiation but this power must be kept within stylistic bounds. If the SL goes beyond the reality level the group has accepted, or is seen to be too willing to adopt either an unacceptable variation, or a variation beyond the group's resources to develop, then he/she may well become isolated and experience ego difficulties. From the point of view of the group the SL may be a source of threat as the SL's fundamental involvement in style might lead him/her to exhaust the possibilities of one style and turn to another. Thus the dedication of the SL to style is both a source of strength to the group and a potential danger to the order the style symbolises.

An SL must always offer competence, preparation and articulation in demonstrating the present stylistic order. The SL requires an effective material base in order to possess the money to buy merchandise. Where the youth cultural style is new, the SL's need of such a material base is reduced because there are no pre-selected items of style to purchase. A new style allows the SL an increased capacity to experiment without necessarily having to buy the accepted expensive clothes of a style. In the case of a historical youth cultural style, the SL will require money to buy the pre-selected elements signalling the style. In general, the SL requires a foundation in an economic base which allows for both choice and experimentation.

Cultural ransacker (CR)

The CR is preoccupied with importation. He or she is concerned to look outside the existing group structure, to absorb ideas and meanings which can be introduced into the group. The CR finds pleasure and purpose in both invention and transferral. The CR monitors the stylistic relations of the youth cultural form. An important difference between the SL and the CR is that the SL's priority is the demonstration of youth cultural style, whereas the CR's priority is stylistic authenticity and discovering how style structures work.

The CR monitors authenticity, searching out new features of a style, and to tries ensure that the group is not seduced by false elements of style. The CR not only monitors the style but attempts to develop the style through knowledge of stylistic boundaries. Inside the group the CR demands stylistic authenticity, outside the group the CR will search for both 'new' and 'old' items which emphasise stylistic authenticity. In a sense the CR is the *bricoleur* of the group. Whether the youth cultural style is contemporary or historic the CR requires an effective economic base. To be able to investigate, experiment and monitor stylistic relations and innovations, the CR needs money. The CR can disturb the style solidarity of the youth cultural group by too great an insistence on invention, discovery and reversal. Such actions may create hostility in the group and bring the CR into conflict with the peer group spokesperson whose concern is essentially with social solidarity, and with the SL whose concern is with style solidarity. The CR may become a potential threat to the youth cultural group.

The CR, then, imparts elements of styles, practices and ideas, and so invigorates the cultural form as well as acting as a guardian of its authenticity. The attraction for the CR is the investigation of other styles and the accumulation of knowledge of stylistic variation.

Peer group spokesperson (PGS)

The PGS is the voice of the group, often loud, and always potentially domineering. He or she will claim the right to speak for the youth cultural group. The PGS requires an audience. He/she will be the first to protect and assert social solidarity. A PGS will also attempt to resolve other members' problems to ensure that a consensus exists. It is difficult for a PGS to admit that he or she is ever wrong. Any sign of uncertainty could be a danger to social solidarity. The PGS rarely speaks of their personal feelings because priority is always given to the social context of the group and its members.

The PGS can disturb rather than facilitate social solidarity through the drive to be dominant (albeit in the group interest). Such actions not only create tension within the group but between the specialised positions. At the same time the PGS demands that other members show consideration for others and allow all to make a contribution. However, the PGS's two roles of domination and promotion of cohesion can disturb the social solidarity of the group which the peer group consolidator will need to repair. On occasions other specialised positions will join together to control the dominance of the PGS. Such actions, however, will need careful consideration in order to avoid injury to the PGS's pride. A humiliated PGS is a danger to group solidarity. In this case the PGS may keep a low profile for a short time and is susceptible to an occasional sulk. When the PGS is active, group social exchanges become ritualised, extrovert and rumbustious. A function of the PGS's cohesive role is the distribution of symbolic awards to ensure that everyone is 'mentioned in dispatches' and to facilitate internal strength and confidence.

There is a potential tension between the style leader and peer group spokesperson on the one hand and the cultural ransacker and peer group consolidator on the other hand. For the former positions (SL/PGS) may create a false self assurance and identity, whereas the latter two positions (CR/PGC) may well have to negotiate the tendency to ritual exaggeration on the part of the PGS and the SL.

The PGS is a somewhat conservative force within these youth cultural groups, essentially affirming or rejecting ideas or practices brought into the group. The PGS is a social form and the initiating or introduction of the symbolic by a social form is not likely to be acceptable to the other specialised positions. The PGS, through the play of positions of which he/she is a part, contrives to be dominant in the practices of group solidarity.

Peer group consolidator (PGC)

The PGC is a social form whose practice is essentially concerned with facilitating the social solidarity of the group. The PGC can therefore be regarded as a specialist in 'repair' strategies. These strategies are applied to defuse actual or potential threats to the harmonious social relations of the group. These threats can come from a variety of sources, for example disputes between members, disputes over style, disputes over status, and disputes between specialised positions. In order to carry out reparative practices the PGC has to have access to a grapevine of gossip, rumour and local histories which provide an important information base. The PGC will be likely to take all sides into account in a dispute, and to demand honesty, insisting that little remains underground to poison social relationships. He/she is likely to use three strategies and choose between them according to the situation: provocation, eccentricity and humour. Whether one or any combination of these strategies is applied, the purpose will be to celebrate the group structure, friendship or culture at the expense of difference and tension. The PGC's major concern is to deal with discrimination and injustice by monitoring and repairing social relations, practices and rituals.

As a social form the PGC has a dual role, to strengthen the youth cultural group when at ritual play in its public face and to unify the group in its internal private face. The PGC is given direction and support by the PGS especially when carrying out the two social roles of strengthening the public face and facilitating unity in the private face. The PGS and PGC share a degree of conservatism with regard to stylistic initiation or innovation. However, both social forms powerfully direct the youth cultural group's public display i.e. its promenade. The PGC is accepting of authority, as a result of his/her confirming and affirming roles.

There is a cross form alliance between the PGC and the CR, as both recognise the threat of symbolic and social exaggerations creating internal divisions in the group. Although there exists a cross form alliance, it is the PGC who is more likely to realise that the CR is the most threatening of the specialised positions to the solidarity of the group. This is because the CR's concern is with the meaning and structure of stylistics, not the social display style but at the level of understanding principles of authentic style itself.

Symbolic and social forms

The specialised positions within a youth cultural group work to strengthen and develop the social and symbolic relations of the youth cultural form. A youth cultural form has a specialised semiotic which is regulated by the two symbolic forms, the cultural ransacker and the style leader. Further, a youth cultural group has social ordering positions which are regulated by the two social forms, the peer group consolidator and the peer group spokesperson.

The symbolic forms function to introduce, develop, use and identify stylistic variations within the specific aesthetic of the youth cultural group and to revitalise the practices of the youth cultural style's aesthetic dimension. The style leader and the cultural ransacker regulate the aesthetic of the specific youth cultural signature which makes its particular form distinctive. (See later discussion of signature). There may be relations of symbolic struggle between the CR and the SL arising out of their respective specialised practices; conflicts arising are however, limited and do not represent opposition between these forms.

The social forms regulate the public and private social relations of the youth cultural group. The social forms function in affirming, confirming and repairing the youth cultural group identity, social relations and practices. There may be occasional relations of social struggle between the peer group spokesperson and the peer group consolidator, however, these relations tend not to be oppositional because the priority of both social forms is collective solidarity. No stylistic variation can be legitimated and become a practice without being first sanctioned by the social forms.

Tension can exist where the symbolic forms attempt to seduce the social forms into accepting a particular stylistic innovation or variation. This creates space for struggles, reveals instability and introduces the potential for a clash. The specialised position a member occupies is not pre-determined or static. Unity is formed out of a constant striving towards an ideal coherence in which rupture is however, inherent. Developing and applying each of the specialised positions requires different sets of skills. A specialised position can be understood as a range, or set, of specific practices which an individual will take over on the basis of a relevant skill. The person is not the position: the practices performed must be understood as demonstration of a specialised position. The specialised positions will not always operate their practice, but only when the situation demands.

In a youth cultural group can there exist non-specialised positions? Within the youth cultural group there are non specialised positions because of the existence of *marginal members*. At meetings or gatherings not all members of the youth group will be present. At particular events, incidents and on various occasions marginal members will be present.

Within a youth cultural group there may be two or more members who occupy the same specialised position, for example two PGSs or two CRs. Two CRs can make a symbolic alliance within the group or two PGCs can form a social alliance. However, there may also be internal struggle (not opposition) between two members of the same specialised position. Further, it was found during the ethnography that where certain specialised positions were absent, the occupant of another specialised position would attempt to monopolise the absent position(s). The consequence of this was not to distort the group structure but rather to reveal the potential struggle between specialised positions in making claims on other specialised positions. For example, where there is no SL present, the PGS may make a symbolic claim that he/she will not be able to substantiate. The PGS may be corrected when the SL is present. The important point is that each specialised position will attempt to dominate and, on occasions occupy, additional specialised positions. But an individual cannot sustain indefinitely the occupancy of more than one specialised position: one person performs one specialised position. However, where the occupant of a specialised position attempts to occupy more than one specialised position, the group members will react against this because they will recognise the display as presenting a danger to both social and stylistic solidarity.

Hierarchy within youth cultural forms

Each specialised position within a youth cultural form shares with others a relation of equality. Specialised positions are equal in the sense that each is required to contribute to the social and stylistic solidarity within the group. However, each specialised position is not equal in terms of the potential of each member to specialise. Therefore, the basic division of labour between symbolic and social forms creates a dynamic but 'edgy' sense of group democracy.

There is a division of labour in terms of *functions*, between the symbolic and the social forms creating oppositions and tension arising out of revivifying and reparation practices. There is also a division of labour, in terms of *status locations*. The four specialised positions (SL, CR, PGS, PGC) are prestigious forms and will themselves become objects of status and power, for competition and domination by group members.

These specialised positions do not form a hierarchy from bottom to top. The issue of hierarchy becomes one of relation, that is, every position has a status. But members might attempt to dominate and occupy other specialised positions than their own to increase their status and power. Where a member successfully dominates both the social and symbolic forms she or he will emerge as the leader, under these conditions the youth cultural group becomes a gang with one identifiable voice and one leader. A gang has only one division of labour (leader/led), in contrast to the youth cultural group which has two divisions of labour, one for social solidarity and the other for stylistic solidarity. Within a youth cultural group leadership is vacant. The leadership position is subject to the relations within and between the two divisions of labour. The dominant direction from within the group is not through leadership but from the relations between the two forms of social solidarity and stylistic authenticity. Leadership is not a central controlling relation inside the youth cultural group because the different specialised positions regulate, repair and control the relations, rituals, practices and communications. The chair of leadership remains vacant because of the two requirements of solidarity and authenticity which overrule the dominance of the leadership position by any one specialised position.

Having outlined the relations within the youth cultural forms it is important to show the contrasting relations between the specialised positions, especially between the social and the symbolic. Two crucial social relations of disturbance in the youth cultural group's solidarity are, on the one hand, the capacity of the PGS to disturb the social through an excessively domineering presence, and on the other hand, the capacity of the CR to disturb the style through importing new ideas. Group solidarity has the potential to be fractured at the level of style and at the level of the social. This affects the relation of the SL's position towards stylistic solidarity, and the relation of the PGS's position towards social solidarity. Thus to sustain and create stylistic and social solidarity there are a series of controlling, oppositional and alliance relations within and between the social and symbolic forms.

The PGC and the CR monitor and revitalise the social and stylistic relations which are real and potential threats to group solidarity. This is in contrast to the SL and the PGS who promote the social and stylistic relations of ritual exaggeration which 'promenade' the solidarity of the group in its public face. The CR is primarily concerned with stylistic authenticity. This means he/she will monitor stylistic practice and ensure that a 'reality principle' limiting ritual exaggeration at the level of style is maintained. If a practice is not authentic to the style, the CR will insist that the danger threatening identity and solidarity is opposed.

The cross form alliance of social solidarity and stylistic authenticity between the PGC and the CR is accomplished through the 'reality principle' which sees ritual exaggeration or fantasy as an oppositional threat to group solidarity. Therefore, within the group there is potential conflict between: the peer group consolidator and the style leader over social solidarity and the cultural ransacker and the peer group spokesperson over stylistic authenticity. The cross form alliance can cause conflict between the two dominant relations of social and stylistic solidarity, while at the same time the alliance both regulates and monitors dangers to group solidarity and authenticity.

The social relations of the face

The model of the social relations of the face describes the three different social relations of a youth cultural group; private face, between face and public face. The three faces refer to the different levels, types and range of interaction within and between youth cultural groups. The private face describes the internal relations of the group. The between face refers to the type of interaction which occurs between rival, different, oppositional and similar youth cultural groups. The public face describes the external relations of the group. (Dunphy 1963, Labov 1982, Kochman 1983).

In both the popular media and the previous literature on deviance and education attention has been concentrated on youth's public profile. Youth appear to have only one mode of social relation i.e. revolt. McRobbie (1980) states "Few subcultural writers seem to be really interested in what happened when the mod went home after a weekend on speed" (p.38). She points out that previous accounts have been concerned to emphasise only one element of youth behaviour, what I have called here the 'public face'. This face is presented for public reading whenever there exist opportunities for recognition. A further point which reinforces McRobbie's criticism is that studies of youth are concerned only with youth as deviant stylists, ignoring the fact that young people have to engage in situations other than those strictly related by membership of a youth cultural group. An individual is also daughter, son, pupil, sportsperson, shop assistant, parent, apprentice, unemployed person, trainee manager and so on.

Private face

The private face is strictly an in-group social relation. Rarely will outsiders be permitted to view this face because it may reveal internal uncertainty. The issues of hierarchy, both within and between the divisions of labour of social and stylistic solidarity are here in play. From within the private face, the youth cultural group works out its internal positions, practices and relations. Here there will be potential and actual internal promenading by group members as alliances and struggles occur between the specialised positions.

The purposes of the internal group promenade are different from those of the formal public promenade. Ritual within the internal promenade celebrates the group structure, history and potential. In contrast, the ritual of a public promenade is more flexible and allows for perhaps greater dramatic ritual street theatre. During the private face the group is present only to itself. Discussions are not suitable for outsiders to hear. Communication in the private face is played out against a backcloth of implicit assumptions and tacit understanding, and regulated by the negotiated procedures the group has developed. This contrasts with the more formalised ritual communications of the public face (Bernstein 1959, Douglas 1970, Labov 1972).

From the researcher's perspective access to the private face is not just difficult or time consuming but also dangerous (Thompson 1966, Patrick 1973, Blackman 1983, Campbell 1984). To gain an interpretation of the inside of a group means in some senses that one has to surrender to the group because of the group's exclusive practices. Difficulties arise because the researcher necessarily has to uphold two perspectives; to maintain and monitor internal group relations, and at the same time assess the internal group relations from an outside position. Keeping one's mind on two positions, the world inside and the world outside, can be dangerous within a participant observation context because the hosts might interpret the researcher's behaviour as at best ambiguous or at worst threatening.

Between face

The between face operates and is in play at a variety of levels and ranges of communication, for example:-
In relations with known outside groups either sharing stylistic practices or having a rival or oppositional stylistic practice. In relations with unknown groups sharing a stylistic practice or having a rival or oppositional stylistic practice. In relation with other groups, individuals or institutions.

Outside groups are those within the locality which are known by the members of the group but are outside their territory and stylistic practice.
Unknown groups are those which the members of the group do not know, i.e. when the group move they may meet groups in regions where the territorial domination is either unknown or not established.
Other groups and individuals are varied groups ranging from younger children's groups to adult-work groups. Other individuals are those persons who are in contact with the youth cultural group. Institutional relations refer to relations between the group and members of institutions where the group does not have control; that is where control lies with the institution, for example, the police.
    A youth cultural group will have a different set of procedures for meeting a known or an unknown group of the same stylistic practice, from those procedures regulating a meeting between a known group or an unknown group with a rival or an oppositional stylistic practice. For example in the case of a known or an unknown outside group sharing the same style or a variant of it, there is likely to be an agreed procedure of interaction. However, potential both for negotiation and for conflict between such groups

is present, even though they possess an underlying similarity of style. The potential for negotiation will be less when meeting a known or unknown group with a rival or oppositional stylistic practice. The potential for negotiation will be present but if the difference between the youth cultural styles is too great conflict may result.

The difference between meeting groups with a similar stylistic practice and groups with a rival / oppositional practice was revealed by one of the mod boys. He described how he would greet an unknown mod sharing a similar stylistic practice. He said

> Right upon seeing a mod, whether here or some other place I would always cross the road and ask where they were from. About the scooters - how many, whether there were any mod parties or conventions going on, you know everything mod. Sometimes it's a good laugh but occasionally, I reckon 'Bullshit!' I know I do it myself. But that's great, that's what it's all about, being neat. The impression.

Paul shows that when meeting groups or individuals who share a stylistic practice, the communication is on a number of levels. The level of hostility is very low but there exists a powerful rivalry to 'out mod' through posture and front. It could be argued that a general pattern of communication exists between youth cultural groups, determined by whether the groups share either a style or a variant of it, or are in a rival or an oppositional style. However, there may be conflict between similar styles arising out of history, territory and identity.

Public face

The public face is the sign that the youth cultural group will offer for public reading. The public face is the face much exaggerated and even distorted by the media and agencies of social control (Taylor, Walton and Young 1973). In the language of deviancy, this can be described as the presentation of youth as a folk devil evoking moral panic (Cohen, S. 1972). The public face is the youth cultural group's ritual promenade in its most observable form and encapsulates both truth and fantasy.

The public face is shown when the youth cultural group display themselves for maximum public consumption. The public face is a strange mixture of reality and fantasy in ritual exaggeration, where the most important function is to feed public consumption and assumption.

All three social relations of the face are continually in flux. They can all operate within a single context as occurs at a festival, party or social gathering. At other times there may be a movement from the private face to the public face when a situation makes possible a ritual promenade. The regulation of the social relations of the face occurs through specialised positions within the youth cultural group.

Specialised semiotic of the youth cultural group

The theory of the specialised semiotic acts as a means to examine the internal practices of the youth cultural group, thereby showing the rules which supply a style with coherence, order, meaning and possibilities. The specialised semiotic can be defined as the system of signs which applies to a particular youth cultural style. In effect the semiotic operates like a language of stylistics. It does not comprise the style itself but rather is the medium which orders and gives meaning to the elements of the style and allows the style to be communicated. A particular youth style can be summarised through its signature. The signature is what we shall call a condensation of the position and practices of the youth cultural group holding a legitimate site within the field (Bourdieu 1984).

In a similar way to that in which grammar orders language so the specialised semiotic provides an ordering structure through which elements of style operate and can change or develop. The semiotic allows the potential for the incorporation of new stylistic features or for certain features to become obsolete (Polhemus 1994).

The production and reproduction of the specialised semiotic occurs within the youth cultural group but it is fundamentally shaped by a two-way interaction between the youth cultural group and the musical artists associated with the particular style (Ross and Rose 1994). The musical artists project and articulate the ideas and experiences of the youth cultural group. But also - through a range of media including film, artistic or photographic images, dress, song lyrics, musical performance and public appearance - the musical artist provides models, ideas and practices which influence the youth groups and contribute to defining the youth cultural style. The film Quadrophenia by The Who (1973/1979) provides an example of the two nature of this interaction in that it is the youth groups which provide the material for the film and it is their experience to which it gives expression but in articulating that experience in a certain way the film provides style models and ideas which in turn influence youth cultural groups themselves (Frith and Goodwin 1990).

The youth cultural groups' specialised semiotic has three relational practices:-

Choreography: which has two facets, dress and appearance and techniques of the body.

Narrative: which has four facets, music, literature, drugs and linguistics.

Circulation: which has two facets, territorial movement and social sites.

The various aspects of these three relational practices are examined below.

Choreography

Dress and appearance

The style of a specialised youth cultural group is readily recognisable by the selection, contrast and combination of clothes worn. Dress and appearance have various working features, including clothes, skin markings, hair styles, make-up and accessories. Youth cultural groups have varying sets of practices and repertoires of meaning which are revealed by their articulation of the aspects of dress and appearance. The difference between the take-up and combination of these items is the critical factor defining opposition through style.

Youth cultural styles have substantial power to transform an object and specialise it to a style. Objects and accessories possess meaning only in relation to their specific use within the youth cultural style. The dress and appearance of a style contain hidden messages (Barthes 1977) some of which are restricted to insiders i.e. to members of the youth cultural group. The clothes' or objects' 'normal' signification becomes subordinant to the meaning imposed and developed by the youth cultural style. Hebdige (1979) suggests that style contains refusal, and amounts to a gesture of defiance imbued with meaning to challenge the social order. Such an interpretation raises the question of how far these new definitions and meanings imposed by the style actually represent a cultural penetration into bourgeois order. An object or item of clothing may have a new definition from the perspective of the working class youth cultural group; however, the group's position within the class structure does not necessarily threaten the stability of 'respectable society'.

The symbolic importance of skin marking, hair styles, make-up, clothes and accessories are that they signify a summary of the youth cultural style's practice, position, coherence and meaning. The dress and appearance of the youth cultural style contain the repertoire of artifacts which have possibilities and potential to be actualised. In the youth style wardrobe the meanings are multiple signifiers.

The items of clothing belonging to a style are embedded within particular meanings specific to that youth cultural style. There exist few items of clothing which different youth cultural styles share. Interestingly, one example is the Doctor Marten boot or shoe worn by female and male punks, mods, skins, new age travellers and ravers. However, the appearance and meaning of the DM's is significantly different because each youth cultural style adapts it to their own stylistic presentation (Knight 1982, Hebdige 1988).

Techniques of the body

I propose to examine five positionings of the body. The most central is posture which supports gesture, walking, dancing and fighting. Sexuality is powerfully interwoven within the techniques of the body (Mauss 1936). An important question which arises is whether sexuality can possibly be separated from style or whether such an analytical separation is meaningless. The body is presented in and through posture as the carrier for promenading both style and sexuality (Shilling 1993).

Posture and gesture

Posture has a range of possible meanings through an arrangement of bodily positioning. Posture within youth cultural style is called intentional communication (Hebdige 1979, Hewitt 1986b). To pose and oppose are the dynamic features within and between youth cultural groups because of the necessity to promenade. It could be argued that all youth cultural styles have different variations of

37

posture, as each has different varieties of dancing which derive from diverse musical styles. Differences in posture are associated with differences of clothes, meanings and objects within specific youth cultural styles which require different positionings of the body (Parker 1974, Redhead 1993). Where a posture states a position, a gesture holds rhetorical and perhaps dramatic purpose (Birdwhistle 1970). Both posture and gesture are up front communications which are specifically non-verbal. Gestures have an immense variety but only one meaning when accompanied by a specific posture. It would be difficult to argue that there could be variations of gesture between youth cultural groups but I would suggest that certain youth groups specialise in specific forms of gesture. Patrick (1973) points out the significance of posture in relation to style, not only in terms of a secret language but for movement, the ability to 'look sharp' and to be prepared for engagement or confrontation (Hall 1959).

Both posture and gesture are significantly different according to the youth cultural group's social relations of the face. Within the private and public faces posture and gesture take on different social and symbolic meaning. In the private face there will be internal promenading to group members; here gesture and posture will be on a different level from where the public face is promenaded by the youth cultural group. Here the two specialised positions of SL and PGS concerned with ritual celebration have a larger public profile with respect to posture and gesture, but the two specialised positions of PGC and CR which keep in check forms of ritual exaggeration will also operate to control forms of posture and gesture.

Three facets of mobility: walking, dancing and fighting

Walking can encompass elements of both posture and gesture. In the early 1960s it was often pointed out that mods had a particular way of walking. Mods swayed their shoulders and took short steps quickly with their feet slightly turned out. If their hands were in their pockets they would have their thumbs sticking out (Barnes 1979). The mods' way of walking, I would argue, possibly relates to their style of dress and specific clothes. Such movements attempted to ensure minimum creasing and maximum neatness. Anybody who knows mods will have heard the story about a group of mods being thrown off a train or bus or out of a cafe because they would not sit down, as the action would result in creasing their clothes.

Further, the quick movements of mod walking are significantly linked to the drug taking habit of 'sniffing' or 'dropping' sulphate or 'bombers' which ensures pace setting.

Dancing is probably one of the most provocative communication rituals of posture through the positioning of the body. Each youth cultural style has its specialised form of dance, from bop and pogo to hip hop and acid house, which are related to the different musical styles. For example forms of dance linked to cultural styles range from 'headbanging' rockers playing cardboard guitars or manic pogoing punks to wide variations of mod dancing from the block to the hitch hike depending upon whether the music is R and B, soul or ska. Mungham (1976) does not focus upon the meaning of dance in relation to the meaning of musical style or youth cultural style. Instead he investigates the social and sexual encounters at the dance hall as a site for female and male courtship rituals (Leonard 1980).

Popularly the dancefloor is considered as a site where girls take a dominant role. However, it is probably more precise to argue that an equal share of the dancing which is specific to particular youth cultural styles is done by both sexes. Disco dancing is more predominantly female and breakdancing is more predominantly male (Toop 1984). Both types of dancing are very competitive and individually related to performance. Different types of dance within youth cultural styles can be complex and demand a tightly skilled performance, such as rock and roll jive dancing by teds, or northern soul dancing by mods, whereas in other youth cultural styles the dexterity of dancing may not be a priority; instead group celebration overrides individual performance, as in the rockers dancing stomp or punk pogo dancing. The significance of a dance within certain youth cultural styles may be greater, for example break dancing and hip hop are specific dance performances of electro music which have a dominant position within the enlarged category of soul music (Gilroy 1993). In contrast, dancing within the major youth cultural styles, such as ted, mod, rocker, skin and punk, is only one particular facet within the specialised semiotic, not the crucial element.

McRobbie (1984) sees dance as a social experience which extends to three relations: image, fantasy and social activity. Her interpretation of girls' dance within the youth cultural style of punk is that,

It inoculates the girls both against some danger by giving them a sense of confidence, and against the excesses of sexual discrimination by giving them a lifestyle which adamantly refuses the strictures of traditional femininity (p.149).

Hebdige (1979) first suggested that punk dancing appeared not only to challenge the heterosexual interest and physical contact in dance but "Resembled the anti-dancing of the 'Leapnick's'" (p.108). (See Melly 1972, pp. 64-65). The meaning carried by punk music results in forms of dancing which are relevant to the values within punk style (Laing 1985) Further, forms of dancing within a musical style are deemed to be masculine or feminine only by reference to various elements which link music to the social structure including, the inner meaning of the youth cultural style, lyrics of songs, social activities and the context of the dance. Dancing is not only related to sexual display, it is also designed to draw the attention of members of both the opposite and the same sex through demonstrations of dexterity and skill (Thomas 1993).

Fighting is the most dramatic and potentially the most brutal technique of the body. Within deviancy literature there exist few accounts of direct observation of fighting. There are numerous second hand descriptions of conflict and its meaning. Both Patrick (1973) and Campbell (1984) note the practical fieldwork problems of danger, fear and lack of access. Thompson (1966) produces an insider account of how fighting is central to the posture and status of certain youth cultural groups, while Daniel and McGuire (1972) provide conversations among skinheads about how they understand confrontation as a 'natural' part of their culture (Poxon 1976).

Narrative

A second relational practice of the youth cultural groups' specialised semiotic is narrative. This section includes the role of music, literature, language and drugs.

An introduction to music and youth

The primary narrative of the youth cultural group occurs through music. I would suggest that within the musical style exist the relations and practices of the youth cultural group, inscribed through the lived practices of the bond between the artist(s) and the youth cultural group. In the last ten years there has been extensive analysis of the meaning of popular music but few of these interpretations have been linked to a qualitative empirical study of youth. Since the publication of Resistance Through Ritual (1975) the culturalist approach, based upon secondary sources of data rather than direct observation, has dominated the interpretation of the relationship between youth and music at the level of meaning (Brake 1980, Redhead 1990). A major problem in the studies listed above is the assumption that the relationship between the youth groups and musical artists is defined, clear and known. Frith's (1978) important argument that "Music's presence in youth culture is established but not its purpose" (p.39) has been continually avoided. However, since the late 1980s there has emerged a valuable series of ethnographic studies which have attempted to address Frith's question (Jones 1988, Henderson 1992, Back 1995).

Early attempts at a sociological understanding of the relation between youth and music (Murdock and Phelps 1972, Corrigan 1973) linked music to social class without an analysis of the meaning of musical styles or youth culture. The purpose of music was thought to be closely tied to identity, primarily only useful to the youth group as a reference point for different background activities (see as an early analysis Becker, 1951).

In the late 1970s a major barrier to understanding the relation between youth and music was the diversion into the aesthetics of high culture (Shepherd, et al 1977). Drawing on Adorno, Marxists in the main have seen the popular music industry as based on mass produced commodities which serve to maintain the dominant relations of musical production; the meaning within popular music thus functions to keep the working class from realisation of their class oppression (Frith 1981, Wicke 1982).

In the 1980s two different, if not unrelated arguments have dominated sociological analysis of the relations between youth culture and music. On the one hand is the proposition that music represents cultural and political positions. Since the Miners' Strike and Live Aid (Street 1986, Widgery 1986) musical artists have been subject to detailed academic scrutiny, and over-theorisation by academics, some of whom have somewhat elitist notions of class struggle (Cohen 1980). Here the main proposition is that punk changed the context of reception for popular music. On the other hand, it is asserted that popular music is back in the hands of big

41

business and that youth culture is dead and politically impotent, reduced to commodity selection and thus compromised (Grossberg 1986). Here the proposition is, 'it's as if punk had never happened' (Rimmer 1985, Lipstiz 1994).

One of the few investigations into the relations between youth groups and music is by Willis (1972, 1978). He constructs a tripartite model of a theory of cultural forms called socio-symbolic homologies which demonstrate three relations: indexical, homological and integral. His interpretation of musical style is as a symbol of meaning for the youth groups whose preferred music holds what he calls "objective possibilities". Willis (1972) states that this interpretation is "developed from literary criticism via ... cultural criticism" (p. LXXVII). The music is understood as a symbol for a cluster of values held by the youth cultural group. His structuralist model allows the relations and practices of the youth cultural group to be assessed in a new way through his modification of Levi-Strauss' concept of bricolage. Willis (1978) argues, that the subordinate group, namely youth, have agency to act on objects, values and meanings within limited spaces "which have been ignored by the dominant culture except for their obvious uses" (p.201). In the last analysis he is drawn back into Marxist categorisation of dominant and subordinant cultures with their respective art forms. Willis (1978) argues "The obvious potential for a meaningful relation with important cultural items will already have been exploited by the dominant culture" (p.201).

Thus within youth studies which focus on music a major concern has been to establish how and to what extent popular music can be considered as art, and the way popular music is understood by youth themselves has been a secondary rather than primary focus. This perspective was further developed in the 1980s and 1990s through post-structuralist and post-modernist analysis which resulted in less concentration on youth culture and a greater focus on the levels of meaning associated with consumption of styles as individual art (McRobbie 1994).

'The band is the bond' relations between youth groups and musical bands

The forms of relation examined below may provide the basis for a model to interpret the relationship in youth culture between youth cultural groups and musical bands. It is possible to separate these relations only at an analytical level; empirically they are inter-dependent.

Identification: Here the band and the youth cultural group dress within the same stylistic boundary. For example, the musical bands below dress in a specific youth cultural style:-

Gong	Hippie
The Clash	Punk
Stray Cats	Teds/rockabilly
The Jam	Mods
Joy Division	New wave
Iron Maiden	Heavy metal
Public Enemy	Hip hop
The Orb	New age

For the band to display the same overall youth cultural style both presents and represents a symbolic relation where the items of clothing, accessories and skin markings embody reciprocal values and meanings. Identification through style establishes a fundamental rule of authenticity of style and meaning. To share similar items of dress and appearance announces that both band and youth group share values, practices and meanings associated and embedded in the style the youth cultural groups display and promenade (Thompson 1972).

Forms of identical dress provide unity and support to the meanings upheld within the youth cultural style which are publicly celebrated through the band's musical style, live performance and material products. In the study, the mod boys would dress in mod clothing both past (original) and present, and especially in those items displayed by The Jam and The Style Council. The new wave girls would not only dress in the style of the new wave and punk bands but elaborated their own creative response to, and development of, that style.

Projection: The band operates within a musical style which presents a largely cultural and sometimes a political position. Bands have the means of public representation through production of commodities for an audience, for example, records, cassettes, videos, magazines and books. It is through such products and interviews in the music and mainstream press that the band can project their cultural or political perspective. Chambers (1981) argues, "We might say that pop music becomes also good 'to think with' it participates in the construction of an effective ... relationship to daily life. It indicates a potential and deeply loaded mode of representation in which the active appropriation of the music - the marrying of musical styles to cultural positions - involves cultural production" (p.38).

A result of this is that the youth cultural group will actively select a band from within the musical style. The youth group's choice of band and/or musical style, will be the band whose projection and meaning within the musical style are most relevant to the youth cultural group's identity. For example, within the study here, the new wave girls' choice of musical style was punk and new wave which provides a critical perspective on women's oppression within patriarchy. At a structural level the girls' choice of music related to the meanings within the lyrics of the songs and the meanings of the youth cultural style, both of which actively supported the girls' values and practice in everyday life. The message in the music of the band becomes more than just "good to think with" because the band seems to share the experience of the youth cultural group. This is demonstrated by one of the mod boys in the study. Gangster said,

> For Paul Weller to pick out the sort of things he does,
> I look through (the lyrics: SJB) and I think, yeah, that
> is the sort of thing I think about, and I mean Christ,
> you know, to be able to think through people's
> minds and pull out things like that.

Condensation: The sound produced by the band is a specialised sound from within a specific musical style, which in seconds expresses to the youth cultural group the condensed meaning of their identity. The band's production is not arbitrary but is structurally related both to the meanings of the musical style, lyrics, audience and context of reception, and to the youth cultural style. Musical style expresses identity, it is a territorial marker for both band and youth group. The sound becomes a carrier of meaning, particular to the youth culture, where the musical style's meaning is conveyed directly to the listener. The specialised sound represents a condensation of meaning (Prett 1984).

Celebration: The band, through their recorded material and especially through their live performances, provide a means and site for ritual celebration which allows the youth cultural group a space to display identity publicly through the promenade of the youth cultural group's public face. The gig is the most intimate site in the relationship between band and youth group. During the 1990s there has been a significant change within rave music as DJs and producers have now started to take their previously studio-bound sound out on the road. The audience collectively celebrate the unity of the youth cultural style, while the music of the band integrates the audience and band into a complex symbolic exchange and celebration ritual. Whatever the medium - record, compact disc, video, interview or photograph - where the band and youth group are captured together the medium becomes a resource for ritual. The photographic representation of the two-way interaction between band and youth group provides an immediate context for ritual celebration by the youth group. Whether the celebration occurs in public or private it bonds both the members of the band and the youth group together.

Production: This refers to the material products which the band produces, such as records, cassettes, videos, books and magazines; other items associated or linked with the band are reproductions such as clothes, accessories, motor scooters, bikes, cars, musical instruments, drugs etc. Musical bands within different musical styles will differ in the quantity and quality of both their productions and their reproductions. The youth cultural group has access to the band's cultural production through interviews, papers, fanzines, magazines, records, live performances and fan clubs. The youth group may initiate the production of their own cultural items (Willis 1990). The youth cultural group will act selectively on the features within the youth culture. For example in the study some of the new wave girls would sometimes sing in local punk/new wave bands and in particular Sioux also wrote song lyrics. In contrast, the mod boys formed their own official scooter club with bank account, newsletter, badges, patches, and scooter magazine with national contacts.

Authenticity: This refers to the reciprocal relation between band and youth groups which bonds both in an exclusive mutual identity. The relation is based on the oppositions of 'selling out' or 'credibility'. A band does not speak solely to a youth cultural group because of the need to appeal to a wider audience in order to gain a living (Negus 1992).

There exist two markets for the band, the symbolic and the economic. Within a symbolic market the band will share a close relation with its audience based on the principle that they have not 'sold out' or betrayed the youth cultural group. Few bands manage to retain the symbolic market when they transfer to an economic market because through commercial success in chart placings the band becomes accessible to a wider audience. For the youth cultural group there is a fundamental micro-relation when the band is in the symbolic market, for them it is *their* band. In the early stages of the band's career the youth cultural group has bought the recordings and been at the first gigs, thereby establishing an exclusive relation. The two markets create a dynamic tension for both the band and the youth group because both desire success and the spread of the style. Where the band exists within an economic market there may still exist relations of authenticity with the youth cultural group, depending upon the management of the band's symbolic potential, resources and history. It is the following of the youth group that gives the band the opportunity to move from one market to another but the youth group has difficulty in supporting the move from the symbolic to the economic (see articles in Ross and Rose 1994).

Literature

Among the most recent expanding areas in publication is the production of glossy literary and photographic texts on youth cultural styles, underground cults, musical artists and musical styles (Polhemus and Procter 1984, Reid 1987, Stuart 1987). An important feature of punk was its literature, with the fast and cheap production of chaotic fanzines which brought information directly to the audience from those who where involved in making the music. 'Sniffin' Glue' became one of the major punk fanzines, Mark P (1978) states, "All you kids out there who read Sniffin' Glue don't be satisfied with what we write. Go out and start your own fanzines or send reviews to the established papers. Let's really get on their nerves, flood the market with punk writing" (See Boston, (1978) p.9)

One similarity between the mid 1960s underground press and the proliferation of punk fanzines in the late 1970s was the attempt to relate music to youth cultural issues, through an alternative approach to both music and youth in opposition to the traditional coverage in the mainstream press (Boston 1978, Frith 1983).

The 1960s counter cultural magazines like OZ and IT and the 1970s 'punkzines' like 'Sniffin' Glue' and 'Ripped and Torn' gave priority to independence and diversity, by ruthlessly attacking the established mode of big business control over the music industry and youth (Frith and Horne 1987, Fountain 1988). Numerous writers who contributed to or ran their own fanzines are now journalists on the established music press, and also, the fan clubs of certain bands produced their own magazines.

A further consequence of the literary explosion created by punk was that other youth cultural styles developed their own fanzines for mods, skinheads and rockabilly rebels. Punk had the effect of revitalising other youth cultural styles. Many aspects of the youth cultural groups' specialised semiotic have been documented in the massive publication of pop books, novels, films, records, videos, magazines, papers, and fanzines on 'new' and 'old' styles. Further, throughout the last three decades academics have entered into the published world of youth cultural literature and these texts have been read by members of youth cultural groups.

This presents a situation of 'cultural slippage', especially where the book is based on an ethnographic study. Youths can identify previous youth cultural groups' practices, positions and relations to interpret their own practices. The immense documentation can be used as a cultural benchmark, to be invoked to validate a claim concerning the original legitimacy of a youth cultural style. Also, the literature may be produced by the youth cultural group themselves; this was the case in the study where the mod boys published their own scooter magazines and an occasional newsletter. In addition, the availability of films and videos can be used by members of the youth cultural group to investigate visual texts for inspiration, accuracy and validation. The social event of a group of rockers watching 'The Wild One' or 'Easy Rider', or a group of mods watching 'Quadrophenia' or 'Absolute Beginners' becomes a collective celebration of symbolism (Rees 1986).

Language

A youth cultural group frequently possesses an argot, that is a language used whereby the group can keep their practices secret. Argot holds a contradictory position in relation to the youth cultural group's promenade. On the one hand, argot ensures that the group's private face, its relations and identity remain hidden, but on the other hand the group's public face demands attention through display and exaggeration which prompts analysis of its secret practices by non-members of the group (Labov 1982). The youth cultural group presents a specialised communication to outsiders who are not given access to information which explains how the group processes of communication are agreed and acted upon. The youth cultural group's possession of a secret language acts as a common backcloth of assumptions whereby meaning need never be made explicit. Each of the specialised positions within the youth cultural group has an equal capacity to 'adlib' verbal exchanges, amongst only group members who know the grid of references (Dunphy 1963, Douglas 1970). The secret language enables the youth group to learn patterns of communication through the internal group structure. Items such as abbreviations, slang words or phrases, or the redefinition or inversion of normal words amount to a subversion in language use, which underlines the contradiction between the group's secret code and the public promenade. The discovery of a youth cultural group who utilise the potential power of a secret language, bouncing ideas and meaning off one another, makes it possible to show how such groups have a developed sense of narrative (Kochman 1972).

For a researcher, the argot of a youth cultural group may be particularly troublesome. The specific problem is whether to ask for an explanation of certain phrases or word meanings, or to wait until the meaning becomes clear.

Drugs

From the 1950s onwards it has been recognised that particular drugs are tied to specific youth cultural styles, for example; beats smoked 'pot' (cannabis), hippies took acid (LSD), mods used 'speed' (amphetamine sulphate) (Chambers 1985). Since the debut of the punk youth subculture in the late 1970s such rigid distinctions have begun to blur. However, certain drugs continue to be associated with particular youth cultural styles, for example cannabis is used among youths linked to the festival culture of travellers and also to some extent in the different types of independent dance music where the drug is used as a relaxant i.e. 'to chill out'. Ecstasy and 'speed' are more strongly associated with the active dance based youth cultures deriving from hip hop and house to rave and techno. Therefore, it would be misleading to assume that specific drugs are no longer associated with particular youth cultural styles, but we need to clarify the particular drug based activities associated with these youth cultures (Merchant and MacDonald 1994).

The popular face of youth culture is traditionally defined by its symbolic acts in public and this behaviour tends to get exaggerated, because a central theme within youth culture is display for public consumption. In addition there has been an increased use of multiple drug taking as part of a life style which is defined as poly drug use. 'Poly abusers' tend to combine a whole range of different drugs alongside excessive alcohol consumption (Coffield and Gofton 1994). In this study both youth cultural groups were involved in small and infrequent drug taking, largely of cannabis as a social drug or amphetamine/LSD as a dance/outdoor drug. For both groups their drug use could on some occasions be described as poly use, although usage was largely defined by particular drug availability and the context or location for the use. Usage in all respects was highly controlled and intellectually defined as a part of their recreational and stylistic practices: drug use was not chaotic but selective and made on the basis of preference (Coggans and McKellar 1994).

Circulation

Circulation is the third element of the youth cultural groups' specialised semiotic. This section considers social sites and territorial movement.

Social sites

This refers to the place or location where youth cultural groups gather. In general, youth cultural groups share types of social sites, although the practices which occur within a site will be specific to the youth cultural style. There are significant variations in practices within social sites by youth cultural groups according to their respective signatures. For each youth cultural group the practice of listening to music will be different, as a result of the different musical styles and the different meanings present within songs (Middleton 1990, Moore 1993).

A number of social sites or locations are common to different youth cultural groups such as members' houses, cafe, gig, club, dance, rave and public house. Each youth cultural group will have their own 'territorial haunt' and specific practices. Although all groups share types of sites, certain locations can become 'social institutions' and develop their own sense of history, for example rocker pubs or skinhead cafes.

For every youth cultural group the party is a central social site which is both a social and symbolic event. At a party a whole host of practices are engaged in by members of the youth cultural group. The gathering represents a display of collective solidarity where symbols, values, practices and rituals are harnessed to promenade the authenticity of style. At a mod party the music played will be specific to the musical styles of mod. No rival or oppositional music will be played. The music at a party is both a rule of circulation because it regulates the flow of activity, and also a musical celebration of the values and meanings relayed through the musical style and the song. The practice of listening or dancing to music will differ according to the youth cultural styles' specialist musical style (Willis 1978). Different musical styles both create and demand different sets of social relations and social contexts, which orchestrate the play of interactions. The party can occur at regular and different sites but the symbolic value of the venue will differ according to its location, whether it is at a parents' house, hired hall or youth's flat.

Conventions and specific youth cultural club events are another significant element within the celebratory practices of a style, which include displaying and sharing modes of clothes and dance, promenading and viewing machines associated with the style eg. scooters or motorbikes, collecting records or listening to music. (Hebdige 1981, Blackman 1983, Walker 1984). These occasions are organised and occur on both a local and national basis, through related clubs.

Territorial movement

The members of a youth cultural group define territory through their stylistic authenticity and legitimacy. Territoriality operates within and through the youth cultural group's style because the style presents direct meanings, values and practices of territory. Owing to the mobility of youth, territory is not solely determined by those who occupy the material environment. Members of a youth cultural group 'carry' territorial practices when moving from the classroom to corridor, or from street to public house. Territory involves certain forms of behaviour such as fighting and ritual insult, and a youth cultural group which occupies an area other than its own will operate its specific territorial practices.

Territorial movement refers to the symbolic and physical construction and usage of space by individuals and groups. Territorial mobility exists because a group controls territory and through movement can occupy new or different space. It is possible to see territoriality in action. For example, in a school a youth cultural group can move inside and outside available school space and determine what occurs. Dominance over a social space means the control of activities which occur and the meaning of such activities. It is crucial to the operation of territorial practice that the other participants already know the extent of the territorial power possessed by the youth cultural group. Robins and Cohen (1978) maintain that the functions of territoriality are linked to the area in which one lives. In the case of youth cultural groups there are territorial practices which are operated as the group moves from and to different and changing situations.

In the study here, both the mod boys and the new wave girls possessed different territorial space but both possessed the capacity to cross boundaries where different types of territorial practices were required, in order to dominate and control the social space. The youth cultural group's ability to define and operate a set of territorial practices is more important than its physical presence as a means of holding territory. In other words, a public display by a group who holds territory which is described in terms of its end result, such as confrontation or violence, directs attention away from the internal relations of the group, its structure, resources and context in the local community. Overemphasis on the public face of a youth cultural group's territorial clash ignores or does not allow for an understanding of how the group conducts its day to day relations.

In contrast, it is possible to understand moments of conflict as arising from times of specialised rituals, for example Bank Holiday vacations at seaside resorts or local derby football matches and also from situations where territory is neutral, ill defined or has not been appropriated by a youth cultural group. Here a challenge may be offered, but this would not be a time of ritual. Such confrontations whether non-ritual or ritual are defined by the parameters of capture or flight and result from differences of identity and territory.

Signature

The discussion of youth cultural forms has so far moved through a series of analyses of different features of the youth cultural forms: specialised positions, social relations of the face and the specialised semiotic. An inevitable consequence of this analysis has been the fragmentation of the sense of unity, coherence and identity which members of these forms experience. Further, from a more theoretical point of view, we have no means of talking about these forms other than through the features distinguished or the names these forms give to themselves. I shall now introduce a concept which it is hoped will integrate the different features of the analysis and at the same time point to the conditions of unity, recognition and legitimacy operating in the youth cultural forms themselves.

The concept of signature

The signature is a specialised multiple signifier indicating the lived practice and history of a youth cultural group. Its practices, positions, powers and relations are condensed in what I shall call the signature. I have argued that youth cultural form can be regarded as positions in a youth cultural field and that these positions can be defined in terms of oppositions and complementaries (Bourdieu 1984). Signature refers to the distinctive, recognisable and legitimate realisation of the style or, more formally, to the legitimate range of practices of any one position in the field or to that of an emergent challenger.

In the case of a painting, the signature enables the image to be named and placed in a historical and contemporary position with respect to other images. The signature confers legitimacy on the image as being authentic but sometimes this is not necessary, as identity may be conferred by recognition of marks, the quality of paint, brush strokes, texture etc. In the case of the youth cultural group there is no one author and there is no one image although there is, as in painting, a development of style. As in the field of art so with youth cultural forms, there are fierce disputes over authenticity and legitimacy and over 'selling out'. And just as in art so the youth cultural forms recognition and identity can be at the metonymic level; a social feature of dress, a gesture, movement or word. Similarly, as in art, the youth cultural form signatures may become marketable commodities (Benjaim 1970).

A youth cultural signature enables a style to be identified within its own history and the history of the field of youth cultural style. Such recognition is revealed by the relationship between the degree of constancy of the style and its integrity over time. Signature guarantees authenticity, legitimacy, even authority and so enables a style to be placed in its historical context as well as its contemporary positions. A signature serves as a signifier for a particular position and refers to the unity, inner coherence and speciality of the style. In the same way that the signature of a great painter by itself intensifies the impact of a painting so the signature of a youth cultural style focuses the style's effect. In the former case there is an author but in the latter case there is no author only a collective sign written as a collective name; punk, skinhead, or mod. The signature enables both members of the group and other groups in the youth cultural field (together with singletons) to identify the inner coherence of their positions, practices and specialised semiotic.

Since the 1950s there have been a limited number of positions within the field, from teddy boys and beats to the contemporary punks and ravers. What factors establish the legitimacy of a specialised group and sustain a youth cultural signature? Firstly, a youth cultural style requires a specialised semiotic. A youth cultural style is not simply the public display of an image, it involves the development of a specialised semiotic practice and informal rules of communication and rituals. A youth cultural group develops internal specialised positions which regulate its stylistic practices and social relations to ensure both collective equality and its authenticity. Secondly, the youth cultural group has a specialised musical style. The bands which typify the musical style influence the cultural style of the youth group and the band members may come to be regarded as authors of the semiotic of the youth cultural style.

The signature expresses creative potential and energy, it summarises the practices of the youth cultural group and its contemporary relations to other groups. In the earlier sections I identified the specialised positions which monitor the signature: those of the symbolic forms, the style leader and the cultural ransacker.

Three temporal aspects of signature

I shall distinguish temporal aspects of the signature, in terms of whether it is an historical, a variant or an emergent signature.

Historical signature

The historical signature refers to youth cultural styles and practices from the past such as rocker, mod, punk and others. These specialised styles were emergent signatures at the precise time of their arrival but have acquired historical legitimacy, authority and authenticity. The historical signature is relayed through a myth of origin. For youth the style has a history and within that history exist levels of heritage. It is important to assess the coherence and integrity of a style across time because the ideological basis and positions may alter.

A youth cultural group will emerge as a spectacular style with multiple signifiers. That is, the style is realised through a wide range of characteristics. However, over time the elements of the style may undergo a process of selection, reduction or hardening. Thus there may well be a selective focusing of the original force and potential. Crucial factors which cause a simplification of the style may well be a consequence of the mass marketing of the style as a commodity.

Two processes which affect the historical signature are dilution and incorporation. Dilution refers to the gradual reduction over time in the range of the elements of the original core group, for example mod becomes reduced to short hair, loafers, Fred Perry and a parka, or skinhead to just 'number one' cropped hair, stained Levis and DM's. The youth cultural style begins to lose its range and subtlety. Incorporation refers to naturalisation and domestication of a style. Concretely, both processes can occur together as the youth cultural style and musical style are utilised in commodity advertisements.

However, we should point out that there is often a dynamic relation between the fixing or freezing of the style over time and the bricoleur activities of the youth group members. On the one hand a youth cultural style may receive public attention which makes it accessible, but on the other hand this does not necessarily neutralise the youth cultural group's power of innovation. Public appropriation of elements relating to a style does not render the style inert because the potential of the youth cultural group's signature does not rest on any one manifestation.

Variant signature

The clearest empirical examples of a variant youth cultural signature can be illustrated by the mod revival of 1978/80, the rebirth and update of the Ted style by the rockabilly rebels, and the new style 'Oi' skinheads in the early 1980s. These signatures are variations of a historical practice generated by a specialised position in the field. A variation does not indicate that a style is 'second hand' or non-authentic, only that the signature does not perfectly match the original from which it derives. The style of a variant signature is likely to be more determined because of its past historical context.

A variant signature is a reaction point between the past historical context of a style and the contemporary arena of the local context. Variants are the means whereby signatures are revitalised and made relevant to changed conditions, practices and economies. In general a variant style is bounded by its past and there will be less local significant stylistic innovation. The variant signature is likely to be strongly regulated by commodity forms, such as musical artist products, and to be more sensitive to media direction and orientation.

This is not to say that the variant signature will not add new features to the original style but clearly its basic attributes are defined by its history and those will be dominant. The variant arises from a specific context which revivifies the style to express contemporary relevance and to relate to the changed social and economic experience of the members. The impact of youth unemployment has influenced the relations and practices of the youth cultural group. On the one hand unemployment places a barrier between stylistic consumption and display through lack of work and money. On the other hand, youth style or practices may not be halted by lack of finance. During the youth riots of the 1980s the direction of attack has not been the town hall, DHSS office, police station or banks, but, as Hebdige (1982) points out, "the video and hi-fi shops, the boutiques and the record shops" (p.18).

A variant signature moves between the past and present and will be influenced by new technology, eg. video, CD, specialised fanzines, computer networks and other developments which may occur in future in the presentation and communication of a style, and also by changes in socio-economic conditions such as high unemployment.

Emergent signature

An emergent youth cultural signature represents an attempt to appropriate and develop a new specialised position within the field. The condition for an emergent signature to arise is that it must be in potential opposition to positions already existing within the field. An emergent signature will seek and gather new and varied accessories, designs and clothes contrasting with, and as an alternative to, what is already present. In the field of youth culture there will be opposition towards an emergent position as it will be perceived as a threat by other positions. The emergent signature will have to promote its difference to establish its legitimacy and its opposition will be the basis of its authority and authenticity.

The field of youth culture is an arena of opposition and difference. An emergent signature's spectacular features become the cutting edge of its originality which rips into existing styles to create and re-create struggle between all positions. An emergent signature scorns the historical and at the same time establishes conditions for vitality within the field. This in turn creates opportunities for a number of variant signatures to develop because there is no one dominant style.

For a position to develop and maintain itself within the field, the emergent signature requires youth cultural groups with their own specialised practices, positions and rituals of communication and with the development of a specific musical style. An emergent style will be multi-contextual, have a significant local orientation and be less directed and influenced by the media than other signatures. The signature will be read by rival, oppositional and complementary youth cultural groups as a summary of meanings, practices, rituals, identity and purpose. The creation of an emergent signature establishes a condition where historical signatures have to reassert their legitimacy in the face of a change in the field of youth culture. For example since punk arrived in the late 1970s, youth cultural styles of the past have enjoyed a new, although often only momentary lease of life during the 1980s and 1990s. An emergent signature announces its own legitimacy but also sets up the conditions for previous historical signatures both to be revitalised and to develop variant signatures for a different generation of youth.

3   Patriarchal games and ritual jousting

Introduction

This chapter presents an analysis of social, sexual and cultural relations, conflict and opposition between the new wave girls and the mod boys. The aim is to provide an interpretation of the way in which patriarchy affects the relations and practices of the two groups both as members of an academic elite within school, and as members of promenading youth cultural groups. The chapter is arranged in four parts. Section one presents data from an informal discussion between the two groups in the careers office at school. Section two presents data from a discussion with both groups in the house of a new wave girl. Section three examines the patterns of communication and interaction in the data by applying the theory of social forms and specialised positions. Section four is a summary of how the two youth groups are differently positioned by patriarchy.

The participants and their specialised positions in the first discussion were as follows:-

Mod boys: specialised position

Paul: style leader (SL)
Rich: style leader (SL)
Keef: peer group
      spokesperson (PGS)

New wave girls: specialised position

Clare: style leader (SL)
Cathy: peer group consolidator (PGC)
Sally: peer group spokesperson (PGS)
Debbie: cultural ransacker (CR)

At the outset there are two important differences to note between the groups; the girls' group is bigger by one, and the boys group lacks the specialised positions of CR and PGC. The presence and absence of specialised positions in each group may give rise to different forms of communication both within and between groups.

This discussion took place after I had shared a variety of experiences, both private and public, with each group. In general, the only time when these two groups were together in school, excluding lessons, was at break in the fifth year area, and then only briefly. Over a period of weeks I had observed and taken part in many of these interactions. I thought it may prove useful to bring the groups together for a longer discussion. The intention was to arrange a conversation to see relations and negotiations in action, within and between the two dominant groups in the school.

Potency and parents

The beginning of the discussion shows the girls at ease, where they have twice demonstrated their own sexual assertiveness. The boys are a little unsure because they are in such close proximity to these girls; here Rich identifies an opportunity to gain some sympathy and focuses the conversation on himself.

21 Rich	Everybody takes the piss out of my nose . I don't understand what the joke is with my nose.
22 Debbie	Oh Rich, we don't want to hear about your nose.
23 Rich	OH SHUT UP , Debbie. It's a social gathering you OLD BIDDY.
24 Cathy	Do you remember when we used to have bike rides and that ?
25 Sally	That party. Did you enjoy it? I thought -
26 Cathy	It was really good . Your mum kept coming in and checking under the sheets.
27 All girls	Laughter
28 Sally	I was just fighting to come (to reach orgasm : SJB) Everyone was under the blankets and mum kept coming in and lifting the blankets and looking underneath to make sure no one was doing anything.
29 Keef	What do you mean by doing anything?
30 Debbie	Oh! What do you think ? Oh!
31 Rich	You thick twat (to Keef: SJB)

Rich expects the girls to respond to his feigned feelings of insecurity about his nose. But they do not and he becomes aggressive. In turn, the girls exclude the boys by talking among themselves. The girls' unity is assured in their celebratory laughter and asserted collective outrageous behaviour. They demonstrate their power and skill in using their sexuality openly as a symbolic resource of exclusion, opposition and independence.   The talk of sexual relations continues but this time the boys attempt to gain the upper hand.

33 Keef   They all seem - parents - to want to get in on it , you know, they don't want to leave you alone. Want to join in. They think you are bringing them (girlfriend: SJB) home, so they can share them and all.

34 Sally   They (my boyfriends: SJB) always play with my brother. He's always disturbing us. He starts nattering and gets his bloody game and everything .... My mum just walks in through the door. Doesn't knock, that's most embarrassing.

35 Keef   Because if you've got someone, you can't take them upstairs with you or in your bedroom. Okay it might sound a bit bad but you've got a record player.

36 Rich   Yeah

37 Keef   You want to doss up there so you have got to take them somewhere and they (parent: SJB) just go fucking mad.

38 Sally   They do keep coming in even now!

39 Debbie   I've been banned from taking boys into my bedroom.

40 Sally   So have I !

41 Cathy   Aaaahhhh , aaaahhhhh (imitating sexual sounds: SJB)

42 All girls Laughter

43 Rich   You think , at your age , you shouldn't be doing it at sixteen, if you get boys in your bedroom!

44 All   Laughter

The girls are asserting their equal right to take boys into their bedroom but Keef makes the context and relation ambiguous. The girls are indicating their independence and sexual development. They are asserting their potency in an explicit manner especially through the cinematic phrase of being 'banned' from allowing boys into their bedrooms. Both groups are now playing with the theme of sexuality, each trying to surpass each other's expression of potency.

45	SJB	What about taking the girl into the bedroom , upstairs?
46	Keef	That's unheard of.
47	Debbie	Yeah! Exactly. I live in a bungalow!
48	SJB	They don't get suspicious or anything?
49	Keef	DON'T GET SUSPICIOUS (said in disbelief: SJB)
50	Clare	Have you ever tried it Keef?
51	Keef	'The old cloak!'
52	Clare	No. Really have you ever been upstairs together?
53	Keef	Yeah.
54	Clare	What did your mum say?
55	Keef	She does her NUT.
56	Clare	What afterwards or while?
57	All girls	Laughter
58	Keef	The first time she goes like -
59	All	Laughter continues.

The girls have ritually humiliated the mod boys peer group spokesperson. Clare's insistent questioning hints at the possibility that Keef is not experiencing full sexual relations with his girlfriend and Keef is unable to tell the complete story because of the girls laughter; the boys are then forced to join in.

Views on marriage and employment

A result of the girls' display of potency, and of bodily opposition, is that it makes the boys a little unsettled. In an attempt to prevent the conversation from deteriorating I introduced the topic of marriage.

60	SJB	What about marriage then?
61	Keef	Whipping
62	Debbie	You're just there to be screwed!
63	Rich	Shut up YOU OLD...
64	Keef	Took the words right out of my mouth.
65	Rich	YOU SULKY COW . You really make me sick you do, you really are bad.
66	Debbie	NO I'M NOT. FUCK OFF. One day a week I'm usually miserable and that's usually Monday.
67	Rich	Not it's not it's Friday, bit of Saturday and Sunday
68	Debbie	OH PISS OFF. You're not exactly like cheerfulness are

	you.
69 SJB	What about women having no careers and the idea that they should just get married?
70 Cathy	CRAP
71 Debbie	Well do you mean at our age - you talking about?
72 Cathy	If it's pointed at you I don't sort of believe in it. But if Debbie sort of turned round and said to me well you know I'm gonna get married and have children and that, then it's up to her. It's up to the individual. But if it's pointed at me I would not go out and do it.
73 Debbie	I probably would get married in the end. But I'm going to do -
74 Sally	There's too many opportunities for girls now anyway.
75 Debbie	Well I think so.
76 Keef	The depression. You can go on the game ! Work in a massage parlour!
77 Paul	There's not many around though.
78 Debbie	I don't know!
79 Paul	Because it's the depression about at the moment.
80 Keef	The recession. It was the depression last week Paul!
81 Debbie	I think at the moment right , it's like there is unemployment, that's because there is women taking the jobs that men could take and bring in the money (interrupted: SJB)
82 Keef	YEAH, THAT'S FUCKING RIGHT
83 Paul	All women do at home is make cups of tea and talk all day long.
84 Keef	That's their day duties Paul!
85 Debbie	While there isn't men working women , okay , can go out to work and the men can stay at home. But it's the man (interrupted: SJB)
86 Keef	WE ARE NOT GOING TO GET ANYWHERE IN THE CONVERSATION TALKING ABOUT EQUALITY .
87 Debbie	SHUT UP KEEF
88 Rich	I'm not talking about equality.
89 Paul	The only things that women are good for is, like...
90 Keef	BURNING!
91 Paul	Is making cups of tea right , a bit of the other and someone to take your aggro out on.
92 Debbie	Oh for God's sake
93 SJB	Do you think that most men are chauvinist?
94 All girls	YES, YES, YES.

95 Cathy	I don't think they are UNDERNEATH.
96 Keef	Ssssschhh. Shut up.
97 Cathy	No. I think they just do it when other boys are around.
98 Clare	He's a big softy really!
99 Cathy	Yeah
100 All girls	Laughter
101 Sally	It's all show.
102 Debbie	Yes he is!
103 All girls	Laughter
104 Rich	Ar , ar , ar . A big softy like that bogroll (reference to a TV advertisement: SJB).
105 Keef	Is there a big softy in your family!
106 All girls/boys	Laughter
107 Rich	I think women are impractical.
108 Clare	No they're not. I think women are more practical.
109 Rich	Oh rubbish.
110 Debbie	If anyone marries Paul. I warn you. He smells.
111 Rich	You (i.e. men: SJB) come home with your wages and you (i.e. women: SJB) say I want my hair done. You don't give women too much money.
112 Clare	Yeah but that's only some, you don't...(interrupted: SJB)
113 Rich	SHUT UP YOU.
114 Clare	NO. Your mum doesn't say that does she?
115 Debbie	No . My mum doesn't say that , my mum just hits my dad.
116 Clare	I know . But your mum (to Rich: SJB) doesn't go out every week and have her hair permed.
117 Rich	No.
118 Clare	WELL THEN . You ' d go to the hairdressers if you had the money.
119 SJB	What if women can have children and a career they...
120 Keef	At this age?
121 Debbie	No, at any age.
122 Cathy	AT ANY BLOODY AGE, YOUR POINT OF VIEW FOR CHRIST'S SAKE.
123 Keef	I don't know.
124 Debbie	Yeah, he's a male chauvinist.
125 Keef	I don't think that it's right . All the unemployment. If all the women went out for work.
126 Paul	They're too fanatical, women, though aren't they.

127 Keef	All that burn your bra business and all this.
128 Paul	When I got my scooter my mother wouldn't let me bring it in the house.
129 All	Laughter
130 Clare	I suppose you expect her to make it a cup of tea!
131 All	Laughter
132 Rich	Take it to bed with you.
133 Keef	Check its oil, take its temperature.
134 Debbie	When it overheats.
135 All	Laughter

The opening moments of the discussion on marriage turn into personal exchanges where Debbie is attacked by both Rich and Keef. The boys' aggression is fuelled by Debbie's comment: 'just there to be screwed'; the challenge is not lost on Rich who resorts to the stereotype of the miserable/frigid 'old cow'. Forcibly, Cathy interrupts to assert that as individuals girls should have the choice whether to marry or gain a career. Both options are seen as an equal vocation, although they give precedence to the latter owing to there being more 'opportunities for girls now'. The boys respond through sexist aggression with rituals of violence; in addition to their allusions to pornography ('whipping'), they imply that the only career for women is prostitution('the game'), that is, that women can only be viewed, and function, through their sexuality. Debbie uses irony to combat the boys fantasies and then attempts to introduce her own formal argument against discrimination against women in employment. Her overall argument is that the fact that men are out of work during recession provides an opportunity for change in social roles since women are in the position of supporting the family. However, her argument rests initially upon a masculinist argument that it is women's entrance into the labour market that has caused male unemployment. This weakness is immediately seized upon by Keef who interrupts and thus prevents her from making her full point. When she does come to the main point of her argument she is again blocked by Keef's shouting which functions to submerge her argument rather than answer it. Here Keef's challenge to the girls takes the form of ritual play. He starts to swear and demand that the topic of conversation on equality be changed. During this exchange Keef interrupts Debbie twice as she attempts to formulate her argument (See Dove 1983). Furthermore on four other occasions the boys explicitly interrupt to prevent the girls from speaking.

The full extent of the boys' promenade of violence is shown in Keef's answer to Paul's question, that the only thing women are good for is 'BURNING'. The boys' argument receives further support in Paul's stereotypical assumptions about women and housework. He claims that women are unqualified to enter the pre-defined male labour market because they belong in a triangle of female dependence; servant, sexual object and 'punch bag'.

In this quotation and throughout the chapter it is possible to see that the girls sometimes take on the boys' language of sexual dominance and use it against them to try to defuse the basis of male dominance. The boys cannot win arguments by mere assertion of their masculinity and sexuality, as illustrated by the girls powerful use of ridicule. The girls' capacity to use the strategy of jousting, makes the boys redirect their strategy to formulate domestic traps. Here they construct 'super' sex role strategies which deflect the girls from speaking about female independence. Instead they are forced to address absurd sexual stereotypes. The girls again use irony to counter the boys creation of domestic traps and the girls are able in some degree to reverse the games in their favour.

The boys' combination of violent expression and sexist abuse is directly undermined by the girls (Cathy and Clare) who maintain that the boys are 'softies'. Cathy breaks the ritualism of the boys by asserting that 'underneath' they are not really as aggressive as their public face behaviour suggests. Both Keef and Rich accept the switch. The boys' response is to switch to a strategy of formal argument, asserting that women are 'impractical' and 'fanatical'.

Cathy becomes aggressive at the boys apparent attempt to divert the conversation;her shouting forces them to return to the focus of the argument. Debbie labels these boys as chauvinists. The boys' games are working 'to wind up' the girls but this does not disturb the girls' solidarity. Keef follows this by invoking media stereotypes and the 'irrationality' of the Women's Liberation Movement ('Burn your bra'), to reinforce Paul's assertion of fanaticism as further support for the exclusion of women from the labour process. Here Paul seizes an opportunity to show the fanaticism of women by reference to his mother's reaction to him bringing his scooter in the house. Unfortunately, this argument backfires and it is his behaviour which is seen by the whole group as inappropriate.

One of the mod boys introduces a narrative of male potency to restore the male image of control.

141 Paul	I didn't get too drunk on Saturday night, did I? My drinking ended halfway through the night.
142 Rich	Ar, run out of money as usual!
143 Debbie	No, he got banned. Someone split on him.
144 Paul	I was in the Red Lion with Dave the other night and he got chucked out and I didn't, did not. Then his OLD BID (mother: SJB) blames me if there's any arguing and that. She went and grassed me up. These two women said "if they see me in the pub again"...that's what the landlord said to me, these two women, her and Norah.
145 Debbie	Nnnnoooooorrrrraaaaahhhhhhh!
146 Paul	She only lives two doors away.
147 Keef	She's FUCKING FLIPPED
148 Paul	She was feeding me stout when I was about five years old. They said if they saw me in there again, they were going to ring the police up and say there's underage drinking.
149 Keef	IT'S A BASTARD THAT IS. THAT'S ALL THAT WOMEN ARE GOOD FOR SEE, SNIDEY GRASSING UP WHEN THEY CAN'T FACE IT.
150 Paul	FANATICAL
151 Keef	PROVES THE POINT. END OF CONVERSATION. Another subject.
152 Clare	No. They wouldn't know... They are just a couple.
153 Keef	They base a couple on the majority.
154 Debbie	You can't judge one person by everyone else.
155 Keef	No. Everyone is different.
156 Rich	NO. Statistically there are more car crashes involving women.
157 All girls	Ha, ha, ha, ha, ha, ha, ha, ha, (forced laughter: SJB)
158 Debbie	My mum is an excellent driver. My mum, to get to London ...
159 Cathy	So is my mum.
160 Paul	My sister took a driving lesson and the bloke who was taking her jumped out of the car.
161 All	Laughter

162 Keef	My mum's the best one. The instructor goes to her, you're wasting your time and your money, and my time - she hit another car in the high street a pig (police: SJB) she reversed into him. Women just can't drive.
163 Paul	They're too highly strung aren't they.
164 Clare	NO. Don't be silly.
165 Debbie	Everyone is highly strung. I'm not!
166 Rich	Ar, ar, ar, no, you old biddy you really are.
167 Debbie	No. I'm not. Sioux is highly strung. (Conversation stops for a moment as the telephone rings. I answer the call which is for the careers officer who is out of school this afternoon. The conversation begins again: SJB)
168 Keef	Inequality!
169 Rich	What are we talking about that for?
170 Keef	That's what our conversation is based round.
171 Rich	Yeah, let's change it.
172 Paul	Yeah. Well they're not for a start are they - equal?
173 Keef	What...
174 Rich	Let's talk about BOOTS and WHIPS.
175 Keef	You're not exactly weight lifters.
176 Sally	IT'S A LOT OF BALL CRAP. WE ARE THE SAME. SHIT! BLOODY BODIES, FOUR LIMBS, AREN'T WE? THERE'S NOTHING DIFFERENT BETWEEN US.
177 Keef	Yeah, But there's strength.
178 Rich	Yes there is.
179 Sally	There's not.
180 Rich	I've got a willy and you haven't.
181 Cathy	Ar, ar, mine broke off when I was three!
182 All girls	Laughter
183 Debbie	But some girls are brainier than you aren't they - Rose, Kerry and that.
184 Keef	Ah but they're hippies.
185 Debbie	Yeah, but they're more brainier than you, aren't they?
186 Keef	They work.
187 Debbie	Yeah.
188 Rich	Who's that?
189 All girls	Well? well?
190 Debbie	She wants to get something with her life.
191 Rich	Who does?
192 Keef	But she can't because there aren't equal opportunities

		for women.
193	Clare	Of course there is.
194	Paul	Everybody realises, don't take on a woman I mean BLOODY HELL!
195	Clare	Would you ever get married Paul? Would you expect your wife to sit at home and make you a cup of tea and get your slippers?
196	Paul	But that's all they do anyway housewives.
197	Clare	I bet she wouldn't.
199	All girls	NO.
198	Debbie	My mum does not. My mum goes out to work.
203	Sally	If you look at my mum and dad. My dad don't let anybody else do the washing up because he's scared my mum is going to leave, you know, bits on the plates. He does the washing up, the hoovering and everything.
204	Paul	She don't do her job properly, does she?
205	Clare	OH NO.
206	Debbie	My mum's not houseproud at all. She couldn't give a fuck about her house.
207	Rich	It's her job though.
208	Debbie	If the Queen came she would say fuck it, let ...
209	Cathy	It's your dad that is houseproud.
210	Rich	If the Queen came round she'd - "cup of tea ma-lady" and all that.
211	Debbie	My mum would offer her a cup of tea, but she, if my mum knew a week in advance that she was coming...
212	Paul	Not even a sherry!
213	Debbie	Oh no, she does drink sherry. My mum wouldn't clean the house up at all. I mean she never goes into my bedroom, she's frightened what she might find. See!
214	Rich	I bet she would clean the house up.
215	Debbie	I bet you she would not.
216	Keef	I bet. Right, I'll phone her up and say...
217	Cathy	She does do it.
218	Debbie	I've seen my mum hoover about three times. Our house is a mess, but it's not dirty.
219	Sally	My dad does it all.

In this episode the boys change their strategy but maintain the attack affirming the basic inadequacy of women. Here they attempt to show women as betrayers and seducers incapable of honesty, trust and loyalty, implied to be the qualities of 'mates'. The boys assume that the pub is masculine territory and this attitude reinforces their argument against women. The girls argue against generalising from a specific case and here Keef agrees: both groups accept the importance of individual difference. This undermines the force of the first argument so the boys switch to a more formal argument to support their position; this time the subject is driving. They again try to establish female dependence arising out of their inability to drive, which they define as a male skill. The girls manage to combat this argument by asserting their mothers as model drivers. But here the boys introduce elements of a game strategy, exaggerating the failure of a mother and a sister as examples of women being 'highly strung', thus incapable of driving. Here the girls' unity is weakened when Debbie discredits Sioux by stating she is 'highly strung' in contrast to herself. This potential moment of lost integrity dissolves as the conversation is halted by a telephone call. The call for the Careers Officer reminds everyone where they are.

The boys attempt to change the subject of conversation. Rich switches to the use of pornographic images and Keef speaks about strength. The girls understand strength to be an ideological concept used against them; Sally says that biologically girls and boys are the same and thus possess the same capacity for strength (Holland 1985). Here Rich introduces the penis as a final element to support the argument about male strength. However, Cathy challenges the male symbol of authority through her absurd comment that her penis broke off when she was three. This joke serves to cut the boys down to size. Her humour is an attack on male control (Douglas 1968). The subversive effect of the comment permits the girls to shift the conversation from a privileging of the body to a privileging of the mind. Debbie invokes some of the boffin girls to support her argument that girls can be more intelligent than boys. Keef does not counter at the level of ability but at the level of youth cultural style. He discredits the boffin girls because 'they're Hippies'. Debbie admits this, although Keef's comment does not lessen the weight of her argument because his attack is on style not on academic ability. His second response asserts that it is irrelevant whether girls are more intelligent implying that it will not get them anywhere since there are not equal opportunities for women. The boys ridicule the girls social and career aspirations, and suggest it is futile to demand liberation. The girls' response to this is to reverse the argument against the boys, by asserting that men are involed in domestic labour. The girls use their own family experience to point out that men do undertake domestic labour in the home.

Introduction to the second discussion

The basic difference between the first and the second discussion which follows is location. The second talk is at Cathy's mother's house. The new wave girls and mod boys sit in the lounge on large soft chairs or stretch comfortably on the carpet floor. Everyone is reasonably close and they all appear relaxed. The participants at the second discussion were as follows:

New wave girls: specialised position		*Mod boys: specialised position*	
Clare:	style leader (SL)	Rich:	style leader (SL)
Sally:	peer group spokesperson (PGS)	Keef:	peer group spokesperson (PGS)
Sioux:	peer group spokesperson (PGS)	Hat:	cultural ransacker (CR)
Debbie:	cultural ransacker (CR)		
Cathy:	peer group consolidator (PGC)		

There are two important differences in terms of the people present at the second discussion. The new wave girls are joined by Sioux (PGS). In the mod boys group Hat (CR) has replaced Paul (SL), this means that they have three specialised positions present whereas in the first discussion there were only two specialised positions. As in the first talk, the girls outnumber the boys but this time by two.The discussion took place at one of the girl's homes because there was no suitable venue available in school.

Sexual knowledge

The early part of the talk took the form of a ritual play and dramatic irony where the girls gave the boys tea and both groups attempted to cadge cigarettes. It is clear from the boys' reluctance to speak that they feel themselves to be in an uncomfortable location. They are subject to the girls' control, so in order to provide a basis of security they begin to talk amongst themselves on crash helmets and then Keef initiates the discussion proper. At the same time there was a sense that the girls were conducting an experiment on the boys to see how they would react at close quarters with them.

255 Hat	I've got four crash helmets.
256 Rich	Keef, do you want to buy my green crash hat for ten pounds ?
257 Keef	No I'm getting a new one for ten pounds, that's my old man, he has asked someone . I'm not being funny.
258 Rich	They're great for parties, great for discos, wear your own crash hat.
259 Hat	I got a fibre glass helmet the other day.
260 Debbie	Oh really!
261 Hat	Full face one.
262 Keef	Now he'll be a right speed king won't he? .... Who saw the film last night?
263 Clare	Oh we kept talking about that.
264 Sally	Where he sucked her tit. Oh it was gross! It grossed me out man!
265 Keef	What about the pig . The pig in the bed, urgh, urgh, urgh (imitating sexual noises: SJB).
266 Cathy	Oh I thought it was brilliant.
267 Keef	I thought it was Paul (mod boy: SJB) quivering weren't it, like he was having an orgasm.
268 Debbie	Yeah.
269 Sally	How much did they pay you ? (to Keef: SJB) I saw on Friday night Saturday morning (TV programme: SJB). It was when Toyah was doing it.
270 Keef	STOP ! er... Friday night, Saturday morning. They got some Deep Throat, some clips of the film.
271 Sally	What's that?
272 Keef	It's been banned. It's by Linda Lovelace.
273 Sally	What's it about?
274 All	Laughter
275 Hat	Sex.
276 Keef	What does it sound like? DEEP THROAT
277 All	Laughter
278 Debbie	Oh Sally!
279 Keef	Gobbling (oral sex: SJB)
280 Sioux	Conversation ' s REALLY gripping (bored tone: SJB)
281 Keef	Has the Humanities teacher split up with his wife ?
282 Sioux	No.
283 Debbie	Yeah

284 Cathy	She hasn't left but they're split up.
285 Sally	Are they getting a divorce?
286 Sioux	Well he hasn't left, his car's still parked outside the house.
287 Cathy	Nor has she, I know, I mean but they're split up. They are getting a divorce.
288 Sioux	I was going to say, because ...
289 Keef	How do you know?
290 Sioux	Because with what Phil told me they weren't living together.
292 Sioux	Yeah, we went past and another teacher's car was round there.
293 Debbie	What Miss Shaw?
294 Sally	No
295 Keef	No, he wouldn't be fucking stupid enough to knock her off. She'd talk all the way through it.
296 Rich	She's nice! The only thing I don't like about her is she's got smelly armpits that smell, and she scratches her crotch.
297 Sally	Urrrrr. Mr. Checkland he's a lecher.
298 Sioux	Urrrr, Mr. Smith smells of BO.
299 Sally	Oh I like him. He's really nice.
300 Cathy	Mr. Smith!
301 Sioux	Oh I hate him.
302 Keef	He's a FUCKING GAY.
311 Rich	I'm sorry but I just can't stand him.
312 Cathy	Well so are you! But we don't all say that you're horrible, do we?
313 Keef	Yeah, we keep it to ourselves.
314 All boys	Laughter

The boys' conversation on crash helmets has successfully excluded the girls. The item, being part of their dress, is a signifier of their specialised semiotic. Part of its potency is the ability to transform the wearer into a 'right speed king'.

The conversation starts properly when Keef raises the subject of the previous night's film in an attempt to capture the discursive space by challenging the girls to discuss openly the sexual theme of the film. The girls show that this is no matter for embarrassment. They are very explicit whereas Keef who initiated this episode hides behind metaphors. Furthermore, Clare states that the girls have already discussed the film, suggesting that they are not naive on matters of sexuality. Keef takes up Sally's challenge, making more direct sexual references, interrupting her and explicitly referring to a pornographic film; this can be understood as a demonstration of the boys' sexual display techniques. He continues, specifying the oral sex in the film, but Sioux's response is made in a tone which has the effect of humiliating the boys. Her deflating criticism, that their 'conversation's REALLY gripping' and her 'bored' tone of voice, imply that the boys lack potency and are inadequate; unlike them she is not seduced by such pornographic fantasies.

The boys' body reference of male sexual pleasure receives no further elaboration as the girls fail to respond; they seem unimpressed. The boys have been silenced. Under pressure Keef drops the conversation on the display of male potency and is forced to offer the girls an opportunity to speak about a real sexual relationship not a fantasised one.

In the ensuing discussion both Rich and Keef attack a female teacher; Keef asserts that another male teacher would have to be "stupid" to sleep with her, not because it would be immoral but because she is sexually undesirable, and Rich attacks her for a lack of personal hygiene. Sally and Sioux retaliate by referring equally disparagingly to two male teachers. Keef deflects the symbolic criticism of the male group; his claim that the teacher is a homosexual, implies for the purpose of his argument that he is not a 'real man'. Here the boys regain strength and their laughter is an expression of this. They are now in a position to reassert their male potency through an oppositional stand to male homosexuality as equated with impotence.

Views on masturbation

In the previous section the boys, because of their rigid understanding of masculinity, defined gay men as not 'real' men, by definition lacking heterosexual potency. In the following section the boys try again to display their heterosexual potency to the girls, this time by their elaboration of a particular boy's toilet behaviour which is seen as sexually ambiguous.

315 Keef   Hat said to me this morning that he (another pupil: SJB) was just standing there, you know and, DIRTY GREAT PRICK.

316 Debbie   He stands there and what?

317 Hat   I told him the other day about Frank Wilson. When he

	has a piss in the toilet, he stands there, right, for about ten minutes , and he's just standing there , pissing.
318 Keef	He's not pissing.
319 Hat	And Keef went in there today , right , and goes "you know you told me about Wilson". He goes, "he stands there and he's not pissing". It's hanging there. He's standing there holding it right and he's just standing there and nothing's coming out.
320 SJB	Who is he ? (This boy was unknown to me: SJB)
321 Keef	He's in our class.
322 Sally	He's a bit weird though anyway.
323 Keef	He's uuur, rrrrrr (sound is accompanied by a gesture indicating a 'limp wrist': SJB). I'LL BREAK HIS HEAD.
324 Sioux	He is weird. He's mum's weird.
325 SJB	He's in the upper ability band isn't he?
326 Sioux	Yes, he's really weird.
327 Hat	I'M TELLING YOU RIGHT . HE'S JUST STANDING THERE.
328 Keef	Hat asked me...
329 Hat	NOTHING COMING OUT. He's sort of standing there.
330 Rich	I think that all relates back to how you kept taking the mickey out of him for having a circumcised willy.
331 Sally	Has he?
332 Debbie	That's not his fault.
333 Sally	In circumcise what does circumcise?
334 Sioux	It's supposed to be cleaner isn't it.
335 Debbie	Yeah
336 SJB	It's also done where the skin starts to grow too large.
337 Rich	Sioux said it's much cleaner and much nicer , that was in the restaurant that was.
338 Hat	Shane this is a good subject of conversation . Do boys wank? (slightly threatened: SJB)
339 Debbie	Do they? All of them?
340 Sioux	I reckon all boys do!
341 Sally	Like my brother today. When I went home, mum, she was talking about my brother, he had a hard on. I said, 'Oh yeah'. She said, "he has one every time in the morning".
342 Rich	W h o ?
343 Sioux	When he wakes up in the morning.
344 Rich	Who said that? What was you trying to say?
345 Sally	Nothing.

346 Rich	That every boy gets a hard on in the morning.
347 Sally	No.
348 Rich	I never do.
349 Sally	No? not...
350 Sioux	Well there must be something wrong with you then.
351 All girls	Laughter
352 Debbie	Do you think there's anything wrong with self masturbation then?
353 Cathy	I don't think there is.
354 Keef	Not if you're locked up in prison.
355 Sioux	NO. There is nothing wrong with it.
356 Keef	In prison though there's gays or thinking about his woman.
357 Rich	Just that I wouldn't do it and I wouldn't do it, and I wouldn't do it, and I wouldn't do it and I wouldn't do it and I can do it (Almost sung, flirtatiously: SJB)
358 All	Laughter.
359 Sioux	You enticing little sod.
360 Keef	Getting personal now.
361 Cathy	Between boys, when boys, sort of, talk about it, it is accepted. But if a girl said that she did it.
362 Sally	It's not, is it? (Cathy's dog comes running into the lounge after being shut in a bedroom: SJB.)
363 SJB	Winston.
364 Keef	Is it a male?
365 Debbie	Yeah! It's got a willy.
366 Sioux	He had it out the other day. I goes "Put it away, you're not coming near me!"

The theme of the discussion is images of male sexuality explored through the topics of masturbation, homosexuality and genitalia. In the previous quotation I identified how the boys were aggressive towards homosexuality in the person of a teacher, and the girls did not agree. This opposition causes the boys problems because their shared assumptions lead to a ridiculing of 'aberrant' or homosexual behaviour.

The boys speak of the 'uncertain' behaviour by a square boffin boy when he stands at a urinal. The suggestion is that his behaviour is not correct in this location; such behaviour might be homosexual. The story is told by Hat in a tone which expresses fear, he shouts and feels threatened.

He gets caught up in his account of the square boffin boy and his penis by the implicit suggestion that he and other mods are involved in voyeurism, perhaps with homosexual intent. Do the mod boys stand in the toilet and gaze at this boy's penis? Is the mod boys' behaviour homosexual? The boys, and Hat in particular, appear to have failed to draw attention to their own potency in contrast to asserted homosexual practices, despite a second more explicit repeat of the square boffin boy's abnormal behaviour. The boys seem to have fallen into a trap of their own making. The girls fail to see the behaviour as passive or homosexual, instead it is described in terms of 'weirdness'; the boy's mother is weird. Rich rescues the boys from the 'dangers' of homosexuality by changing the focus of the discussion to the boy's circumcised penis. Then Hat makes a further switch in the conversation to the potent subject of male masturbation. However, the girls reveal that they know much about the male body. They have information on the penis, circumcision and male masturbation. The boys are threatened (and surprised) by the girls' ready facility to talk seriously about masturbation. The girls focus upon masturbation as a fact of life, whereas the boys now see masturbation as a weakness; a man only masturbates when he cannot have sex with a woman. The boys' define of masculine potency as having heterosexual intercourse. From the boys' perspective, Sally raises a taboo subject when she states that she speaks with her mother about male masturbation. For the boys this is a threatening relation, where mother and daughter are seen as in collusion.

In general, the conversation of the new wave girls is not a game: it is a manifestation of their feminism. It is this which provides the serious basis for their arguments and their refusal to take the discussion at the level of a game. The girls (Cathy) assert that boys can talk about masturbation but it is not appropriate for girls, as this will indicate that girls are both sexually active and can achieve sexual pleasure independent of men. They present a threat to patriarchy, within the terms of which only men express sexual ambition and activity and women are taken to be sexually dependent upon men: it is this which lies behind the boys' equation of potency with heterosexual intercourse. The boys are caught in a dilemma: they are unwilling to admit to masturbation. But why? Because in terms of their potency, masturbation would appear to be unmanly, weak, and perhaps homosexual or even virginal. According to their definition of potency, to engage in masturbation suggests an absence of normal sexual relations.

This conversation follows on directly from the previous quotation. The girls have been questioning the boys about male masturbation so in an attempt to maintain a balance I ask Keef what he knows of female masturbation.

367	SJB	What do you know about girls' masturbation then Keef ?
368	Keef	Ur . I heard two girls talking about it. In fact I had it on tape.
369	Rich	No. A third year girl.
370	Keef	No. A fourth year girl mate.
371	Rich	Oh right ! What do you think of the fifteen/ sixteen year old boy who is having it off with a thirteen year old girl?
372	Sally	I think thirteen year old girls are stupid.
373	Sioux	Yeah so do I.
374	Rich	Yeah so do I.
375	All	Laughter.
376	Sioux	Hat you look EMBARRASSED.
377	All girls	Laughter.
378	Sioux	Who is the thirteen year old girl then?
379	Keef	What Sioux ? Go then Hat tell them who you're going out with.
380	Sioux	Who is the thirteen year old girl?
381	All girls	Laughter.
382	Hat	Keef layed out a second year girl. A second year!
383	Sioux	Who's that?
384	Debbie	What's her name?
385	Hat	What's up with that?
386	Keef	No, who?
387	Debbie	IT'S ABOUT YOUR SIZE Keef!
388	All girls	Laughter.
389	Hat	She might have been a very mature young girl.
390	Sioux	Who?
391	Sally	It can damage you, though if you have it off at thirteen.
392	Hat	Why?
393	Keef	I ain't damaged! Is this where the party was?
394	Sioux	Yeah it was great, we pushed the table here, we had the

chairs across there. That chair was over here as well. We didn't have the telly in here. It was in the bedroom and all the ornaments were put into the cupboard.

395 Cathy   How many were in that bedroom?

396 Sioux   There was- what ?- about nine of us. There was Steff and Gaz on the bed. Gaz was being really funny he was jumping up and down really high. He was going come on Steff you're not usually this shy. You like it like this, he was going.

397 Debbie   It was really funny.

398 Keef   She's getting really exited, she's pushing my leg.

399 Sioux   There was Steff, Gaz, Collen, Tom, Denise, Slim, Ian and Robert.

400 Cathy   There was six in the other bedroom and the rest out here.

401 Sally   I remember waking Shane, and then Paul up at five o'clock in the morning.

402 SJB   What are you two (Cathy and Debbie: SJB) going to get up to on holiday?

403 Debbie   We're going to get up to everything!

404 Keef   What's the legal age for lesbians?

405 Debbie   Twenty one.

406 Sioux   Twenty one.

407 Debbie   I'm not a lesbian, I'm bisexual.

408 Keef   Oh ur who is?

409 Sioux   No I think you'll have to be a pure lesbian.

410 Debbie   YEAH!

(Keef leaves to catch a school bus to go home: SJB)

At issue here is the groups' different understandings of 'sexual maturity'. Throughout this quotation both groups promenade the body with competing and opposing claims, and definitions of potency. From the mod boys' perspective sexual status does not derive from long term relationships: it rests upon a boy's ability to seduce a younger and preferably inexperienced girl. Thus sexual maturity is understood in terms of a boy's success with virgins, as an enhancement of his public potency and the potency of his group.

The boys deliver their account of male potency within a framework of bravado, exaggeration and jousting. When Sally affirms that it may be harmful for a girl to have sexual intercourse at thirteen Keef's response not only demonstrates a complete absence of concern for any younger partner but is also an attempt to claim additional potency through the implication that he was sexually active at that age. However, they are unable to pursue their claims of sexual success and to dominate the argument because the new wave girls hold a different understanding of sexual status. Rather than congratulate the boys on their sexual conquests the girls reverse the boys' claims. Sally states that young girls who have sex are foolish and immature. Also there is a suggestion that if boys choose younger partners, it must be because they too are immature. In the struggle over appropriate age levels the boys are caught within the contradiction of their own promenade of potency.

The boys struggle to maintain group unity; this never fragments, but their performance is weakened by the girls' constant questioning, ritual humiliation and laughter. However, the boys are far from defeated. They do not give the names of their young girlfriends thus secrecy is maintained and with it solidarity conferred by a shared knowledge.

Significantly, the boys suddenly switch the topic away from the investigation of themselves, to one of the girl's parties. This gives an opportunity for the girls to promenade their own behaviour. A new wave girls' party would usually continue through the night and all guests would stay and sleep in various rooms. The chances for promiscuity and myth-building are obvious. However, the girls' relationships with boyfriends were generally long-standing. These boys would in general be two or more years older than them. For the girls, sexual status does not rest upon attracting a succession of younger boys but on the development of sexual relations within a stable relationship.

In an attempt to dislodge the girls from their promenade of heterosexual confidence the boys, through their PGS Keef try to humiliate the girls by suggesting that two of them are lesbians. However, the remark has the reverse effect. The girls speak about lesbianism with ease as they did about masturbation. The girls' public display of moving from heterosexual assertion to this acceptance of lesbianism, effectively draws to an end the boys' interest in the discussion of sexual maturity (Allen 1982).

The boys' display of male potency has not altogether failed, but it has not succeeded in placing the girls in traditional positions of sexual subordinacy. It is the combination of the girls' ability to show group solidarity, to promenade and to privilege the female body and desire which enables them to preserve their integrity and to present their feminism.

78

Positions and communication

This chapter brings together the two youth cultural groups in order to examine the data to see to what extent the theory can possibly explain the patterns of communication which occurred. The data from two informal conversations has been presented almost in full. This provides a context within which to understand the individual parts and to understand more fully the ritual engagement.

A crucial determinant of an interaction is whether a group is playing a defensive or an offensive strategy. The drama between the two youth groups takes the form of ritual insults, jousting and games of humiliation. The specialised positions act according to three rules depending upon the social forms present, (social/symbolic), the setting (or location) and the context (or occasion).

I shall refer to the first discussion as (A) and the second as (B). Next I will specify the line or lines in the discussion. Later I shall look at the more general relationships between the specialised positions in terms of offence/ defence, jousting, exaggeration, games and solidarity.

In the transcript we see the specialised positions play out the major roles of communication: joust, challenge and opposition. Parallel positions in competing groups are often in ritual combat, for example female against male style leader. We can also expect to see the style leader and peer group spokesperson challenge the opposing group's solidarity, or oppose any attempt by others to dominate the talk, but in so doing, they may present a threat to their own group's solidarity. Both positions will themselves try to either direct or dominate the subject under discussion. These are all promenading rituals of exaggeration. The cultural ransacker is preoccupied with intellectual strategies of communication, such as reversing meanings in an argument, or making factual assertions which widen the context of the argument or introduce new concepts. Finally, the primary role of the peer group consolidator is to unite the group, and this may be achieved by rituals of humiliation designed to elicit laughter. Some of these examples show cross alliances between social and symbolic forms. On the one hand there may be an alliance of the style leader and the peer group spokesperson, and on the other hand an alliance between the cultural ransacker and the peer group consolidator. There is likely to be tension between the two sets of alliances. The cultural ransacker and the peer group consolidator have to cope with the exaggeration of the style leader and peer group spokesperson and have to support them when their domination is threatened.

Style leader (SL)

This selection shows the way in which the SL will attempt initially to direct, and then try to gain control of the promenading rituals by directing conversation. In other conversations the style leader speaks more about the specialized semiotic but here their main role is to direct the conversation. At the start of the first talk Rich enters the room singing a song from the repertoire of the mod boys' specialised semiotic.

A. 91-94, 96-98. Rich and Clare joust on whether women have the right to spend their or their husband's wages on a new hair style.
A. 108-113. Paul selects an element from the mods' specialised semiotic i.e. his scooter, to assert the irrationality of women. However, rather than Paul's mother being shown as a "fanatic" the girls reverse the situation so that it is Paul who is the fanatic. Clare challenges him by forcing an image of domesticity on the male scooter. When the scooter enters the household by the boys' own definition, it comes under the control of women. When the scooter is offered tea, Paul and the mod boys are ritually insulted.
A. 116, 119. Paul speaks about being prevented from promenading in his local pub; this is an insult to himself and the public face of the mod group.
A. 131. Rich uses a formal argument about car accident statistics to introduce an argument that women's driving is dangerous.
B. 193, 195. Rich offers to sell his crash helmet to Keef at a reduced price. Keef (PGS) is careful to apologise to the Rich for being unable to accept this bargain.
B. 257. Rich finally manages to move the conversation away from the subject of the square boffin boy's passivity by raising the subject of circumcision.
B. 284. Throughout the two discussions we have seen Rich promenade and practice exaggeration; here he delivers his ritual wind-up almost in song form.

Peer group spokesperson

This selection shows the peer group spokesperson as a powerful and domineering force within both groups. Whereas the style leader will try to direct conversation, it is the PGS who tries to dominate the encounter by acting in a loud, challenging and often aggressive way.

A. 13-15,17-18. Sally and Keef initiate stories on parental surveillance of sexual behaviour. They become the voice of the group on these matters.

A. 62,66. Keef dominates the conversation by shouting and asserts that it is fruitless to proceed any further on the topic of equality.

A. 122,124,126. Keef tries to control the conversation by shouting and becoming abusive. His aggression is directed towards a blanket condemnation of women. The fact that the SL has been prevented from promenading in a public house, is a challenge to the mod boys' public face.

A. 150-154. Sally and Keef joust on issues of physical strength and gender. Sally dominates by shouting.

A. 175,191. Sally introduces the narrative of her father as an active participant in the domestic realm to challenge the boys' stereotype.

B. 199,201-202,204,206-211,213,216-217. Keef and Sally joust and attempt to dominate the narrative on sexual explicitness in two films. He dominates here but he is quickly challenged by Sioux who delivers a ritual insult. Her challenge is to the boys' right to promote pornographic fantasy.

B. 267-278. Sally and Sioux unite to challenge the boys and dominate them by showing 'forbidden' knowledge of male masturbation.

B. 321, 323. Sioux dominates the conversation and speaks at length on the girls' all-night party. This similar to Keef's praise for those involved in the fight (see chapter 4).

Cultural ransacker

This selection shows the cultural ransacker's ability to use and develop formal arguments as a means of breaking ritual exaggeration. In particular, the CR's strength is shown by their skill in transferral of meaning. However, story-telling is not a strength of the CR as is shown by Hat's inability to join in an exaggerating narrative.

A. 58,61,65,67. Debbie uses the reality principle in an attempt to break the boys sexist ritual exaggerations. She attempts a formal argument that women's employment will bring changes in social roles however she is unable to make her argument to full effect.

A. 158-165. Debbie shifts the discourse from the body to the mind. Through this successful transferral she argues that academically minded girls have more scope for employment.

B. 192,196,198. Hat opens the conversation by talking about scooter helmets. He focuses upon the number, type and range of crash helmets he owns.

B. 212. Hat states the reality principle of the film, its subject is solely sexual.

B. 265-266,279. Debbie and Hat joust upon the facts of male masturbation. Both put questions. Hat experiments and colludes with me by offering masturbation for discussion. He transforms the talk about circumcision to masturbation. Finally, Debbie demands that the conversation remain at a serious rather than an exaggerated level. She asserts the reality principle by stating that it is normal to masturbate.

B. 311,314. Debbie does not receive an answer to her question and follows up with a heavy ritual insult to Keef. Her actions break the force of the boys' ritual exaggeration.

B. 330-337. Debbie, in response to my question shifts the context to a directly sexual one. She breaks the boys' masculine promenade by transferral of her sexual potency, from a previous concern with heterosexuality to one of lesbianism.

Peer group consolidator

This selection shows the peer group consolidator's ability to break social exaggeration through assertion of a reality principle. Cathy is the only PGC present in both discussions. She concentrates upon development and use of repair strategies. She is most successful in uniting the group through a combination of humour and ritual insult; this not only affirms but also celebrates solidarity.

A. 4. After Rich has been aggressive towards one of the girls, Cathy draws the girls together by beginning a conversation whose subject matter excludes the boys.

A. 50,52. Cathy intervenes in an aggressive manner casting aside the boys' games and opens the way for Debbie to legitimise individual choice of marriage or career. In this way Cathy preserves solidarity by justifying difference based upon personal choice.

A. 75,77. Cathy uses the reality principle to break the boys' ritual exaggeration. She asserts that the boys are not really as aggressive as their public face behaviour suggests. Her intervention provides a base for unity and the girls go on to argue against the masculine promenade.

A. 156. Cathy applies the reality principle to deny the boys' potency and ritual exaggeration by refusing to accept the terms of opposition. The girls laugh triumphantly in celebration of her wit.

A. 181. Cathy intervenes with the use of the reality principle which the boys choose to ignore. Her observation of the houseproud father goes unchallenged by the boys who prefer to stay with the game developed by Debbie.

B. 288. Cathy unites the girls in a generally agreed statement about female masturbation.

Forms and specialised positions

I have attempted to understand patterns of interaction and forms of communication on the basis of specialised positions (SP). Specialised forms do not play a constant role throughout all discussions. The forms tend to be triggered or elicited by different stages of an interaction. In certain instances a particular SP will control or try to control the whole interaction. Thus it is necessary to understand the context for and occasion of an interaction, especially in relation to which SPs are present and who is on the offensive or defensive.

Important differences between the two groups influence the shape of the discussion. The girls always outnumber the boys by at least one. All SPs in the new wave girl group are present for both talks: they are balanced. For the boys neither discussion sees them with a full quota of SPs: they are unbalanced. In the first talk only the boys' SL and PGS are present; in the second talk these positions are joined by a CR. The latter talk is at the house of a new wave girl - this gives the girls a significant territorial advantage.

When explaining the pattern of communication we can note the effect of the boys' unbalanced social form on interaction. The first talk reveals an excess of exaggerating forms. In the second discussion they are still missing a PGC and have gained a CR or a non-exaggerating position. This has important consequences for their offensive strategy and solidarity.

In the first talk the mod boys are in a dynamically offensive mode, moving rapidly from one ritualised exaggeration to another on a variety of controversial subjects: employment, marriage, drinking, sexual behaviour, parents and driving. They use ritual and personal insults, game strategy, teasing traps, 'wind up' and aggression in their attack on the girls, to which the girls' SPs play and develop a more subtle defensive response. The boys' constant sexist exaggerations force the girls to challenge, joust, and break this ritual. The girls have to specify local areas of experience such as mothers in employment, mothers' driving skills, fathers' labour in the household or mother's lack of concern with the housework, to confound the boys' promotion of sexist misinformation.

In the first discussion the boys' two SL's and the girls' SL are in conflict over aspects of style. It may be that Clare takes on a minor role in the second talk because only one mod boy SL is present. In the first talk Keef (PGS) takes a dominant role in promoting exaggeration. In the second talk his authority is more effectively challenged because the girls have two PGSs which furnishes them with additional resources in moments of ritual attack and defence. Occasionally, in the second discussion when one girl PGS is humiliated the other will intervene, always with the intention of maintaining group structure.

During the second talk the girls begin to move out from a defensive and into an aggressive mode, for example the two PGSs challenge and tease the boys about male masturbation. The PGSs promote their sexual knowledge while Sally also stresses collusion with her mother on the matter. Here we see the boys' offensive strategy in decline; without a PGC they find it difficult to retain unity. In contrast Cathy as PGC plays an extremely active role for the girls in ensuring that group structure remains intact. The PGC is at the centre of both attack and defence strategies. In general, throughout the first discussion the girls operate a defensive mode; it is here that Cathy (PGC) shows how she unites the girls through humour. Her wit is crucial to the girls' solidarity in the following examples, lines 6,21,77,156. In the second discussion she plays a slightly less significant role, which may be due to the additional presence of the two girl PGSs or that this talk occurs in the safety of her home. Throughout, she is sensitive to the boys' ritual exaggeration and will confront it if it has not been successfully dealt with by the other specialised positions.

There are relatively few moments of weakened solidarity in either group as the SPs joust both within and between the groups to dominate the narrative of body references and sexual innuendo. The SL or PGS do not weaken significantly because they are the dominant and exaggerating forms. Weakened solidarity is not a result of failure of the forms but due to a specialised position under pressure. For example in A. 140,142. Debbie (CR) weakens the unity of the girls by criticising Sioux, calling her 'highly strung'. Another example is in A. 189 where Cathy (PGC) damages group unity by admitting that Debbie's mother did do housework. A final example occurs in B. 244,246,254,256. Hat (CR) shows his inability to join the promenade without weakening the public face. However, Hat is 'hoisted by his own petard', revealing the inability of a CR to promenade alone successfully for any length of time. Meanwhile, Debbie (CR) sees her opposite number in a weak position and defuses the exaggeration by jousting and asking questions. Her advantage is that in the girl group all the SPs are interacting. There is no need for opposition within the girl group between SPs because all others interact at given moments. Ultimately, Debbie (CR) succeeds in breaking the ritual exaggeration of male potency by transferring female potency from heterosexuality to lesbianism.

Conclusions

I have tried to show at the level of interaction how two youth cultural groups hold different positions under patriarchy. In this discussion gender issues are at the fore. If social class relations are significant it is probably the way in which they are manifestly embedded in patriarchy. For youth, gender and patriarchy are two fundamental locations of dependence and independence owing to their position in the household.

The basic feature of the discussions are the boys' attempt to place the girls in traditional positions of domestic and economic dependency. The boys present images of masculine hegemony; job, wage packet, public house, driving, strength and so on, as both material and ideological factors which demonstrate female subordination. Discriminatory barriers and hurdles are put before the girls as a means to inhibit their social aspirations. For the boys women are to be kept out of a predefined male labour market and their educational chances are restricted due to a naturalised unequal opportunity.

The dynamic feature of the boys' promenade is their determination to shun serious argument in favour of 'wind up'.

Rather than answering arguments on their own terms the boys change tack and use ritual exaggeration to aviod making proper comments. Each time they are asked a direct question the question remains unanswered as they use various strategies to avoid meaningful discussion. The boys' ritual play of creating stereotypes protects their public masculine identity. The necessity for them to assert myths of masculinity is bound up with their reputations of violence (Ramazanoglu 1989).

In contrast the new wave girls speak openly on topics such as masturbation, male erection, sexual intercourse and so on; their expressive command of this subject matter is disturbing, not only as a direct challenge to masculinity, but also indirectly as a possible threat to the boys' patriarchal power relations over younger girls. The girls effectively break a double taboo, since within patriarchy not only are girls not supposed to possess such sexual knowledge but also they are denied the power of speech on these issues (Shiach 1991) .

The boys spread misinformation which is very extreme, such as legitimating violence against women and portraying women as sexual objects whose role is to serve male needs; in response the girls develop countering arguments to tackle this misinformation, but also their front appears extreme because of the force of social taboos against women speaking about sex. The boys spread misinformation throughout the school community and it is not significantly countered because of the need to maintain the public face. The male image recreates it own logic. However, as a youth cultural group girls show sensitivity to the fact that the boys' do not fully believe in their aggressive arguments and attempt unsuccessfully to expose the contradiction.

4   Rituals of violence: mod boys

Introduction

This chapter is divided into four sections. In part one there is an ethnographic description of one of the mods' outings. This account derives from my field diary. The purpose here is to document in detail the types of activities which the mod boys engaged in when they visited the nearest large town. In part two I present the entire transcript of the mod boys' discussion of the outing which took place in the early evening of that day at a party. The intention here is to show the whole representation of the mod boys' account of the fight which took place. In part three I put forward an interpretation of the successive phases of the talk in terms of the theory of social and symbolic forms (the specialised positions and the social relations of the face), to demonstrate how the discussion moves from the private to the public face. Part four gives an interpretation of the mod boys' fracas with the rockers in terms of the oppositions of style and generation.

Ethnographic description of a mod outing

The previous night the mod boys had been celebrating Keef's sixteenth birthday. They had decided to go on a "pub crawl". In the morning Paul, Keef and Hat had hangovers, so scooters were abandoned for safety reasons and the group waited for a bus to take them to town. They arrived at the bus stop at ten to nine on a frosty morning, and their spirits began to be revived as they talked about the previous night's drunken adventure.

The mods went up to the top deck of the bus and sat at the back, and began talking about the clothes they would buy before they went skating in the afternoon. The bus journey was almost thirty miles, slow and bumpy. About half way, the mods curled up in their seats and prepared to "stake it out" by sleeping until they reached their destination, which was a large town not unlike Brighton or Eastbourne, a traditional south coast English town with a good range of clothes shops.

On arrival in the busy town they rushed along the pavement in search of the first clothes shop. As a matter of course they went into every male clothes shop. The first shop they entered seemed the opposite of anything that could be called mod. They asked a few questions about ties and berets, laughed and moved off. At the second clothes shop Keef purchased a fish-tail parka. Once outside on the street the pace of walking quickened. The next two unisex clothes shops and two modern male clothes shops proved useless for their specific requirements. Paul cried out that his headache had not disappeared, so he purchased some "drugs, yeah Disprins". Outside the shop all the mods joked,

"Hey, what happened to the purple hearts,
the pill-popping youngsters of today".

Although taken for medicinal reasons, each mod "knocked back" a couple of Disprins to make an imaginary symbolic connection with drug taking. The mods decided they would walk towards the older part of town, as the route is via a scooter shop. Another two clothes shops here were tried, one of which was particularly expensive. In the shop they began lifting up jackets, trying them on, gazing at themselves in mirrors, checking over the shirts and asking, "where are the ties? are those the only selection?" They, investigated every item; Paul managed to buy some Levi jeans, Hat a button down shirt and Keef a tie.

The boys combined promenading with relaxation at the amusements. They played a few computer games and looked around "checking out" rival youth cultural fractions. Hat challenged me to a game of pool. Paul (SL) selected the music from the juke box: "Strange Town" and "Eton Rifles" by The Jam and "My Generation" and "Happy Jack" by The Who. The three mods reminisced about the other times they had been to the arcade amusements and also spoke about the party they were going to in the evening. They found the next three clothes shops not to their liking and were now approaching the scooter shop. Paul (SL) asked me,

Paul	Did you see that, last night the scooter shop was on the local news , with all the mod Lambrettas and Vespas lined up outside?
SJB	No.
Paul	Well it was some article on something about street lighting and they passed by the scooter shop. I was just sitting watching the TV and there, right in front of me was the scooter shop.
All boys	Laughter

At the scooter shop Paul inquired about collecting the log book of his scooter as it was under guarantee. Inside the shop all three mods were explaining that next year they would be buying new scooters which would be more powerful than their restricted 50cc machines. They were manipulating the new scooters, looking through scooter brochures and calculating the cost of all additional necessary accessories and possible conversions.

It was almost half past twelve and Keef kept making references to food in terms of his "lack of ability to contain meself from eating the nearest person who walked by". They decided to make their way to the "mod cafe". Again the pace quickened, then Hat said "Hey look, that old rocker over there has a mod patch on his jacket": indeed he had a"Who" patch on his leather jacket. The three mods debated the complexity of this contradiction as they entered a market. They considered the market to be "absolutely boring", apart from the record stall which had "some old soul classics". They joked about flared trousers, "Kipper ties" and large lapels on jackets. About a hundred yards before the cafe they decided it was time to "wind up" somebody.

The three mods prepared themselves and entered a travel agency, with the idea of gaining information about a holiday in Afghanistan. The man and woman behind the counter were extremely perplexed, as the coverage of the revolt against the Soviet occupation of Afghanistan had recently dominated the news. Paul, appearing very neat in his suit, asked for details, stating "It is very important". While Keef added "You see it is to do with our special

89

Geography field trip." Straight faces were kept and grins held back until they were outside, when they burst out laughing. Once in the street, Keef surveyed the brochure he had been given on the Middle East. The walking pace was stepped up by Keef but one more clothes shop was entered. At this small shop Hat purchased some trousers in the "Prince of Wales" check, while Keef protested about the urgent need for food. Every time one of the mods bought an item of clothing it was examined carefully for faults.

Inside the cafe they ordered their meals while fighting mock battles, singing, and chanting and "chatting up" the two girls who were serving. They played only one record on the juke box, "Start" by The Jam possibly five or six times; nothing else was considered suitable. When the food arrived on the tables, although knives and forks were sometimes used, their specific use was for defending the territory of one's own plate rather than for eating. There was alot noise, much shouting and banging as the next chorus in The Jam song was reached (again). The mods managed to persuade the two girls to turn up the music, to the annoyance of other people in the cafe.

Refreshed, the mods left the cafe and began the afternoon session by a confrontation with a "Bible Puncher" in the street. Keef immediately played the role of a heretic and argued on specific points about interpretation of the Bible, the role of Jesus and whether he "made things up". They moved away rapidly when the religious advocate asked them to contribute some money. After this brief interlude of excitement the mods found themselves in Boots, and set about their first challenge which was to visit the record department. But first they lit their cigarettes and walked from the ground floor to the top floor where the records were. Although smoking is prohibited in Boots they were not reprimanded. It took the three mods approximately ten minutes to go through all the CD's, LP's and singles, occasionally stopping at ones they owned or mod classics like Quadrophenia by The Who. Overall, they considered the record selection at Boots to be "pretty poor" as there were "practically zero old singles". When the three mods stepped outside the department store they were almost immediately met by a group of seven mods comprising Hendrix and Header, who had with them two fourth year marginal members of the mod group, a skinhead from the criminal boys and two other marginal members from the fifth year.

The mod group now numbered ten, eight wearing parkas and two wearing crombies. They hastily made a move towards the seafront, firstly, to play on the amusement machines and then to go skating. At the "amusements" most of the mods met up with their girlfriends who decided it was time to join the queue for the skating rink.

I had never been skating before and I was extremely reluctant to make a complete fool of myself on a pair of roller skates, but I was persuaded as neither Paul nor Keef had been on skates before. Inside, the activities at first appeared entirely chaotic. One of the mods and his girlfriend took Paul and I round the ring about three or four times, then I decided to retire for a few minutes. The mods who could skate grouped around those mods who could not and tried to teach them the basic skills.

While taking my short rest I began speaking with a man aged about forty and probably the oldest person skating. I noticed a group of eight rockers towards the canteen end of the building. The rockers moved onto the rink. They were good skaters, quickly manoeuvring in and out of the children and teenagers. I rolled away from the older man and started to go round with some of the unsteady mods precariously balanced on roller skates. Suddenly one of the rockers crashed into two of the mods in front of me. Everybody apologised and got up off the floor. But then this happened three times more in quick succession. The mods were beginning to become unsettled, as most were not good roller skaters and felt in a weak position as the rockers were obviously "showing off - trying it on".

At this particular moment I considered my presence might become too involved as a researcher, so I sat down with a couple of the mods' girlfriends. Tension suddenly returned because on the other side of the rink an incident began. One of the rockers ran into Header but then also punched him when he was on the ground. The mods were galvanised into action and ready for confrontation. Header, who was hit, explained what happened, as the mods gathered round him. I could anticipate what was going to take place. They decided they had been challenged. Meanwhile, the rockers continued circling round the skating rink. Header was upset but Keef was outraged. Header decided to telephone his father. They went to a telephone box, contacted Header's father and explained the situation of the forthcoming confrontation with the rockers who were slightly older than the mod boys.

Inside the skating rink the mods were worried firstly about whether they could "beat-up" these older rockers, and secondly, about what would happen after the incident. The researcher was caught in a very hostile situation: the mods questioned me in terms of, "If it starts, you are with us aren't you?" I said, "If anyone of you appears to be getting physically damaged, badly, I will step in". On reflection, this remark now seems very "cool" but it can be stated that my stomach felt extremely unsettled. The impeding fight was impossible to stop and in any case my position as a researcher meant that I could not attempt either to join in the fight or stop its occurrence. Although I could perhaps have persuaded the mods to withdraw from the confrontation my task was to understand, rather than to manipulate, their behaviour.

After about fifteen minutes, it was signalled that Header's father had arrived. He was just over six feet tall. The rockers were already outside the skating rink. The mods slowly moved out of the doors and I asked the caretaker if I could have my cassette recorder from the cloakroom. I stepped outside and within a second the fight began. The mod boys and rocker youths fought head on. Hat was hit in the face, Paul and Keef went charging in attacking the ring leaders. The rockers were lashing out, kicking the girlfriends of the mods and as the embattled youths swayed to and fro delivering punches, it almost seemed to happen in slow motion. The conflict was over in about eight seconds. Header's father stood behind the mods as they fought, apparently playing no great physical role, but he was there. The two fighting forces separated. The rockers had been punched to the floor and were beaten physically and symbolically. Heavy insult was hurled from both sides. The rockers made more gestures threatening violence, but Header's father then interposed and pushed one of the rockers away - his only significant physical action. The two groups moved about three yards back to reveal the injuries of blood, broken teeth and ripped clothes.

The mods sustained no great injuries except for a few bruises and a cut leg of one of the girlfriends. As a group they moved away from the seafront, slightly numb, presenting their immediate recollection and personal role in the fight. The narrative was spontaneous and breathless. They were shaking, nervous, agitated: it had indeed, been a shared dramatic experience. They decided to leave the street because it would be over twenty five minutes before the bus would arrive. The mods went into a large department store, going straight to the top floor for a coffee and a short rest. After this the group divided into those who were going to catch the first bus and those catching the second. It was considered better to split up as the police were patrolling the town. By half past five everybody was away from the area and its potential problems.

Once they were away from the fight location, and moving towards their own territory, the fear of the fight was transformed into its celebration. Two hours later Keef, Paul, Hat and Header were together at a party given by a sixth form girl. They arrived early, so they grouped around a large oval table in the dining room and began to recount the shared fight experience. The transcript which follows is the entire conversation, until more guests arrived, when the discussion broke into smaller units and the noise level made recording an impossibility.

Celebration and mythologising

Beginning of the discussion. (Phase one of the talk)

Header	Hat was hit by that bloke first, see him run over.
Paul	He hit Hat and he shouted Paul.
Keef	Paul goes oh, ur, Keef. Looked round I see this kid , so we just steamed straight in both together didn't we. Who hit him first you or I? Don't know.
Paul	I went at him but I missed him and he came up.
Keef	When Paul came over I thought he was dead.
Paul	I hit him straight on the nose, he when urrr.
Keef	Because we must of hit ' em about four or five times each really.
Paul	That is when they were standing up.
Keef	I was really wading in with both fists and then.
Paul	And then he crashed, and everyone was going to jump on his head.
Header	My old man reckons their tea is going to be cheaper tonight as they won't be able to drink.
Keef	I was on the ground with him and I thought fucking hell I ain't gonna stay down here. Because you (Paul: SJB) were doing a mental on him. So I jumped up a bit quick and started kicking. See all the blood on his coat. He was getting his head smashed in against the ground.
Paul	I fell over his head.
Mod boys	Laughter.
Keef	Did you fall on the ground then?
Paul	Yeah, I fell over his head.
Keef	Because there was a big mass of bodies.

Paul	Because I jumped on his head with my knees like and kicked him in the head, right and jumped down on my knees and as I landed I fell over like.
Keef	I was just going, I remember when he got up, I got him straight in the kidneys really hard because all his shirt was up, really hard. That couldn't have done him much good.
Header	You wouldn't have thought we'd have won , though they had enough.
SJB	I think they realised , they just didn't have it together.
Header	My father goes I only joined in , he said you were making a good meal of it and he goes I was only waiting in case if any broke off on to one of you.
Keef	I really enjoyed it.
Paul	Yeah, I did, it was a great laugh.
Keef	It might sound funny but I did enjoy it. Paul, you were doing a mental on him, kicking him in the head when he went down you were kicking everywhere weren't you. Did you quarter him on his spine? Should have.
Paul	Yeah, I did.
Keef	I was just stamping on him. It was that good.
Header	When he hit me it really hurt . I really lost my temper.
Keef	Don't want to lose your temper. I was just kicking for pleasure.
Mod boys	Laughter.
Header	Did you see him when he came back again he stuck his head. Did you see part of his tooth break? All white stuff on the ground.
Keef	Spit his teeth out . Kick him in the teeth, arrr arrh that really was orgasmic staff weren't it. Lucky they weren't killed . If you look at it , you could think three kickers.
Header	It was great though we didn't take a beating.
Paul	Yeah it makes a change . I thought we were going to get killed.
Header	So did I, you think when we really started I thought oh God that crowd there.
SJB	Why you could see they had had enough was when your dad got in the car. We were about two hundred yards up the road and they just stood back there, they didn't move. I thought they were going to make a run for us then.
Paul	Yes so did I. That's why I wanted to run along the sea

	front because I mean, you can get outside in that mist, you're virtually alright.
Keef	Because the old bill (police: SJB) came along, right.
Header	The old man (father: SJB) I said when you going to get a new car then. He goes this week I hope. They took me number. Telephone rings, he is in gaol next week. He's got to explain how he got his face on the front page of the local Argus.
Keef	One of them was trying to push your old man about and your old man goes "Leave it out, you've had your fun." He goes ur ur, so your old man starts swinging at him, bang, bang. I felt like jumping then but it did not seem worth it. It seemed all over.
Header	Yeah I was gonna say, when he leapt in at my dad. We had and my dad had his face like that (gives demonstration: SJB) and his face was just going, he hit him then. It was over weren't it.
Keef	I don't know how long it lasted.
SJB	It didn't last very long because by the time I got the cassette recorder, put it down on the pavement looked to see what was happening, these two (Keef and Paul: SJB) were on the ground doing something.
Keef	Did you see us steam in? you missed me steam in.
SJB	Well I saw you steam in because I saw everyone fall on the floor.
Keef	We massacred them didn't we. You've got to admit. He went urrr, I don't know. Paul sort of stunned him, he went back like that, I went oh dear what have I done and he has lashed out first and caught me in the eye. Then we just kept punching his head. Then he went down and we got him.
Paul	It was a good job I didn't have my scooter.

(Phase two of the talk)

Julie	This party, he (her father: SJB) will kill me if this place gets wrecked. It's early yet.
Paul	It's got to start, a night like this, alot of people.
Julie	That's not a cue to start any trouble. Would Keef start trouble? Yes.
Keef	We don't look for trouble. We finish it.

95

Header	Harmless as a fly!
Paul	I was gonna dive in front of him but he kept getting out the way, when he was going round. I was - I slipped over in front of him.
Keef	He sort of kicked you then.
Header	When I got him though, he went mad I really did hit him.
Keef	He caught you a lovely punch first though didn't he? Yeah, he caught you with a swinger, didn't he?
Header	Well, he was coming straight at me. I can't stand up on skates.
Keef	No outside, he hit you first.
Header	No he didn't.
Keef	He did.
Header	I hit him first, I hit him didn't I, then stood back waiting for him to come back forward again.
Julie	THERE ' S STILL FOUR HOURS TO GO WOULD YOU BELIEVE. Remember that. FOUR HOURS.
Header	Don't you remember he came, I stood there.
Keef	I was kicking and pushing.
Header	Kick him in the head , then he goes that's enough.
Keef	Hat he's all right. He was in there. Did you see Lee? He was doing a mental on him, even his little brother was in there kicking away. All the girls were kicking. At least we all stuck together. The mods. Hard. No doubts. Once Paul was going in I couldn't believe it. So I went in and that was the end.
SJB	Everyone was together.
Keef	You think there was skins and mods there.
Paul	There was one skin there and the rest were mods.
Keef	Must send Concrete a picture of five parkas kicking shit out of one bloke. One crombie.
Paul	The "face".
SJB	Two crombies.
Paul	Oh yeah , Lee . You see the "face" stand out from the parkas. Stamping on some kids head.
Keef	You see me kicking, the face and kicking.
Julie	Were the girlfriends and that lot allowed in?
Paul	Yeah they were all allowed in because they were inside when we had the big bundle. I think anyway. Annette (Paul's girlfriend: SJB) whenever there's a fight or

96

	anything, she goes 'let's go inside' or something like that.
Keef	You would have loved it. Hendrix was straight in there. He gets really tired out Hendrix. He was knackered.
Paul	He just fights on the quiet.
Jane	Er , Keef what did your dad say last night when you got home?
Paul	He was crashed out.
Jane	What did your dad say ? he didn't seem very pleased.
Paul	No he didn't, did he.
Julie	He weren't very pleased but he didn't say anything.
Jane	Yeah my dad was not very pleased but he didn't say much.
Keef	Who's going roller skating next Saturday?
Header	I reckon we'll get in free.
Paul	I got in for half as well.
Header	When you said about going back for your fifty pence.
SJB	That was a wind-up.
Keef	I got mine.
Paul	I needed that to get home!
Header	You cracked me up when you said I got to wait for the girlfriend. My dad goes ur - well chose the way you want to die then.

(Phase three of the talk)

Keef	I want a guided tour of the house in a minute. See what it looks like, see what I can see.
Paul	I thought it was a mansion. It has a low ceiling , as it is in The Red Lion (local pub: SJB).
Julie	There's cats upstairs.
Header	Keef kills cats.
Paul	Go in for a bit of the old buggery.
Header	He pulls their heads off.
SJB	What were you doing this afternoon Phil?
Phil	Sod all.
Paul	Masturbating!
Hat	Did you get up at six?
Jane	The dog started barking.
Hat	So Shane said.
Paul	Which one!

97

Jane	Pardon. Look Paul , one more sarky remark out of you.
Hat	That blouse is see-through, that is.
Paul	Is that the girl from school?
Jane	Yes.
Hat	Yeah she's in my class. Vanessa meet Shane. Shane meet Vanessa
SJB	I've seen her already.
Keef	Let's talk about worms - the cats - I'm fucking starving. These cunts (mod boys: SJB) walking round all the shops. Ha, ha,ha -the travel agents.
Paul	We went in this travel agents asked them to go to Afghanistan.
Keef	We got a big pamphlet on it. That was really pissing them off,we went in and wind-up this bloke. Then this bloke in the street selling these pictures - religious notes - load of old bollocks and all this. We had a perfectly riotous day didn't we. In the cafe we were like animals. We were all picking the food up with our fingers -stuffin' it in.
Hat	Some of us that had some food.
Paul	I got one or two chips for lunch!
Keef	Yeah I had chips for lunch, the Jewish bastards.
Header	Which cafe did you go in?
Keef	The mod cafe, we stormed it, like a zoo weren't it?
Header	What after you had been there?
Keef	We were all talking, swearing ...
Paul	That will be the talk at the school , now for about a week, now that will.

(Phase four of the talk)

Keef	Right , we're beginning the party . This is called operation get Header smashed. We're gonna spike his drinks with Disprins okay.
Header	You've got a big mouth Keef.
Keef	Header is gonna be fucking smashed.
Paul	Here's Church the shaven headed youth. You should have been there Churchy.
Keef	We were all stamping on their heads . We're going to Eastbourne soon.
Paul	There's so many skins in Eastbourne.
Header	They hate mods as well.

98

Keef	Bollocks do they. There's loads of mods in Eastbourne.
Paul	There's about seven or more mods along near Eastbourne with scooters because I've been round with them.

Positions and communication

The transcript has been divided into four phases for the purpose of analysis, although the conversation was continuous and is given unedited. The reason for the division is to allow an assessment of the discussion in each phase and between phases, which might also offer an insight into the talk as a whole. Overall, the structure of the conversation can be understood in terms of the mod boys' social relations of the face. There is a movement from the private to the public face; as an audience gathered round them, so it presented an opportunity to promenade. In this section I shall apply the theory of social and symbolic forms in an attempt to see how the specialised positions interact and communicate within this youth cultural group. The participants and positions are as follows;

Symbolic forms: Style leader-Paul. Cultural ransacker- Hat.
Social forms: Peer group spokesperson-Keef.
Peer group consolidator - Header.

Phase one

During phase one the mod boys are alone sitting around a table, there are only a few guests at the party and they are moving from the kitchen into the main room, not staying to listen to the mods. The two specialised positions of the SL and the PGS heighten and promote ritual exaggeration. Both specialised positions demonstrate the solidarity of the group through their individual contributions. Paul (SL) and Keef (PGS) are concerned to document in detail their particular aggressive acts. They outline the immediacy of the fight and how both were united in causing damage. Neither social nor symbolic form was dominant, each contributed equally. In contrast Header (PGC) acts as a catalyst: he stresses the consequences of collective action and breaks the flow of ritual exaggeration by such comments as "Hat was hit" and "you wouldn't have thought we'd have won". The PGC is challenging the ritual promenade of the SL and PGS. Header seizes the opportunity to play his winning card i.e.

the role of his father during the incident. He attempts to steer the talk round to his own role and that of his father but fails to initiate an expansion of the story. Header falters and provokes the theme of doubt.

One reason perhaps why Paul and Keef do not mention the role of Header's father, is that to overstate the contribution of an outsider so early in the assessment of the fight might reduce the group's claim to victory. Paul and Keef carry on elaborating the rituals of violence and are conducting the battle at a leisurely pace; Paul is falling over and Keef has time to stamp: ease of victory is assured in their slow motion accounts. The PGC makes another insertion of doubt by drawing attention to the reality of the conflict. Header shows emotion; he is hurt. He appears to weaken the strength of the group by pointing out that one only feels pleasure but not pain until one is hurt. The PGS responds to this in a manner that intensifies the promenade of violence. Keef has two points to put to Header, firstly the context of enjoyment of the fight, and secondly control during the fracas. The PGS states "Don't want to lose your temper. I was just kicking for pleasure" (Laughter). Keef suggests that lack of concentration through losing one's temper could bring unexpected consequences. The PGS refuses to allow uncertainty to enter the evaluation of the conflict during the private face. At this point Header offers Keef an opportunity of power, by introducing a sexual metaphor of climax "all white stuff on the ground". Keef uses the moment to celebrate the sexual connotation of conquest by asserting that the experience was "orgasmic".

Header manages to gain a momentary alliance with Paul about the reality of the fight. Header and Paul acknowledge the possible consequences and doubts, namely that they could have been "beaten" or "killed". Here the ritual display becomes slightly displaced and Header grasps the opportunity to place the spotlight on his father who will have to get a new car, have his face on the front page of the local paper - or even be put in gaol. Here, Keef aligns himself with the socially important position of the father within the fight. As the dominant social form Keef (PGS) can announce when the fight is over and credits suspension of the attack firstly to the father, then to himself. Significantly, Keef argues that the actions of Header's father are at the end (after the fight); this means that group prowess remains intact, free from outside help. With the private face discussion of the fight now over, a number of girls gather around the mods and Keef asks for an outside assessment of how long the fight lasted. I answer, but suggest that I did not see fully the beginning of the fight. Keef is flabbergasted, so I respond in more precise terms which leads him on to the triumphant summary that "we massacred them".

Paul SL introduces two stylistic elements in phase one of the discussion. Firstly, he invokes the symbolic romanticism of the mod's last stand on the beaches. We can see images of the film Quadrophenia in Paul's statement "run along the seafront" and "get out in the mist" which is supported by Keef's point that the police were close behind. Secondly, Paul notes another element from the film that "it was a good job I didn't have my scooter with me".

Phase two

During phase two of the conversation the mods are joined by five girls who are listening and making occasional comments. Julie who is holding the party becomes concerned by the discussion of violence and wonders whether the mods might cause further violence. The interruption by the girl marks the first change in the discussion, where the mod boys move from the private to the public face. The girl's fear of the boys' violence fuels the mods' desire to promenade. Paul responds with a ritual exaggeration that a fight at the party is a certainty, "It's got to start." Another girl asserts that the boys must show more control and she points out that Keef's behaviour is unpredictable. Keef (PGS) sees his opportunity to combine his reply with an assertion of their ritual victory. He states "We don't look for trouble. We finish it." Then Paul begins the fight sequence again. Immediately, there is a disagreement between the two social forms of PGS and PGC. Keef and Header take part in a joust about the interpretation of the battle. It is possible to explain the difference of opinion between the two social forms as, firstly, an issue between the PGS and PGC concerning dominance. Secondly the play for dominance strengthens the youth cultural group when promenading in its public face, for it maintains the level of tension and keeps the fight at the centre of the discussion.

One of the girls intervenes shouting at the mods, pointing out that "THERE'S STILL FOUR HOURS TO GO WOULD YOU BELIEVE". The mod boys' public face has dominated the discussion. Then Header drops his disagreement with Keef and the latter (PGS) begins to award praise. He distributes medals for bravery and concludes by confirming the social solidarity of the group "The mods. Hard. No doubts". Everyone has made a contribution to the victory. Keef is slightly over-zealous in his account and makes an incorrect style assessment. Paul (SL) corrects Keef's statement; they are not in disagreement and the PGS goes on to secure his social dominance by making the link with an elder mod called Concrete by suggesting sending him a picture of their battle. The SL here invokes mod hierarchy by arguing that he is "the face" and the other mods are "parkas". Keef does not challenge the SL's symbolic order, but continues to document the violence of the fight.

The public face of the mod boys' display of violence is interrupted by the girls, who try to redirect the boys to the non-violent subject of their girlfriends. Keef is asked questions but he refuses to be distracted from keeping the fight at the centre of the discussion. Paul answers for him. After further interruptions the mods find it difficult to maintain their audience and begin to joust amongst themselves.

Phase three

As we reach phase three of the conversation more guests have arrived at the party. Some are standing next to the mods at the oval table while others move between the kitchen and the main room where music is beginning to be played. Discussion of the fight is dropped. Keef and Paul speak about the site of the party and assess what they might possibly do here. One of the girls tells the boys that there are animals upstairs; her statement is both advice and a warning.

However, the girl's comment about cats leads to a series of sexual innuendoes, and a "wind-up". It is a clear example of the mod boys' public face in action. Header (PGC) affirms the "wildness" of the PGS's behaviour. Header states that Keef "kills cats". Paul alters the level of ritual insult to assert sexual deviance with animals, "go in for a bit of the old buggery", then he suggests that one of the girls present is a "dog" (i.e. slag). Furthermore, a boy arrives in the room and stands next to Paul who aims a powerful sexual insult at him by maintaining that the boy spent the afternoon "masturbating". Hat then enters the conversation. He and I both ask factual questions which begin to dismantle the play of ritual in the group.

In the room the noise level is rising and the space is becoming crowded: people are surrounding the mod boys as if they are holding a news conference. Keef (PGS) seizes the opportunity to maintain the epic by addressing the assembled crowd with a summary of incidents throughout the day. Keef's narrative of the adventures leads to a brief exchange during which the public face of the mods speaks about their behaviour at the mod cafe which they "stormed" and where they were like "animals" in a "zoo". Finally, Paul asserts the importance of the fight, by claiming that it will be the talking point at school for a week.

Phase four

By phase four it is nearly nine o'clock in the evening, the kitchen is full of people and in the main room people are dancing. In the dining room the mod boys are extremely crowded by other guests and communication between them is becoming difficult. The PGS announces he has the power to start the party. Keef decides to turn the party into an event, "to get Header smashed" (i.e.out of control). This creates a final ritual joust between the social forms in their attempt to keep the air of violence apparent. Could the mod boys fight amongst themselves? The mod boys' SL announces the arrival of the SL of the anarchist punk group, "Here's Church the shaven headed youth". Keef addresses the anarchist punk, makes a summary of the fight and states the next challenge. Paul (SL) asserts that the problem in that town is a complementary but rival youth cultural style. Header argues it is too dangerous to challenge them because "they hate mods". In response, the SL argues he knows the mods who have scooters and Keef affirms that numbers are available.

Oppositions: style and generation

Here we are going to change the level of analysis in order to focus on how the oppositions of style and generation regulated the interaction of the fight and its celebration. There are four generations at play in the account of the fight:

Mod boys aged 14-16 : boys
Rockers aged 17-19 : young men
Father aged 39 : domestic adult
Elder mod "Concrete" aged 29: style young adult.

103

It was the young men, the rockers, who provoked the fight at the skating rink. They deliberately crashed into the mod boys who were knocked over and punched. The mods offered no immediate challenge, so from the rockers' perspective the mod boys appeared "easy". They identified the mod boys as invaders of their territory and took steps to point this out to them. From the positions of strength and territory the rockers understood the situation as one where they were slightly older and would win.

The rockers' physical challenge was initially directed at the level of style; as the mod boy was punched the rockers shouted "fucking mods". The second insult was directed at both the person and the style; they screamed "fucking mod wankers". The combination of heavy verbal insult and an initial physical challenge set the scene for a fight.

As the rockers were older than the mods, this gave the mods the right to bring in an older generation i.e. the father. Header's father was telephoned and came to the seafront by car. The call was made by the PGC (Header) and the PGS (Keef). The two social forms combined to ensure that the fight would not be lost. During the confrontation Header's father did not play a directly physical role, although towards the end of the fight he appeared as a n "anchorman", holding back but ready to act if required. However, the father was not needed to take part in the actual fighting. The key to the call for the father is perhaps based on the fact that he is older than the rockers. The style of the father is irrelevant. This opposes the initial age opposition of the rockers as young men to the youth of the mod boys. The mods successfully out-manoeuvred the rockers in this subtle game of age oppositions.

In the transcript the mods refer to the young men - the rockers - as "kids". This is a reversal and a denial of the rockers' male potency in terms of style and age. The style label of rockers is never applied. The mods concentrate on a ritual display of violence and it is the PGS who announces the victory of their solidarity "The mods. Hard. No doubts". By referring to the young men as "kids", the mod boys have successfully introduced an age reversal to their credit: here the reversal is potency versus infantalism.

From the mod boys' perspective the fight is a celebration of masculinity. The episode is held together by the contradictory relationship of dependence and independence. The mod boys celebrate their independence through the youth cultural group; the public fight is a good example of such independence. The youth cultural group is going out on its own and here regards any dependence on the family as threatening their own independence. However, because of the potential danger of the conflict inherent in the imbalance of age, a link is made along the male line to contact the father. This represents a line of male potency, where the mod boys require physical support. They sacrifice a degree of independence by enlisting a parent. The father joins with the boys in their romance of violence. This links the two male generations of boy/men and son/father. The father has momentarily been released from adult dependence to become a guardian of the young warriors, the mod boys.

The second line of male potency is revealed by the mod boys' call for recognition of their prowess from the elder mod "Concrete". The elder mod joins the boys' fracas through the PGS's proposal to send a photograph that captures and celebrates their violence and secondly, celebrates the social hierarchy and strength of the "parkas" within the mod group. The mod boys' victory is passed upwards to the elder mod, illustrating the way in which each generation has to revitalise and develop its own "myth". In the transcript Keef speaks of the elder mod in order to validate their response. "Concrete" is pictured by the mod boys as someone who has seen it before. Keef asserts that the elder mod must give respect to the young mods because the mod boys have made the grade, they fought and blooded the rockers on the beach.

The oppositions and differences then are as follows: firstly, the age differences are transformed by style(s) into oppositions, and secondly, the age differences and style oppositions are transformed into oppositions of potency. In reality the mod boys (the warriors) maintain potency opposition with the domestic father (guardian), whilst they remain domestically dependent. In fantasy the mod boys maintain potency opposition with the elder mod Concrete (stylistic guardian) whilst they remain stylistically dependent. The mod boys' independence is only challenged by their own initiative to call for a guardian (domestic or stylistic). Their independence is a measure of the distance between the mod boys and the two adults. Distance is defined as the shortening or lengthening of potency oppositions of (a) the Domestic and (b) the Stylistic. The mods were in a relation of domestic dependency with respect to the father and stylistic dependency with respect to the older mod Concrete. However, the terms of domestic dependency are reduced by the mods' own prowess and the same prowess both links the mods to Concrete and demonstrates their independent claim to be the 'new mods'.

Conclusions

It is possible to identify four repetitive themes in the mods boys' rituals of violence : victory, death, violence and potency. Throughout the fieldwork I observed the mod boys in a number of different confrontations but none were as important or as symbolic as the fight with the rockers at the seafront. News of this fracas spread rapidly. In their own territory the mod boys went on a promenade, they were "king" and even the local older rockers acknowledged this as a victory. From the mod boys' perspective the unexpected occurrence of this conflict brought them together in terms of both solidarity and style. They had played out their own version of the film "Quadrophenia". Paul (SL) who bought the book "Mods" (1979) by Richard Barnes remarked "Well, Shane we did it by the book". The mod boys had accomplished their own "myth" at the seafront and had an elder mod with whom to celebrate.

The ethnographic data details the relations, practices and communications of the youth cultural form in private and in public. In applying the theory of social and symbolic forms, the specialised positions, I arrive at an interpretation of the description and the transcript. The style leader and peer group spokesperson celebrate and engage in the ritual exaggeration of violence and "front". The peer group consolidator attempts to bring reality back to the conversation by stressing consequences and doubts, although his disagreement with Keef during the party heightens and supports the mods masculine potency. At the party the boys try to maintain tension and an aggressive atmosphere. After exhausting the descriptions of their fight they either "wind up" the audience or ritually joust amongst themselves. The mod boys put on a performance.

5   Rituals of integrity: new wave girls

Introduction

The data in this chapter is a transcript of a conversation from a cassette which four new wave girls made one evening alone. The girls are Sioux, Sally, Lynne and Cat. The note in the field diary states that one morning Sally gave me a cassette saying:

> We made this tape the other night. We thought you would like it because you're studying us and doing tapes. So we did one for you. Can we have it back sometime; we thought we'd help you, suppose. You coming for the walk?

The girls often made tape recordings of their "gatherings", indeed they were much involved in documenting events and feelings. They wrote long letters, poems and songs to each other, drew and painted pictures and photographed certain occasions. The girls who made this cassette reveal in their talk a combination of specialised positions within their youth cultural form. Not all specialised positions are present and the breakdown is as follows:-

Sally	Peer Group Spokesperson	Social form
Sioux	Peer Group Spokesperson	Social form
Lynne	Cultural Ransacker	Symbolic form
Cat	Cultural Ransacker	Symbolic form

The presence of the two PGSs should ensure that they dominate the discussion; it is their perspective which is being put forward. Both the PGS's and the CR's are without their respective complementary social and symbolic forms, the PGC and the SL. This exclusion is important because when all four positions are present, alliances and oppositions should occur and contradictions of interpretation arise. The question arises of whether by excluding or limiting the participants in this conversation the PGSs deliberately structured the event to their advantage. The venue for the discussion is Cat's parents' house. The site of the recording is Cat's bedroom, and the time is late evening before the girls go to sleep. She has assembled the girls together to do the recording but it is the PGS who announced the intention to give me the cassette.

Lynne   You going to play this tape to him?
Sally   Yeah.

Context: an important issue is what the girls were telling me by making the tape. A partial explanation may be that they were already heavily involved in documenting personal and group history and that the arrival of a sociological researcher gave a new dimension to this work. Throughout the fieldwork I collected a whole series of letters, poems and pictures from the girls. I was permitted access to old letters and they frequently discussed the historical changes that had taken place in the group. Other groups in the study did not share such an interest.

What was their motive? The message on the tape is predominantly that of the girls' two PGSs. Perhaps, as the dominant voices in the group, they wanted to express their feelings and attitude towards the research and the researcher. In this respect the tape merits attention because of the investment put in it - it represents an attempt to influence the collection of data on themselves.

This chapter is divided into two sections. In first part I shall look at "conversational choreography", that is the elements of the girls interaction and conversational style. In second part I present an interpretation of the girls' rituals of integrity and attempt to show how the meanings of such practices are socially and culturally related.

The choreography of conversation

This refers to the way in which a conversational style is brought off. Choreography is used to highlight the significance of shape and design, the role of participants in contributing to the shape, and the elements of which it is composed. In the case of this conversation the style is narrative in the context of the private face of the group. The choreographic elements I distinguish are onomatopoeia, banter, epic stories, jokes and chorusing. During conversation or story telling all or some features of the choreography may be present. Conversational choreography is a ritual format of expression within the girl group, it reinforces group ties and positions, is a declaration of the bond of friendship, and offers opportunity for creativity.

Onomatopoeia

Onomatopoeia refers to words which phonetically are associated with the referent that is signified. The use of onomatopoeia in the conversation may be considered an attempt to recapture the excitement, absurdity, humour and pleasure in the present by recalling the 'soundtrack' of the original event.

Sioux	Is that my coffee Cat?
Cat	Yeah.
Sally	It was really funny today Sioux. Hilarious.
Sally	There was this sewing machine here okay. Then there 's this plug to pull out here and there's all Cat's assessment here, Sioux.
Cat	And you know what happens.
Sally	Yeah, I pulled this plug out boommpp and the coffee went sttuummmm.
Sioux	Sttuuummm.
All girls	Laughter.
Sally	Went sttuummm all over Cat's assessment and everything and all over her Basement 5 words.

Here the sounds of "boommpp" and "sttuummm" become signifiers of pleasure giving the story zest and immediacy. On the tape the coffee story is the first subject of discussion. It is about Cat and it is in her bedroom that the talk is taking place.

Sally relates the account of her clumsiness as a humorous event. There is no malice in Sally's damage to Cat's assessment. Sally also indicates that the spilt coffee went over Cat's words to an album by the cult reggae/punk band Basement 5. Thus we note that the CR was studying the words to the music during a classroom lesson. This was frequently done by other cultural ransackers in the girl group. Debbie would carry around the words of songs which would be learnt collectively and reproduced by the whole group at moments of ritual significance.

Banter

Banter is a form of hierarchical play where power relations may be tested between those holding equal relations and between those holding unequal relations. Banter directed upwards in the authority line, is more dangerous and so a little more unusual than that between equals or directed downwards in the line of authority. Such verbal communication is highly competitive and can be understood as a series of quick-fire improvised soundings, where individuals attempt to out-do each other in wit and absurdity. Elements in banter are puns, voice impersonation and rhyming couplets.

Sally	Now I've gone all anaemic . Not anaemic, what's the word? I've got stomach ache.
Sioux	I've gone insipid, he, ha, ha.
Sally	I've got a bit of shrapnel in my leg.
Sioux	I've got a bit of nut in my teeth.
Sally	Remember my hip, Cat. I got a bad hip (impersonation of character Benny from Crossroads: SJB).
All girls	Laughter.
Sioux	That means I can't walk down the stairs.
Sally	Yeah . That ' ll be alright. I can't walk down the stairs.
Sioux	Ah , have you got that beetroot ? voice impersonation again: SJB).
Sally	I can ' t remember what bloody beetroot you on about.
Sioux	I dug it up from the garden the other day.
Lynne	No. They were potatoes.
Sally	Were they potatoes.
Sioux	They were beetroot, they were purple.
Sally	You sure it was potatoes.
Sioux	You don ' t get purple potatoes unless they ' re really

	cold. Tatters in the mould, cold. Ha (clap of hands. SJB) Get the pun. Ha, ha, ha, ha, ha, ha, ha, ... One lump of coal or two. Oh doesn't matter. That's what you have with a cup of char, hi, he, ha, he, he, ha, ha.
Sally	Does anybody get these jokes?
Lynne	No.
Sally	You know that apple I ate . All the bad bit. I think it must have had a maggot in it, it's just come back up my throat.
All girls	Laughter and screaming.

The two PGSs engage in ritual jousting. The pitch and flow of the voice is manipulated to give the impression of hesitation, then of excessive urgency. The performance is filled out with onomatopoeia and extra sounds such as slurping, tooth sucking and absurd laughter. There is voice impersonation of the character "Benny" from the soap opera "Crossroads" and also non-verbal communication. This type of narrative style which the group has developed gives rise to its own brand of humour; such conversations were common within the group.

A parody of domesticity was frequently played out by the new wave girls. These interactions were sometimes developed into small dramas, for example they would put on make-up and conventional female dress and walk to the high street to buy an ordinary household item, such as jam or sugar. On these occasions the girls would adopt "bingo accents" of women and screech in a ferocious manner about the price of food.

In the quotation there is a momentary disagreement between the two PGSs as they battle for dominance of the narrative. Sally questions Sioux about her absurd jokes and ridiculous laughter. The function of Sioux's laughter is a part of the girls chorusing: she is trying to sustain the level of competitive banter. Sioux's capacity for laughter and her repertoire of different forms of laughter was legendary within the girl group especially her impersonations from the film "Carry on Camping" and her impression of the "dirty old man".

There is little contribution by the CR's to the competitive bantering. They have great difficulty in initiating the social discourse of the group. The continuous flow of the PGSs prevent Cat and Lynne from speaking, they are reduced to making interruptions rather than elaborations. Cat makes no comment. Lynne makes two factual comments which are both negative.

111

Firstly, she states the vegetable was a beetroot not a potato and secondly, she answers "no", that Sioux's jokes are not understood. Here, Sally cleverly uses the CRs' desire to introduce reality to stop Sioux's banter. This makes room for her to tell an amusing tale which ends in laughter.

Jokes

Jokes were a regular feature of relations within the new wave girl group. In general, jokes were told inside rather than outside the group, although there were exceptions to this rule. The jokes which I consider should not be evaluated in themselves but as a further mode of self expression. I shall present four jokes told by the girls, the first three came from this tape, the fourth was told during another discussion.

Joke 1

Sioux	I got a really good joke right . There's two Hippies. One goes "Hey man turn on the radio". He goes "Radio I love you".
All girls	Laughter.

Joke 2

| Sally | It ' s really good . You heard the one about the Princess and three Irishmen. Three Irishmen screwing a Princess. One comes to draw it out. But it got stuck in the exhaust. Ha, ha, ha, ha (coughing: SJB). |
| All girls | Laughter. |

Joke 3

Sally	Have you heard this other joke ? You've probably heard it. About the Durex and three men working round a hole. He drops the china tea pot. He goes "Go and get a new one and make sure it's pyrex because they last longer".
Sioux	Yeah. He, er, goes pyrex, pyrex.
Sally/ Sioux	Pyrex, pyrex, pyrex.
Sally	Durex.
Sally/ Sioux	Durex, durex, durex..
Sally	So he goes into the. If we've all heard it, it's not worth telling it is it ?
Sioux	Tell it to the tape recorder.

Sally	He goes to the oh where, what do you call it.?
Sioux	Hardwear thing.
Sally	That's it hardwear. He goes "Can I have a durex please"(change of voice to indicate a man: SJB) He goes "Sorry mate, I think you need, um in the chemist". So he goes to the chemist. "Can I have a durex please and the chemist goes "What size do you want?"
All girls	Laughter and giggling.
Sioux	Ha, ha, ha, ha, ha, ha, ha, ha. How do we do it? Haa, haa, haa, aaa, aaa, aa, aa, haa, aaa. Haa, haa, haa, aaa, aaa, aa, aa, haa, aaa.
Sally	Ne he, he, he, he, he, he, he, he, he, he, na, na, na ner ner ner ner ner er er. It's a lorry!

Joke 4

Debbie	There's these two convicts and they've just escaped from where they were in jail and they're walking down the road, and this girl comes along on her bike. She's a quite a nice girl - schoolgirl (ironic tone: SJB) And she goes to one of the blokes. "Oh can you mend my puncture for me? One of them goes, "Yeah, alright then." He goes "I'll catch you up." One of the blokes goes off and one of them stays behind and mends her puncture. He mends it for her and she lies on the grass and takes her shorts off and says "Alright you can have anything you want for mending my puncture ." Ten minutes later this bloke catches up with the other guy and he's pushing a bike. The other goes "Did you mend the puncture ?" and he goes "Yeah". And he goes "What did you get in return?" He goes "She took her shorts off and said I could have anything I wanted. So as the shorts wouldn't fit, so I had the bike!"
Sioux	Oh Christ (Laughter: SJB).
All girls	Laughter .

Each of the four jokes carry racist and sexist attitudes, and it is a feature of many jokes, very much like the functioning o f stereotypes, that they short-circuit critical thinking (Perkins 1979). Thus jokes can reinforce and support stereotypical understandings. A crucial element in the target of these jokes is that the subject does not have a legitimate position or social role. Thus, in each joke the major categories are hippie, immigrant (Irish), roadworker and convict, which represent low status positions in society. The categories can function as terms of abuse because they are from subordinate and oppressed groups.

However, there is another category which is common to these jokes, that is, the jokes are about men. From this different perspective the significance of these jokes is their possible potential to challenge views of male omnipotence. These jokes make fun of men, making them fallible and undermining the notion of male sexual control . What is the symbolic meaning for the girl group in telling such jokes? Douglas (1968) offers an insight,

> The one social condition necessary for a joke to be enjoyed is that the social group in which it is received should develop the formal characteristics of a 'told' joke: that is, a dominant pattern of relations is challenged by another. If there is no joke in the social structure, no other joking can appear! (p. 366).

The dominant pattern which is attacked in these jokes is male control of sexual meaning. The girls' jokes portray the male as sexually absurd. One man tries to chat up a radio, another sticks his penis in the exhaust of a car, a third shows ignorance by confusing 'pyrex' and Durex and has to answer about the size of his penis, and the fourth fails to have sex when it is offered directly to him. These jokes follow Freud's (1916) definition of the joke in terms of the weakening of conscious control in favour of the subconscious; the juxtaposition of control against that which is controlled. In Douglas' terms the girls do not propose another set of relations, although their attitude to boys, boyfriends and men is clearly spelt out in chapters nine and ten. The new wave girls' anti-patriarchal practice, close physicality and 'lesbian' displays are a challenge to men which follows Douglas' thesis that a joke is told when it offers a symbolic pattern of a social pattern. The girls collection of jokes, puns and stories tended towards showing the foolishness of men. They were the only female group in the fifth year to tell jokes of this type which had a sexual meaning.

It would be an exaggeration to argue that these jokes represent a challenge to male sexual dominance because I heard similar jokes told between boys within the school. However, the same or similar jokes could and did have a different meaning when told by girls.

Epic narrative

One type of conversational style particularly associated with the PGS is the epic story or narrative. An epic story is a long tale which combines both a humorous and a serious element. In the example below we see the gradual build up to an epic story told by Sally concerning embarrassment and one of the boffin girls.

Sally	Have you ever seen any of Shane's work?
Sioux	I can't read his writing.
Lynne	He won't let anybody else see it because he's written about us lot.
Sioux	Yeah . I think he wrote about one of the boys showing his bollocks off at the party.
Lynne	I know he's written something horrible about Ellen Smith (boffin girls: SJB).
Sally	Yeah, he said that in French. Right we was coming into the lesson on Monday. Oh you have French with us. He came in and he's yacking on about Ellen Smith.
Sioux	And we was really laughing and somebody goes "Shane, Shane."
Sally	It was me . I was going "Shane, Shane, there's Ellen Smith going bright red."
Lynne	Oh no!
All girls	Laughter.
Sioux	And I really laughed.
Sally	It's the same in English Literature. Right, we are doing Chaucer. Anyway Ellen Smith is reading and she goes "Chaula clit" (Chauntecleer: SJB), she goes "was a cunt". And we all pissed ourselves laughing. She goes "cunt-cu-countryman (stutters: SJB) like that, it was really funny at the time. Actually, it's really randy because they're saying that you know, that the Nun's Priest tale, it is a priest and the old inn keeper, because they're all telling stories and that. The inn keeper goes, "um, well if you weren't a holy man. If you were a worldly man i.e. you weren't a priest. I bet you'd be sexually potent, you'd be a right little raver". It's really explicit and Chauntecleer rides Pertelote twenty times every morning. And Mrs. Holland (teacher: SJB) is going all into it. She is going all like this, "oh, oh,

115

oh"(imitating the sounds of sexual enjoyment: SJB). I can't keep from laughing.

The girls are talking about the social relations of fieldwork. Lynne (CR) asserts the reality principle when she maintains that the researcher will not let outsiders read the field diary. Their personal and private information is secure. This leads them to speculate about what I may have written. She interrupts, to state that she "knows" the researcher has written something horrible about a boffin girl. This leads Sally to develop and expand upon the theme of embarrassment.

The central point about the story is amusement at someone else's expense and therefore the superiority of the new wave girl group. The boffin girl is embarrassed, according to Sally, by my talking about her in the classroom and she becomes embarrassed when she inadvertently utters words used to refer to female genitals. Sally asserts that Chaucer is of interest not just because it is a set text but because of its descriptions of sexual attitudes and behaviour. Her epic has an autobiographic format, the narrator is both participant and observer. The delivery of the story is crucial because it must be exciting so as not to be subject to interruption. The epic story is part of the PGSs repertoire for social dominance of group interaction. It is also a marker of their vocal competence and their ability to capture and hold the group's attention.

Chorusing

Chorusing is produced when the girls together sing, shout, vocalise or make a variety of noises. Chorusing usually occurs at the end of a comment, discussion or an accident, it acts to celebrate, castigate, humiliate or purify a meaning or an action. If a statement by one of the girls is ambiguous, creates vulnerabilities or weakens solidarity, chorusing will occur to remove the negative reverberation and return the group to its original position of strength. Chorusing can also be seen as territorial, when the girls sing or chant songs of their chosen musical style. This cassette signs off with a burst of the new wave girls chorusing.

Sally	I keep wanting to sing something.
Sioux	Yeah, come on, what shall we sing ?
Sally	'Christine, the strawberry girl'.
Sioux	What about the 'Red Light'. "She falls into frame

116

	without the fashion of doubt. But the Polaroids ignited upon seeing their subject. Boomp and the aperture shuts, too much exposure". I really like this bit when it goes "wur, wr wu ways, into focus, flat lips glossy kiss."
Sally	It's horrible isn't it, glossy kiss ur, ur.
Sioux	"But emotion drips down the sleepy young doorstep" Yeah, I like that one as well. "Nocturnal habits are surveyed with interest, so crawl into cars. Ignore any colours and in our radiance. It's time for our neighbours". I think that's a really good song.
Cat	It's good yeah.
Sally	I tell you what I've got the hang of now . F-I-R-E-I-N-C-A-I-R-O, F-I-R-E-N-C-R-O, (letters enunciated in a song: SJB) Oh God I said it wrong.
Sioux	F-I-R-E-I-N-C-A-I-R-O, F-I-R-E-I-N-C-A-I-R-O, F-I-R-E-I-N-C-A-I-R-O. And the heat disappears and the mirror fades away. Hey, we're going to see The Cure. What the hell are you doing?
Sally	Taking my socks off . God, I'm slowly becoming more naked and naked.
Sioux	Oh Sally!.
Sally	Perhaps not.
Sioux	Oh Christ!
Sally	They don't smell, just drifting down the side.
Sioux	Don't be so disgusting!
Sally	We seem to be the only two people in this conversation. The rest have gone to sleep.
Sioux	How now you brown cow? Talk to me you silly slag!
Sally	Oh I know what we can sing. Um "I called you yesterday" I can't sing. I need somebody else to sing with me.
Sioux	(Coughing noises: SJB). Clear me throat.
All girls	"Tried to call you yesterday . You were at the Monday Club or a communist demonstration. Who cares? You're going somewhere everyday. Vegetarians against the clan, every woman against every man. Never one to one, what's wrong, what's wrong with one to one. Just once, just me and you. Cause one to one is real and you can't hide, just for you that three's a crowd".
Sally	Da, da, da, da, da, da, da, da, da.

Sioux	I like the next bit though about waving a banner.
All girls	"I agree with that you say . But I don't want to wear a badge. I don't want to wave a banner like you. I don't mind it, if you do. You're beautiful when you get mad. Or is that a sexist observation. Oh one to one."
Sioux	Oh I know what we can sing Sally. "Mother of Mine".
All girls	Laughter
Sally	"You gave to me".
Sioux	Fuck this and fuck that. I don't want a baby that looks like that.
Sally	Oh baby (End of cassette: SJB).

The girls consider four songs to sing, 'Christine' and 'Red Light' by Siouxsie and the Banshees, 'Fire in Cairo' by the Cure and finally they decide to sing 'One to One' by Joe Jackson. Why did they sing this song? Because the song fits their sentiments and presents an understanding of the relationship between categories as distinct from persons. In the song the categories are firstly, political, secondly, gender and thirdly symbolic. The girls' sense of integrity is realised at the level of the song's discrimination i.e. people are "beautiful" and categories are "ugly". The words of the song are "good to think with", in that the meanings coincide with their cultural relations and practices (Krige 1968).

In the conversation Sioux mentions that the girls as a group are going to a forthcoming concert by The Cure. She makes a claim that a particular song by "Siouxsie and the Banshees" is "really good", this is acknowledged by Cat (CR). When the girls stop singing Sioux shouts 'Mother of Mine', which was one of their night-time walking songs, it was often sung when they were drunk and in good humour. Sioux (PGS) signs off the tape with a ferocious delivery from one of her own songs called "The Baby". It is clear that the girls are tired when Sally states "the rest have gone to sleep". The songs are performed as a collective goodnight both to themselves and to me.

Integrity

The new wave girls' rituals of integrity are a concentrated marshaling of symbols and practice. The rituals amount to a kind of economy in expressing personal affection, feelings and meaning. These rituals are a carefully developed means of communication constructed within the private face and extended to public face interaction. In chapters nine and ten I identify, firstly, the girls close physicality, that is, their intimate private and public bodily contact, and secondly, their use of the female body, its representations and its signifiers to challenge male power relationships through an anti-patriarchal practice. In order to develop the analysis further the use of the term integrity, here, refers to the proposition by Daly (1978) that radical feminism "is affirming our original birth, our original source, movement, surge of living. The finding of our original integrity as re-membering our Selves" (p. 39).

The aim here is to use the concept of integrity on a social basis to offer an insight into understanding the new wave girls' conscious actions and behaviour. Integrity refers to the socially genderised female physicality; the integrity of the female body is seen not in terms of an addition or an exclusion of parts or functions, it is an integral whole, a unity from which no part may be taken. For the new wave girls the body is a site of power whether with reference to the sexual or the physical. Their rituals of integrity are expressions and actions which use physicality and sexuality openly as a symbolic resource; as part of their whole cultural practice and relations.

On a metaphorical level the girls operate a cultural positioning of their bodies. They celebrate the positional structure of their group, whereby the group makes it possible to speak of the body, to think with it and through it. Integrity then is the use of the body as a means to create a code independent of the dominant gender code (MacDonald 1980). The girls speak about their legs.

Sioux	Oh look at those legs (To Sally: SJB).
Sally	They ' re classic ! They'll go down in the history books.
Lynne	We ought to start a rugby team because we all have fat legs.
All girls	YEAH.
All girls	Laughter.

This is a spontaneous group joke which plays on the conventional expectation that girls should have 'slim' legs. They are highly amused by the contradictions which they perceive here and indulge in a heavy irony. It is Lynne (CR) who has introduced reality by pointing out that the girls have "fat legs" but she also brings in a reversal. They could take part in rugby, an essential male context of competitive physical violence.

119

The new wave girls create a collective identity through individual experience, assessment and interpretation of bodily problems. In terms of conversational choreography this means that bodily tales may come in a variety of forms; stories, jokes, puns or ordinary conversation.

Sally	When I'm in the toilet having a fag (at home: SJB) and I'm flicking the ash when I'm having a cigarette. I'm flicking the ash when it goes sssch, sssch, schsssssch. I go (cough twice: SJB) or something. I try to time my shits to land at the same time as the ash goes down. But my shit velocity sometimes is greater than the ash.
All girls	Laughter.
Sally	And I miss - close .
All girls	(Burping noises: SJB)
Sioux	All you've got to do is fart now.
Cat	That'll be no problem.
Sally	Oh do you remember that night you stayed at my house, we went down to the beach that night? Do you remember with Cathy and Bloc as well as Mick? When we came back to my house do you remember? I was doing one after the other. I had a whole tin of baked beans.
Lynne	What about when were at camp then?
All girls	Laughter.
Lynne	Sitting there burping having saveloys.
All girls	(burping and farting noises: SJB).
Sally	There's all these farts.
Sioux	You should've *taped* it.
Sally	We're sitting there , all got our sleeping bag flaps out, five of us are all there like drunks slurping away at this cider.

The girls are in a humorous and nostalgic mood, relating stories about ritual bodily behaviour. Collectively they celebrate the dramas of bodily functions, suggesting that the body may be out of control; hence the inability to control "shit velocity" farting and burping. The stories of the body, whether in control or out of control, reveal how the girls share the body as a practice; it becomes socialised within the group. The mutual appreciation of the "body out of control" not only binds them together, it shows their capacity to promenade. Paradoxically, the ability to apply this idea actually

120

shows their control and use of the female body to deal with sexual contradictions. All the girls accept that they have the same bodily problems and functions - there is no differentiation.

Socially, passing wind is more commonly identified as associated with masculine behaviour. Women who fart in public are usually looked upon as not conforming to the stereotype of feminine behaviour. The girls' ritual capacity to fart in a group situation expresses solidarity, and is part of their integral voice. However, it seems that within the youth cultural group, the CR has to introduce or point out their farts.

Lynne	Arrrr , you missed it I just farted.
Sally	All together, arrrrrr.
Lynne	Oh, they missed it. Cat just passed wind.
Sioux	Oh God!
Sally	Was it really Cat? We're getting into all recriminating things here!

The PGSs Sally and Sioux would fart loudly and without warning and it would be greeted with the gesture of laughter and possibly a story of "greatest farts". Here Lynne states that her own fart went unnoticed. The social significance of farting is honoured only by the social form, hence, Sally's cynical joking response. Indeed, Cat's fart has to be remarked on by the other CR. This results in Sioux's comment of "Oh God!" Cat is exposed and gently reprimanded by Sally PGS. The distance of the CR from the social practice of farting is further shown by the fact that Cat's fart is disguised by Lynne as "passing wind". It can be argued that farting is a gesture of the position within the group and can only be credibly authorised by the social forms.

In this section these examples of their flatulence could show how they have become colonised by male bodily practices rather than freed of them. However, from a different perspective, their rituals allow them the "socially unpermitted": that which disturbs the expression of the feminine becomes in some sense the expression of the feminist. The girls commonly recall past events of "outrageous" party behaviour.

Sally	I've been sick in the sink.
Sioux	Right I ' m in the queue , right till it was my turn and I

121

	thought "I can't wait any longer" because it was my turn. I went into the bathroom and I got some toilet roll.
Sally	Oh no!
Sioux	And I went to toilet in the garden.
All girls	Laughter.

This story is a celebration of non-conformity to traditional feminine toilet behaviour. It is more usually men who go to toilet in the garden rather than women. Sioux's tale is an announcement that their behaviour is expressive, it is a summary of their integrity. Her actions are not only individual but also an integral part of group ritual. Rituals of integrity also involve physical touch and suggestion.

Sally	That's nice, let's turn the light out. Then I can masturbate without anybody watching me ...
Sioux	I could just eat . I could just eat , um , marsh-mellow.
Cat	We haven't got any sorry. No.
Sioux	Now let me think.
Sally	I could suck a marsh-mallow.
Sioux	I could suck something else! He, he, he, he.
Sally	Cat's - tit Not even funny.
Sioux	I'd have to suck Cat's because neither of you two have got anything to suck, so, ha, ha, ha, ... What do you clean your navel out with?
Sally	Fingernail.
Sioux	What do you clean yours with Cat?
Cat	Fingernail.
Sioux	I do mine with a cotton bud.
Sally	Oh, I just let it clean itself.
Sioux	I don't. I bet if you stick your finger in your belly button and smell your finger it will stink.
Lynne	Urrrr.
Sally	Urrr. I'm going to try it. Oh God! It's lovely! Haa, ha, ha, (screeching: SJB)
Sioux	I didn't hear a word of that Sally. What did you say?
Sally	I goes, it's sending all pains... I think I got...
Sioux	Oh God! She's got rheumatism in her stomach.
Sally	I think I'm turning into a hypochondriac.
Sioux	Yeah, my stepfather is a hypochondriac. I swear it.
Sally	It doesn't smell.

Sioux	I like picking my belly button.
Sally	I like picking my nose better.
Sioux	I like picking spots, great big yellowy ones.
Sally	Oh I haven't got any.
Sioux	Well you're alright.
Sally	Lovely!
Sioux	I like getting big juicy spots, especially on the back of my neck.
Sally	Oh Sioux that's really disgusting.
Sioux	It's horrible. They really hurt.
Sally	Just think, wake up in a pool of puss in the morning.
All girls	Urrrrlah.
Sioux	Puss drops keep falling on my head. Puss drops keep running down my neck (singing: SJB).
Sally	Puss drops keep rolling down my back (singing: SJB)

Here we see the new wave girls playing with taboos in a competitive style. The PGSs engage in banter and ritual jousting. Sally invokes masturbation and the idea of sucking "Cat's tit", while Sioux raises the stakes by remarking " I could suck something else!" In general, they deal with aspects of the body which are beyond their control such as illness, fear, dirt and spots. These aspects are taken up within the girls' rituals of integrity and dealt with in play and humour. Choreography, in particular, the chorusing at the end serves to overcome any sense of individual vulnerability resulting from sharing intimacies by offering a unity of experience. Danger has been minimised and collective action demonstrates sisterhood.

Conclusions

In this chapter I have applied the theory of social and symbolic forms, the specialised positions and the social relations of the face, in order to analyse the girls' conversational choreography and rituals of integrity. I have tried to show how the elements of the new wave girls' narrative style of interaction function in the private face. Choreography is central to the girls' communication when promenading as a youth cultural group. The language of ritual arises out of a combination of elements. To sing as a group, to provide enjoyment together, gives the girls a strong sense of belonging. Chorusing and free association expresses and reinforces

123

group ties and shared assumptions. Joke telling and singing have a comforting, almost religious function, offering consensus and solidarity. Their choreographic practice is different in the private and public face. The conversational style realised through the specialised positions carries their rituals of integrity.

The social basis of the girls' integrity is their group relations which create a space for individuals to engage in practices which can be considered as anti-patriarchal (See chapters 9 and 10). The girls' celebration of their own sexuality as natural becomes the communal responsibility of the group, and it is through this wholeness that they begin to collectivise the female body and thereby re-member themselves towards a position of integrity. However, outside the context of the private face of this girls' group, the context of patriarchal culture forces them into a position where they are made to respond to and challenge masculinity. The collective action taken by the girls allows them to confront the contradictions they meet daily, although the ground rules of this confrontation remain on male terms (Lees 1993).

The discussion of the girls' rituals of integrity has illustrated their self conscious celebration of the female body as natural. In other conversations they spoke openly about bodily functions and were not embarrassed by their bodily fluids. The girls demonstrated their power and skill in using the gendered female body and their sexuality openly as a symbolic resource of exclusion, opposition and independence. The new wave girls understood farting or menstruation as a natural expression of their female body and did not assess them as unclean, separate or even "unfeminine": rather they understood the body in terms of integrity - an original unity from which no part may be taken (Daly 1978).

6　　Boffin girls' culture

Introduction

The boffin girls were a pupil group, usually known as "conformists" by other pupils in the school. This chapter is organised in four sections:

The boffin girls pupil friendship group: discusses the different sets of relations within the group and tries to clarify how the internal group dynamics affect the girls' pedagogic successes and bodily.
The boffin girls' work ethic: initially outlines the principles of action of the girls' work ethic, choice, discipline and competition, to identify the rules which the girls use to maintain their future middle class status.
Official pedagogic practice: builds on the analysis of the work ethic in order to describe more fully a model of conformist group relations and practice.
The boffin girls' structured pedagogic practice: discusses the girls' interpretation of how they employ their particular pedagogic practice, the difficulties they encounter and the attitude they expect the teachers to have towards them. I will focus upon the girls' understanding of examinations as "ordinary", and present the girls' view of sexual discrimination within the curriculum. Finally, I show what the boffin girls understand as their weakness, and in particular their experience of sexual vulnerabilities. The concern here will be to outline how the boffin girls' pedagogic practice is put into operation in the context of the school. I hope to show, that the

boffin girls' relations, practices and communication work within a structured pedagogy which has three features, first, principles of action, second, a site of resources, and third, an outward display of academic status and style.

The boffin girls friendship group

The membership and relations of the boffin girls were described in chapter one. This chapter provides an interpretation of how relations are managed within the boffin girl group. There were thirteen girls in the overall boffin group, which was divided into three smaller groups, the core group of five and two other groups of four respectively. I choose to focus upon the core group of boffin girls because, unlike the two other groups, it did not fragment. The two other groups often consisted of pairs and girls who changed their friends (Meyenn 1980).

The middle class boffin girls not only belonged to the same social class but also, importantly, regarded one another as intellectual equals. The boffin girls' recognised aim was to gain formal qualifications, and all the girls were prepared to sacrifice pleasure to ensure pedagogic success. The girls' explicit marker of deferred gratification was their special parties to celebrate passes of O'level examinations. When a boffin girl was successful in taking an examination early, the group would organise a party. This demonstrated that the boffin girls had clear rules which not only divided work from pleasure, but prescribed that success at school should be rewarded by pleasure outside school.

There were no divisions inside the group arising from educational aims, about which there was a consensus. The basis of division within the pupil friendship group was their acknowledged sexual vulnerability. This refers to their lack of information and experience in heterosexual relations. This division within the female friendship group was based on the judgements of other girls concerning their physical maturity and attractiveness. Common phrases used by the boffin girls to refer to this internal division were "she is more mature" or "she is more immature". Information, news, stories, jokes and gossip on bodily and sexual issues were high status within the female group and this information appeared to be divided into either "body" or "rumour" news. The operation of the division meant that girls assessed as mature would receive body and rumour news, whilst boffin girls understood to be immature would have access only to rumour news.

The boffin girls' work ethic

In a discussion on jobs in the local labour market and school examinations the girls display their pedagogic expertise and middle class values.

Rose   The higher your qualifications the better chance you've got of getting a job.

Kerry   And of what area you want to work in.

Rose   Depends, because, I mean, I know some people. My dad does interviews down the power station. He said some people with degrees have been on the dole for two years or more. But that is only because they, alot of people do try to get higher jobs than they should and it depends generally on what you want to go into. Because alot of people think I want to do this job, go and get a degree and then there are not any jobs for it. And because they have got the degree they will not go for lower jobs. The more qualifications you have got the best chance of a job. I mean around here, if you have got no qualifications, I would say you would probably get a job, but not the sort - probably would in the end.

Monica   Would be! This area!

Rose   You would probably get a job as a farm labourer or something, but I would not class that as a good job.

Kerry   It's not good money.

Rose   It's not good money that's what I mean. But you have to have qualifications.

SJB   What do you think of the people who don't want to do any exams, they just want to get out?

Ellen   STUPID

Rose   I think it is stupid. But it's their choice is it not? It's their choice.

Kerry   They have made their choice, that they're not going to do any exams, so they're going to leave school. So they probably will not be able to get a job, they will be walking into the state. And so they are affecting

127

everyone because they're going to have to support them later on. It is their choice not to do any exams but they will sort of say, "Well I don't want to do any exams, so I'm just gonna depend on the state". And you have to support them.

Here we can begin to see aspects of the boffin girls' work ethic, especially in relation to one of their principles of action, choice. In the following discussion they elaborate their social class based distinctions, in terms of education as a preparation for mental and manual labour.

Rose	I think everybody is given the same chance in life. I mean, we all go to school, we all go to, you know, we all get the chance of a long education. You have got some people can do manual labour and some people at the top inventing things or running the country.
Mary	That's the principle though, everyone does, sort of their best.
Rose	Yeah I know, but somebody who is just lifting things and putting them in one place, you cannot give them as much money as some people who are really using their brain, really thinking and taxing themselves.
Mary	You could say that people were taxing themselves doing manual labour, just as much as mental.
Rose	You could, but you have got to have some *rules*.
Mary	Some people have to be more equal than others.
Rose	I mean those people who are running the country have got a heck of alot more responsibility.
Mary	Yeah. I mean people are always saying that there is not any class distinctions nowadays. You don't have the upper crust.
Ellen	You do.
Mary	You do and you have to.
Rose	But some people work hard and get their money. I think 'good luck to them'. But other people just inherit it and that and I do not. I suppose I am jealous. But you know, I do not like things like that where people have got all the money.
Mary	But the thing is nowadays alot of the sort of class discrimination - is intelligence as well, because we are in the upper band and top class and we are doing O'

levels and things like that. Other people tend to think we are snobs just because we are clever.

It is possible to identify what I shall call the boffin girls' work ethic, that is, their three principles of action: choice, competition and discipline, which the girls apply in learning environments inside and outside the school. These explicit rules of learning are applied by the girls not only to their own approach, attitude and ability in school but also to their assessment of other pupils. I shall now briefly specify the elements of the boffin girls' work ethic.

Firstly, in terms of choice, we can see that the girls regard it as the right of every individual; they suggest that pupils should have the right to choose whether or not to take an examination. The school seems to be understood as a site of resources to gain qualifications, where pupils have an equal opportunity to learn. The boffin girls perceive school as a neutral institution For them, the combination of being middle class and also the school's top pupils has made them somewhat blind to their own advantages, when they assess how rational their decisions are in contrast to those of other pupils without such advantages. They maintain that working hard in school to achieve success is a rational decision based upon choice which is equally available to all.

Secondly, in terms of discipline, throughout the fieldwork, the boffin girls expressed the view that to pass examinations pupils require self discipline; this results in more qualifications, hence increased opportunities. The girls understand the operation of the labour market as being responsive to their acknowledged ability. They believe that their disciplined approach to school subjects will create parallel results and opportunities when they enter the labour market. The points mentioned concerning the type of degree and work available, reveal that the girls' principles of action are subtle and sensitive to potential change. They state that qualifications are central to finding good jobs, with good money and responsibility. Those pupils who do not want to take examinations are assessed as not accepting responsibility for their actions, since it is felt that ultimately such persons will be supported by social services. The two quotations show the strength of the influence of order and rules on the boffin girls' behaviour; it is within this regulative framework that the girls learn.

Thirdly, with respect to competition the boffin girls celebrate their pedagogic achievement of passing school examinations. They identify the world of work and the world of school through two different models; firstly, in terms of the mental/manual labour division, and secondly, in terms of the two systems of meritocracy and inheritance.

However, their liberal principle of choice creates a momentary opposition between equality and competition when Mary suggests the equality of the two types of labour. They are caught within the classic sociological division between achievement and ascription. They support the notion of mental labour, because of their position in the school pupil hierarchy, but they cannot accept a system of inequality which may operate against the criterion of intellect. The boffin girls argue that elites in society are acceptable only if they owe their position to the rules of competition and hard work which permit those with most mental capacity to be at the top. During the discussion I noticed that all the boffin girls smile and nod in agreement with Mary's assessment as she successfully transfers the model of work, mental labour and meritocracy to the world of school. Here, the elite in the fifth year of secondary school is the boffin girl group, who assert that they owe their dominant position not to wealth or social class but to their intelligence and work ethic.

Official pedagogic practice: a model of conformist group relations

This section attempts to draw on the principles of action outlined and to elaborate the boffin girls' site of resources, that is, their official pedagogic practice which is that of a classic seminar form. The boffin girls' within-group relations can be described as a site of celebration, resource and exploration of the structured pedagogic principles (SPP) of the school, supported by the class position of their families. Their SPP condenses into a work ethic whose essential components are individual choice, competition and discipline, and it is this ethic which is both dominant and dominates these girls' practices. However, as we shall see, this ethic provides both the condition of their resentful subordination to their family and their subordination to teachers, and yet also offers the conditions for their release from both. We can summarise diagrammatically the boffin girls' group practice as follows:

Figure 1:   *Model of conformist behaviour*

1. principles of action
choice   discipline   competition
(work ethic)
2. pedagogic practice
seminar form
(resource site)
3. style
pedagogic promenade
(status display)

The seminar form is a site of available strategies and resources where the girls can rise above the limited and mundane nature of personal assertions, and enter into debate on important issues. Throughout the fieldwork I took part in and observed many instances of the boffin girls' official pedagogic practice in action. The subject under discussion would vary but the seminar form would remain the same; arguments for and arguments against to show the differences within and between competing opinions.

Pedagogic promenade

The boffin girls' pedagogic promenade was the highest form of their official pedagogic practice. The seminar form was the basic relay for the promenade but before it could occur the girls set a high standard on contribution, in fact, it could be seen as representing a rehearsal for the examination room. During the pedagogic promenade, the simple statement of an opinion would operate against its logic, in order to display the articulation of different, oppositional and contradictory levels of argument. The structural format of this display of competence, style and status meant that priority was given to the abstract level of argument. The rule was to support each side and try to resolve the problem by suggesting a possible balance. The girls removed themselves from assertion of an opinion and concentrated upon the validity of one scheme against another.

This boffin girls' pedagogic promenade begins with the topic of competition within capitalism.

Rose   No , the nationalised industries are (running the

131

	country down: SJB) because people don't tend to work so hard as much because there is not so much...
Kerry	Output.
Rose	There is no competition.
Kerry	Because they've got the Government to support them.
Rose	No competition, so they do not need...
Mary	I think we ought to have a certain amount of each (nationalised and private industries) don't you?
Rose	No. But I mean, perhaps we have alot of nationalised industries; there's rail, the coal board is nationalised.
Kerry	British Leyland was.
Rose	British Leyland was a nationalised company. But I mean alot of firms, more than half the people.
Kerry	There is no incentive now because , you know that if you do not make a profit, then, you are going to get the money anyway.
Rose	Yeah . If they didn't know. If they (the workers: SJB) know that they haven't got any competition, they think we're the only ones in this country making this; so they think don't need to work as hard because they are the leaders. But if they had competition, they would work hard. Because they'd think well this firm next door is making the same thing and if we make twice as much as them, well it's better, we are going to sell more, and we are going to keep our jobs.
Kerry	Apart from that if you are not nationalised, you have got to work and you have got to make a profit to keep the company there.
Rose	But when you've got say, like British Leyland... I mean they'd have been much better just keeping their companies on their own. Because you have competition, alot more competition.
SJB	Why do you think competition is better?
Ellen	Because they are going to say if we are nationalised , they are going to need, the country needs us. And if we want more money we will go on strike, we have got to pay it because we are all depending on it. So they are more likely to go on strike, if they are nationalised.
Rose	But the thing is , it depends , because if you ' ve too much nationalisation people do not work. If you have got too much private industry then the owners get the

	upper hand because they know that people have to work to survive. Therefore, the bosses just exploit them. They do not pay much money and things; you have got to...
Mary	Have a balance.
Rose	I mean, not all the time, but sometimes I think unions are right to strike because some people are poorly paid. And they are right. But some people are not prepared to and say no we can't afford to strike we have to go back to work, we need the money. But then when it comes to the union pay, they expect to get the pay as well which I don't think is right.
Mary	I think sometimes when companies sort of go on strike for a reason, it is a good reason. And then other people think oh well they got away with going on strike. And then they go on strike, just simply to say they want the pay rise that they don't really need. So I think there are too many people who are trying to cash in on the Government through strikes and things. It is not doing any good at all to those people who really need it.
Rose	I think when Labour was in government, they suggested wage increases of 5% or 6%, and the Tories had a right go at them. Now the Tories are in they are suggesting wage increases of 5% or 6% and Labour...
Kerry	But the thing is to pay for the extra wages that everyone is paying out to the Government. They've got to rise the taxes or the prices or something to get more revenue to pay the excessive wages. That is a vicious circle.
Mary	The Government are cutting back and people are complaining about it. It's better than borrowing more.
Rose	Yeah. That is what I am saying, Governments, just sort of, they do the same thing if they are in power. But both of them are sort of contradicting each other. Whatever they say about the other party, they have said it once, they have done it, they have tried to do it themselves. But when the other wants to do it, they just say no, you should not. It's all wrong.
SJB	Do you think that's the main problem?
Rose	They do tend to run each other down.
Mary	What we just said about industry, there has got to be

	competition I think there has got to be competition in government as well.
Kerry	Only at the moment I think they should get together.
Rose	No , you are never going to get them working together, because they have got no, they have got different ideals.
Kerry	Yeah . But at the moment they are just , they are working for themselves. I don't think either of them are really working for the country. They are trying to get one up on the other, using the country as a, ur. Apart from that, you cannot deal with the situation, what is it, four years you get in power, usually isn't it? You cannot deal with the situation, if it is pretty bad, in four years, because then, say the government is going to be changed, and if you are left, you are going to go over to the right. You are going to use a totally different set of ideas and methods and it is just not going to do anything, it is only going to make it worse.
Rose	That ' s just it , because, I mean, Labour get in, but I'm not saying I'm Labour but I'm not Tory. I mean if they had carried on Labour could have probably got us out of this recession. But then if you leave the Tories there, they probably could as well.
Mary	Whatever one is in , they will use their own method.
Rose	If they are left for a long enough time they will get you out, both of them.
Mary	But the thing is people get upset about all the cut backs and everything, whichever government is in power, so that people will vote the other way to stop them doing it.
Rose	I mean, I don't think the Tories did better or any worse than the Labour Government.
Mary	They are just doing it their own way.
Rose	Yeah.
Mary	I don ' t think that really we know until it has sort of worked.
Kerry	I mean like France they have got seven years with their President, don't they, which is better, that's if it is a good President.
Mary	But if it is a bad one, I don't know, that's ...
Rose	But the thing is in this country if there is a pretty bad

	Government they do tend to sort of get alot of stick and they do get out earlier.
Kerry	That's because it is a democracy.

The pedagogic promenade is hesitant at first but once the girls move into their display of status and style the strategy of argument and counter argument becomes increasingly complex. They construct a discussion through competitive contributions by building up assertions and perhaps also bringing in other relevant issues to widen the debate.

I shall identify the four arguments, counter arguments and the proposed balance and then I will make an interpretation of the boffin girls' pedagogic promenade. The *first argument* is that workers in nationalised industries have little incentive to work hard because there is a lack of competition. The first counter argument put forward is that private industry exploits workers by paying low wages because employers know that the workers have to sell their labour to survive. The first balance is that there should be a combination of each type of industry, in the public and private sectors. The *second argument* is that employees strike because their wages are below subsistence; inadequate pay forces workers to take industrial action. The second counter argument put forward is that other employees strike for wage rises which they do not require as they are not poor. The second balance is that the government deals with pay increases through taxation, it is a "vicious circle", nobody wins. The *third argument* is that Labour and Conservative parties have different and oppositional methods, ideals and policies. The third counter argument put forward is that whatever party is in power, it is only interested in retaining power, not in the people who voted for it. The third balance is that possibly the different political parties could work together or Mary's proposal of introducing "competition into government". The *fourth argument* is that whichever political party is in government it could overcome the problems of the economic recession. The fourth counter argument put forward is that a longer time in power might be worse if the government is bad. The fourth balance is that government can be voted out because Britain is a democratic society.

The pedagogic promenade displays the boffin girls' underlying competence. From their perspective they have presented the factors involved, giving more significance to the development of the argument and its structure than to content or personal experience.

It was only as a result of extensive fieldwork with the boffin girls, both within the formal and informal spaces of the school and outside school, that I realised that the pedagogic promenade was a general model of analysis applied by the girls which could be activated readily. The same general structure was employed time and time again by any number of the boffin girls as markers of their position.

An important feature of the seminar form is that the girls' personal opinion has a tendency to become displaced by the assessment of argument and counter argument. The operation of this official pedagogic practice permits the girls to stand back from the subjectivity of their response to the issues involved, and releases them from the necessity to formulate their own opinion on these matters. The seminar form allows for discussion on important problems a discussion to which they can contribute within the safety of their pedagogic competence. The seminar form operates by articulating the grounds for, and in so doing creates, the boffin girls' pedagogic promenade, that is their display of status, style and speech. In general, the boffin girls have accepted the ideological message of pedagogy i.e. the appearance of neutrality, and it is upon this basis that they display their pedagogic competence.

If we look at the pedagogic promenade from another angle we could suggest that takes the same form as an examination essay. The candidate does not give a personal opinion but writes about the issues and problems relating to the question from a number of accepted different sides. In the above quotation the girls distance themselves from the arguments under discussion through their position in pedagogy; personal feelings are not considered relevant. The neutrality of discourse has priority; their acceptance and application of the ideology of pedagogy shows that their assessment of an issue is both rational and ordered.

The pedagogic promenade is the high point in the display of the boffin girls' competence but it also shows that the girls are dominated by a pedagogic form. This is the intellectual relation which they have acquired from their parents, from the school and from their peer group (Delamont 1973, 1983). The outcome of this intellectual relation is that the boffin girls are subordinate to pedagogy. These points will receive attention in the following section.

The boffin girls' pedagogic control: a self generating practice

I shall now examine certain features of the boffin girls' structured pedagogy, in an attempt to show how the girls are dominant in, and dominated by, school processes. The essential proposition will be twofold; the girls' pedagogic practice is a self generating form by means of which the girls process any subject and articulate its relation and meaning, and it also shows that they are subordinated to pedagogy.

In the example the girls discuss someone they consider to be a bad teacher; this throws light on their work ethic and their independence from the teacher.

Rose   I think in English, I mean if the teacher is bad I'm not saying it doesn't make a difference, but it doesn't make as much difference as with alot of subjects.

Kerry   You don't need to understand it.

Rose   You don't need to understand it. It is the sciences mainly that...

Ellen   And Maths.

Rose   Maths is a science. Yuk! It is a science. I mean some arts subjects, I think Sociology, you need some understanding don't you or is it all learning? Alot of the arts subjects are just learning and even if a teacher cannot teach you, you can get a book and sit down and learn it, you could pass.

Kerry   Just churn it out in the exam.

Rose   Yeah, because if you are brainy enough to do O' levels anyway, you could pass. I'm not saying, you could get an A or B but you would pass the O' level. But in the sciences I think the teacher has to be able to get it over to you because you have to understand it. That's it, in sciences the teachers are not very good, they tend to be not that good teachers.

The girls are confident of their ability to learn and understand any school subject, to pass examinations and gain certificates. They here display distributive rules of learning, they make a division between arts and science subjects which require different pupil strategies. They say that pupils require a teacher in order to understand science subjects, whereas pupils do not have to rely on the teacher in arts subjects, because these can be learned for exam purposes without being understood. The girls assert that as a result of this, individuals can learn arts subjects by teaching themselves assuming that the pupil is "brainy enough to do O' levels anyway". In science subjects this strategy of self teaching becomes an essential aid to passing the examinations, owing to the more difficult nature of science and the increased likelihood of teachers not being able to teach it well. This is a clear example of the strength of their work ethic; through its principles of action the girls maintain that it is possible to pass examinations without relying on teachers.

Subordination and recognition

This section concentrates on the boffin girls' perspective on teachers, and special attention is given to the manner in which the girls are subordinate to pedagogic demands. However, I shall also focus on their demand for an adult teacher-pupil reciprocal interaction. The boffin girls maintained that where reciprocal relations were not developed between teacher and taught, there would be no space for potential praise and reward, and this would result in a less effective educational setting.

Rose   Some of the teachers treat you like adults, don't they.

Kerry   You have to be able to relate to the teacher because you have got to respect a teacher as well.

Rose   They teach you, Mr. Willis teaches you as an adult doesn't he.

Kerry   Yeah

Rose   As equals, because you know, you have got lessons, lessons come first but if you have finished it or you have finished the experiment, they talk to you about other things. It's not just all lessons, you know, your subject all the time. But other teachers, they sort of look down on you, they teach you as children rather than as equals.

Kerry   Other teachers are good, Mr. Willis, if you have got break or something, you finish an experiment and other people have not, he will come up and say, 'did you watch such and such on telly last night'. They've got a relationship with kids outside the lesson as well as inside it.

138

The girls emphasise that it is encouragement rather than direction that is needed from teachers. At times it seems that the girls are subservient to the teachers, but the girls also demand a relationship based upon equality. It is clear that pro-school pupils like the boffin girls do not simply conform to the school values and norms. The girls use their ability to win time in the lesson which gives them status as achievers. Then they use this time to gain further status as adults by engaging in conversation with teachers on equal terms about matters unrelated to school, for example television programmes. They use their intellectual position in the school to create a social relation within classroom time. These middle class girls expect the teacher to contribute as much as they are willing to do, whereby the girls are given a reward for their performance by the creation of an adult relationship with the teacher inside and outside the classroom.

In one sense, the boffin girls perhaps had a rather inflexible approach to learning. Consequently, where they did not receive the appropriate method of teaching they often became disruptive. During classroom observation of the boffin girls it was possible to see a number of different strategies which they would employ to manoeuvre the teacher back to structured learning. The girls would move on to the next section themselves, then they would ask questions about what was coming up in future and finally they would start to display deviant behaviour and wait for the teacher to notice that they were not paying attention. However, they were prepared to accept that teachers cannot always make the lesson interesting and that they may have to learn boring facts.

Kerry   The teacher can't always make it interesting because you have got to do what is on the curriculum. And if that is boring well that is tough. It is just the way the teacher teaches it that makes it interesting. It is up to them. But you can't do interesting subjects; if the class finds one bit interesting you just cannot do that all the time, because you have got to do the other stuff.

Kerry argues that her interest in a subject and the learning of the subject, do not always coincide. She shows acceptance of the school's structured pedagogy. In general, for the boffin girls pedagogy came before pleasure, to the extent that Kerry suggests it is up to the teacher to make the subject enjoyable. Superficially, their acceptance of the structure of schooling appears to be almost one-sided, the school system dictated to the girls. But at a deep level, their acceptance of the school structure was based upon the spaces it gave for their acknowledged status and skill to be won and celebrated. The girls were able to position themselves as observers and assess the structure of schooling in a manner not available to most pupils.

Teachers who did not offer an adult relation and who treated the girls like children did not receive full co-operation from the school's top examinees. For example during my classroom observation of one history lesson the teacher continually refused to acknowledge the girls' demands for an equal/adult pedagogic relation. In this lesson, one of the boffin girls was dismissed from the classroom and told to sit outside, something which was without precedent. In this case the boffin girls decided to do other work which they considered more urgent, during the lesson, and displayed their disapproval by sustaining a persistent murmur. This teacher failed to establish the correct learning environment and this resulted in forms of deviance by the school's top examinees.

Ordinariness of examinations

The boffin girls who had already passed a number of O' levels a year early in the fourth year, were familiar with examination processes and procedures. They were confident, perhaps slightly arrogant, about revision and examinations. The girls reduced considerably the fears usually associated with sitting formal examinations.

Rose	When you've got other examinations you cannot spend ages working on one exam, you've got other examinations.
Kerry	Like the mocks we've just done. We had all the subjects in a week.
SJB	Did you do much revision?
Kerry	You couldn't, you could do about two or three hours on each examination.
Rose	Unless of course you revised before.
Ellen	On all O' levels they want to give this extra homework to get us ready.
Kerry	They say 'You have got to have a biology weekend' or something, this weekend. And then everyone (teachers: SJB) says that, so you have got piles of homework.

Ellen	We've got three sociology essays (this weekend: SJB).
Kerry	It just depends which subject you put as your most important, that you do the work first and spend the most time on.
Rose	It tends to be the ones you like. I mean I spend all my time doing history because some of it is assessed , and all others just go.

For the boffin girls revision is just a process of preparation for the examination, they suggest that there is a considerable amount of work to do but that they just divide the time by the number of exam subjects and work out a schedule. They point out that there are favourite subjects and priorities i.e. assessment, but subjects for examination are simply there to be taken. The girls can be rather dismissive of an examination, as one of the girls shows.

Rose	I cannot stand it (statistics: SJB) I mean I could pass it if I work. But it is just so boring, I cannot bother working. It doesn't bother me, if I get it because it is just sort of, to me, it is an extra O' level.

For the boffin girls the "speciality" of taking examinations had been inverted into an ordinariness. However, they do not underestimate the importance of passing examinations. The crucial difference between their approach and other pupils' approaches t o examinations was that the boffin girls were able to define the whole process as mundane, and each stage had been rationalised. Their common concerns and rather insular position in the school provide them with maximum opportunity to share their resources.

SJB	Do you swap your homework?
Rose	Shall we answer that one (Joke: SJB).
All girls	Laughter. We do.
Rose	We do copy.
Kerry	'I haven't done my homework today can I copy yours?'.
Ellen	We do copy.
SJB	I saw some of Sarah ' s homework round Alison's house that was being copied out.
Monica	Oh yes.
Rose	We do not copy. We pool our resources, that's how I put it.
Kerry	Yes.

Rose   But I tend when we have tests and things , I tend not to revise because I think then you can work out what you know and what you don't know. A week later you have forgotten it all, because you have just learned it the night before and I, it is just stuff you remember for a couple of days and not much longer. For the mocks I revised some but not much because I wanted to see what I knew.

The right to swap homework within the boffin girl group is based on one principle, which is that each girl is expected to conform to the group work ethic; otherwise there would be no access to the group's intellectual resources. This process is understood as a method whereby the pupil gains access to the knowledge required to pass examinations. The test is interpreted as a test for the pupil which allows her to evaluate her ability. The test is not defined as an imposition by the school upon the pupil. The boffin girls' employ their pedagogic practice to understand critically the meaning of the examination (Aggleton 1987). The subjects are learned, revised and then mostly forgotten, as the boffin girls move on to their next pedagogic challenge. Even though they are dominated by formal schooling, they exploit it instrumentally to achieve their own aims.

Sex and pedagogy: genderised subjects

Sexual divisions within school are well documented at a variety of levels: at the level of teachers, pupils, curriculum, decision making and extra curricular activities (Weiner 1985, Holly 1989). The term 'genderised subjects' refers to those subjects where certain assumptions concerning modes of appropriate sexual behaviour operate. These assumptions of the school and of its teachers, tend to create relations of opposition and subordination between boys and girls which lead to further sexist discrimination between pupils. Pupils' notions and stereotypes of appropriate self and opposite sex behaviour become an important means for them to assess which subjects to choose. This is because the pupils' position in school will be partially understood according to the subjects selected by their peers. Here the girls point out that in male defined areas of the curriculum, they are given a lower status because they are not male.

Kerry	Because we did home economics, needlework and 3 D - technology, which was sort of metalwork and woodwork, because they sort of had boys and girls together. They (teachers: SJB) did not think we were capable of doing anything too difficult. So they used to make really SIMPLE things in all of it and EVERYTHING.
Rose	I don't know . In 3 D, technology we made quite good things.
Kerry	I mean I made a clothes rest and it is still working.
Mary	But they were really simple things.
Rose	Yeah I know.
Mary	We didn't ever make things like pokers (for a coal fire: SJB) or anything like that did we.
Ellen	No. It was nice getting a lump of wood and sawing it into a certain shape and you know...
Rose	Yeah, but you had to learn.
Ellen	Drilling , you had a piece of wood and you had to drill certain sizes of holes.
Kerry	Those pendent things we made in metal.
Rose	I enjoyed making those.
Mary	Yes, doing it.
Kerry	Yes I enjoyed making them but they were...
Ellen	USELESS.

The boffin girls display enthusiasm about the lessons within the male preserve of a technical subject. At first they appear reticent to acknowledge that they were placed in a subordinate position but then the girls argue that they were permitted to make only simple things. The girls realise that they suffer discrimination, their stay within this male preserve was only temporary. The subject contents made available to them reflected the girls' low status which reinforced their marginal position. The girls made "useless" things for decoration rather than for practical use (Measor 1984). For the boffin girls, the school's top examinees in both arts and science subjects, such sexual discrimination is illogical because they can use their skills and apply them to any subject.

The boffin girls experience a contradiction of their patriarchal relations. No matter how intelligent they are or how many qualifications they may have, some things will be put beyond their grasp because they are girls. The school in which the boffin girls have so heavily invested, is now seen as actually withdrawing potential credit from them (Whyld 1983).

Sexual vulnerabilities

The boffin girls' sexual vulnerabilities are a consequence of their acknowledged lack of information and experience of love and heterosexual sexual relationships. The girls' uncertainty is understood by them as an important gap in their knowledge. In this section I shall concentrate firstly on the boffin girls' problems concerning sex education, and secondly, on the official sex education talks given separately to the female pupils and their effect on the boffin girls. Here they outline the crux of the problem, which is limited access to different types of sex education.

Ellen	We do not do general studies.
Kerry	We didn't get the choice.
Ellen	I think we ought to learn it though.
SJB	Do you think that?
Ellen	Yes, I think so. Everyone has got a right to learn.
Mary	There is so many people sort of making their , forming their own opinions and that, and then they say you are brainy, you should know all about it, but alot of people don't. Because we do English literature we do not have any sex education. No, we do sort of in biology.
Kerry	I mean you do in biology, but.
Rose	We don't really do it in biology though.
Ellen	In biology you do alot about your genes.
Mary	No. We've been doing contraception.
Rose	We are going into that this weekend as well Ellen .
Mary	He said, we will spend a little while longer on it , but it is nothing really.
Kerry	It is better than NOTHING.
Mary	I think it's nothing you don't really know already I know about, you know. We do sex education every year drawings, pictures and things like that.
Ellen	My life. Sex education was so sickening, ur,ur.
Mary	But you don't really know anything much about it.
Rose	They don't teach, you know. They learn all about, sort of, what, I don't know...
Mary	Biological value of sex.
Rose	Yeah. We learn that. They sort of... No, also they learn

	other things (in general studies: SJB) as well as sex education.
Monica	If you have it rammed down your throat every twenty minutes.
Mary	Yes but, um, not in, but, biology things like that you sort of...
Rose	We should...
SJB	Do you think they (teachers: SJB) look on it as purely biological?
Mary	Yes. I think we ought to...
Rose	It is not in biology.
Mary	It is only with Mr. French. He is a little better because he is sort of blunt, he gets to the point and he is daft.
Rose	The head of the science department is a bit like that, as well, isn't he Ellen.
Ellen	Yes. Everybody...
Kerry	You should be taught about the emotional side of it as well.
Mary	Yes.
Kerry	What to expect.
Rose	They do learn alot of other things in general studies as well as that.
Mary	About not to be pressurised into doing something that you think you might, or if you think it is right.
SJB	Mm.
Rose	But we did not get the choice to do general studies.
Mary	No.
Kerry	No.
Rose	We just had to do English literature.
Mary	I don't know that it's better to do general studies but I think we ought to know more.

From the unfinished sentences and half comments it is possible to see that the boffin girls reveal many of their uncertainties and hang ups. It is clear that the sex education the girls receive in biology is not the type of information they want. At the level of the curriculum, the girls explain that the timetable option allows English literature or general studies. As the school's top pupils they were forced to take Literature rather than General Studies, as the latter was unexamined. The latter subject offers informal discussion on physical and emotional aspects of sexual relations which is closer to the form of sex education that the boffin girls required, rather than sex education in biology which concentrates on the mechanics of reproduction.

The contents of general studies can be developed according to the wishes of the teacher and the taught, and also, at Marshlands general studies was taught by the leader of the Youth Wing who had an established relationship with pupils based on informality and friendly contact. Thus, the boffin girls said on numerous occasions that sex education, as taught in general studies, was what they wanted, because it was made personal and related to their feelings and problems.

A major obstacle for the boffin girls' access to general studies was that, independent from the subject being non-examined, the class contained lower band pupils. Sex education in this context could possibly become a battle ground, because in such lessons the personal would be emphasized and the boffin girls' vulnerabilities here would be close to the surface (Jackson 1978b). In discussions with the boffin girls they acknowledged that other pupils disliked them because of their high status. Thus, from the perspective of the low status pupil, this classroom situation could present an ideal opportunity to attack the boffin girls.

The discussion reveals an important internal division between those girls who they defined as immature or mature. The mature boffin girls had access to both 'body' and 'rumour' news, whereas the immature boffin girls received only 'rumour' news. The mature/immature division applies here where the mature boffin girls are Kerry, Monica and Mary, and the immature boffin girls are Ellen and Rose. The immature girls' hold a negative attitude to the discussion on sex and also attempt to close down the conversation by side tracking the subject under discussion. These differences within the group were quite divisive because they were not related to educational achievement but had their basis in an arbitrary concept of maturity.

Girls' official sex education talks

Separate official sex education talks for female pupils occurred quite frequently from the first to the fifth year, and usually took place after assembly or registration. All the girls were subjected to these regular programmes which presented the school's position on female sexuality. Boys were not present during these sex education talks, nor did boys receive a similar separate talk. During one of

146

their discussions the girls elaborated their feelings on how the school had framed female sexuality in these "talks".

Mary	So in the Lower School, um, sort of, the girls were sort of taken away at registration and things like that and after assemblies and given a GOOD TALK.
Kerry	TALK
Ellen	TALK
Rose	TALK
SJB	What was the talk?
Mary	All about growing up and how we were different.
Rose	They, the boys, were not allowed to hear. But they always found out about it, didn't they.
Mary	Yes. But they, sort of, never ...
Rose	They talk to you in general.
Mary	They mention... They might have told the boys as well. They sort of kept it separate. They made you think of it as something to be hushed up and kept quiet.
Ellen	I REMEMBER. What they talk about, urr.
Mary	I think it should come out into the open. You should be able to talk about it between boys and girls and not get embarrassed about it.

The perception of female sexuality presented in these talks was as follows; firstly, girls should cover up their body and hide their sexuality, secondly, a girl's bodily functions are not to be made public or spoken about with boys, such matters are strictly for females, and thirdly, the girl's body is not her own because it relates to other things, it is better to deny any feelings, especially desires. (Rocheron and Whyld 1983, Holland, Ramazanoglu and Sharpe 1993).

The boffin girls appear to have been asked to accept that there is something shameful about the female body; discussion of the female body had to occur in a separate all girls setting. The formal exclusion of boys from these talks (and lack of equivalent male sex education talks) was assessed by the boffin girls as one factor which promotes the boys' negative attitude towards the female body: privacy is seen as increasing stigma. The boys' rudeness and hostility was thought to be partly a result of their having been excluded from these talks. The separation appears to make the girls think of their bodies as unnatural, not a proper or a worthwhile subject of conversation or that female sexuality is something

147

unpleasant, perhaps even bad (Scales and Kirby 1983, Holly 1989). It could be suggested that the school has induced in some of the girls a fear of female sexuality which prolongs their immaturity (Jackson 1978a). Do the boffin girls have any other ways of gaining access to information about female and male sexual behaviour? In the previous section the boffin girls complained that in school they were denied access to the kind of sex education they wanted. Inside and outside the home the boffin girls' activities came under detailed surveillance from parents. For example, to go to a party or a disco, a girl had to tell her parents which boys (and girls) would be present. The parents then decided whether such male company would be suitable and whether they would allow their daughter to attend.

The boffin girls were restricted in terms of the range and type of sex information to which they had access. The school's formal position in the "talks" presented one perspective, the girls' parents enforced a moral regime of a similar nature, which left their peer group as the only other available source for alternative views upon female and male sexuality (Thomson and Scott 1991). As we have seen, the boffin girls' peer group relations were at their most divisive with respect to sexual and bodily information because access was not open to all. The basis of access to peer group knowledge on female and male relationships was a function of the mature/immature divisions inside the boffin girl group.

Conclusions

In this chapter I have presented an interpretation of the boffin girls' pedagogic practice and an account of their relations and practices in action. We can identify three sites of the origin and continuity of the boffin girls' official pedagogic practice, firstly, the school, secondly, the peer group and thirdly the family; each site shows the girls' social class relation to education. These relations to education, acquired in the school and in the family are mediated through their expressive interpersonal peer group love relations. The school and the family combine in the promotion of middle class individualism with competitive relations and explicit rules for achievement, but in the peer group these relations also become relations of support, collaboration and affirmation. The clearly structured pedagogic practice of the school and the family, denies and attempts to exclude the ambiguities, contradictions and tensions which the boffin girls have to face as a consequence of the normative definition of their age and gender relations, social class position and contact with other pupil groups, and in particular, sexist male groups.

The boffin girls exploit schooling for their own requirements but at the same time they accept the neutrality of pedagogy and the authority of the school. Thus, it may appear that they are subordinate to the school. Such a simple conclusion would be misleading because it fails to investigate the means whereby the girls work within the school processes.

This chapter has also outlined a theoretical model of the boffin girls' practice of structured pedagogy. The boffin girls' intra-group relations can be described as a site of celebration, resource and exploration of the structured pedagogic principles of the school, embedded in the class principles of their families. The structured pedagogic practice of the boffin girls condenses into a work ethic, the essential components of which are individual choice, discipline and competition; it is this ethic which is dominant in the school and dominates these girls' practices. The girls' pedagogic promenade displays their underlying competence, order and consensus; indeed it is a rehearsal for the essays to be written in the examination room. I interpreted this work ethic as the condition both of their resentful subordination to their family, and of their instrumental subordination to teachers, however, it is also the condition for their release from both. Their acknowledged aim is to gain educational credit which will give them an opportunity to enter college or university. Thus, success in school allows these girls to escape from local pressures of parents and boys.

7   Boffin boys' culture

Introduction

This chapter presents an insight into the cultural practices, relations, rules and communication within an upper ability male pupil group. The three sections in this chapter offer an interpretation of the boffin boys' culture in action. The first section examines the boffin boys' friendship group, with particular attention to their rule-based framework of interaction and practices of masculine intimacy, together with their ideology of individualism. The second section builds on this analysis which identifies the importance of the bonds created by their shared attitude towards schooling and achievement. There is a description of the boffin boys' seminar form of discussion followed by an analysis of their efforts to gain social mobility and the implication of these efforts for their class of origin.

The third section presents the boffin boys' feelings and experience as they attempted to move from the safety of their all-male group to establish relations with girls. Here I shall concentrate on the consequences of the rule-bound behaviour of the boffin boys with respect to their relations with girls, their sexual realities and fantasies of that reality, and their strategies for dealing with rejection.

Boffin boys pupil friendship group

The three core members of the boffin boys' group, Howard, Gary and James, were a closed male friendship group. In school it was essential for all aspiring male boffins to be known by or in some way associated with these three individual pupils, or with the eight marginal members. It is possible to distinguish three basic features of the boffin boy friendship group. The first refers to the basis of identity. The second refers to male rivalries. The third refers to their vulnerability.

Identity: the boffin boys denied that they were a collective type or a group possessing an expressive identity, and affirmed the contrary through the presentation of an individualistic pedagogic identity. Howard's specialism within the group was as the controller of pedagogic status, he ordered, allocated esteem, and reinterpreted other boys' contributions. He was the senior friend within the pupil group and there was internal group competition among boys for his time and friendship. Howard was the person to whom love was addressed and he occasionally took on a teacher role.

Rivalry: inside the boffin boy group there were a number of boys who were style singletons, i.e. they possessed a youth cultural style but were not members of a group, and so did not share the social relations of the style. Thus within the boffin group there were individual spaces for style satellite specialities. These different styles, however, only reflected the individualism of the member, not the group, and did not infringe upon the rule that they were not a type. An important opposition within the boffin boy identity was on the one hand the denial of being types, and on the other hand, the forging of an identity in the form of a pedagogic instrumental solidarity as the basis for their interactions in school. Inside the group the boys acknowledged rivalry but refused to enter relations of rivalry with expressive groups because this might adversely affect their aims in school. Being identified as in competition with an expressive group might have meant that the boffin boys would be typed unfavourably by both pupils and teachers.

Vulnerability: there were two external relations which endangered the boffin group's instrumental relation to education, which was the source of their identity. Firstly, James introduced ambiguities and uncertainty into the all male group through his relationship with his girlfriend(s). He brought information into the group about the issues and difficulties of establishing and maintaining an intimate relation with girls. This created individual and group vulnerabilities if this personal relationship became dominant over the pedagogic relation. Secondly, Gary was upper working class unlike most other of the boffin boys who were middle and lower middle class. The other boys considered that any boffin boy, and in this case Gary, who displayed "unsavoury" working class attitudes or behaviour militated against their aspirations to social mobility. Gary's class traits were assessed as being inappropriate especially within an external group setting. Thus boffin boys presented two types of tension and vulnerability firstly, with respect to their social class peer group relations and secondly with respect to their sexual relations; both threatened their pedagogic instrumentalism.

An ideology of individualism: not "types" but individuals

A "type" was understood by the boffin boys as an identity which is expressive and might be in opposition to the school. The boffin boys' assertion of not being types points positively to their behaviour as largely pro-school (Blackman 1992). The boys were seen to identify with the school, and thus were not types. The criminal boys used to say of the boffin boys, "They don't do anything" which meant that they did homework and had no social identity outside the school and home. The boffin boys possessed an invisible social identity which other pupils were ignorant of and which only became visible to me after a number of months, when I was allowed to accompany the boffin boys to parties and discos. However, where features of their invisible social identity surfaced and became defined as a "type" the boffin boys would either deny or reject this interpretation, for example in this conversation about Gary's disco dancing. (Here the boffin boys are joined by two mod boys)

Keef	Gary used to make a right embarrassment of himself, his disco dancing.
Gary	That was yonks (long time: SJB) ago, weren't it.
Hat	You're still disco dancing!
Keef	Jiving!
Gary	Not really disco.
Keef	Used to do head over heels and all that , didn't you.
Gary	No I don't think, not to quite that extreme.

152

Keef	Full twist up in the air!
Gary	Not, not like that.
James	He used to really freak out.
Gary	I used to be a right idiot, I know that.

Gary receives no support from the other boffin boys to overcome this ritual humiliation. He asserts that this type of behaviour is of the past, and he accepts it as a mistake which he has now corrected.

Underlying the boffin boys' understanding of a "type" was also the assumption that this entailed a lack of individualism, for example, as Howard put it "I just like single songs, I do not like types". James states " I do not go dressed out with hair all sticking up, I do not look too extreme". "Types" were associated with practices which could restrict the boffin boys social mobility project. It was on the premise of not being a "type" and the promotion of an image of being a pro-school pupil, that the boffin boys' ideology of individualism rested. Their individualism was maintained firstly, by their instrumental detachment; they saw themselves as having no specialised identity and were not in competition with other pupil groups; and secondly by the rules boffin boys used as basic principles of their practice. They evaluate their actions according to a careful consideration of possible consequences for their aim of social mobility : their prudent practice was the means to this end.

The boffin boys' pedagogic practice and class vulnerabilities

This section will focus upon the boffin boys' pedagogic practice, which in general, refers to their approach to education. Here, I want to concentrate on a particular feature of their approach to learning in school which I have termed the "seminar form". They were in the upper ability band and were recognised by the teaching staff as possessing the ability to be successful in examinations. The data presented will attempt to show their intellectual practice in action.

The seminar form.

The seminar form is a term used here to describe the boffin boys' pedagogic relations; in this group it is Howard who, as the senior friend takes on the guiding role of a professor. Participation in the boffin boys' seminar form involved making assertions and counter assertions and the development of, or the raising of, more and more complex factors of a topic. In the early afternoon I went with the boys to an informal talk on "entering the sixth form". In the late afternoon in a discussion they began to speak about their feelings about the values held by some members of the sixth form at Marshlands.

Gary	They reckon they are right boffins. The ones that go to CND benefits. They go round, oh, oh, oh.
James	Checkland (Sixth form pupil. SJB)
Gary	Yeah . People like that you know , they really think because they are bright, that they are superior to you because they are taking their A' levels.
SJB	Do you think that?
Howard	Because they are . But I do not think they know enough about it to. See, I don't know enough about it. They do not know enough about it to make up other people's minds.
Gary	They are just into this peace thing, you know.
Howard	You can have your sort of ideas of peace , world peace. That is not practical because in the sixties they found that out. But nuclear war is something difficult to determine, if good or bad. The actual war, you know, just shit really, but determines...
Gary	In effect, because if one country has got it, you have got to have it as well.
Howard	See if you're a dictatorship or anything like that , and Russia is really a dictatorship, and um - if they get... If there was not nuclear arms, they (USSR: SJB) are bound just to knock them up. You cannot take the technology away ...
James	The communists are not against nuclear power , are they.
Howard	The idea of communism is all right , but it is just in practical terms that I think it is not.
James	It is the idea that the Government gets all the wealth.
Howard	That is not the idea. The ideas of communism are alright. But after that, you cannot have it, with, it is just human nature to want and to get more for yourself...
James	I think they (USSR: SJB) have got all the facts wrong.
Howard	It is impossible now, you cannot do it (drop the bomb:

	SJB) because it would be a good thing to have nuclear disarmament. No threat of holocaust. But hen you get minor wars that can run longer and cause just as much damage , where you do not get the inherited stuff .
James	You talking about power stations as well?
SJB	Well that can come into it.
James	Yeah , well when everyone talks of nuclear power being dangerous right. Yeah, maybe it is. But all the examples of disaster and everything have been in America. They are differently designed reactors than what we've got here, they are not half as safe.
Gary	I don't think they will ever use nuclear weapons , not in our lifetime.
James	No . I think you do not need nuclear disarmament as long as you have got it there. It is a deterrent. don't think it will ever come to anybody using it.
SJB	What do you think of Britain's policy?
James	Keep it up. Keep it up.
Gary	Thatcher, she has got to say that she has a policy, hasn't she.
Gary	She has got to say that but now she's in line with the USA.
James	I mean the Campaign for Nuclear Disarmament, it has only got one country to say right, I am not going nuke, you know, you say right. Everyone says right. Get rid of nuclear power, and Russia just keeps one blinking, atom bomb back. They jump it on Britain. Bang. And we were good, we disarmed ourselves.
Gary	Without nuclear weapons nobody can do it. So if you are going to have deterrents, so I think...
Howard	There could be a nuclear war because you know they can get away it.
James	It is states that cause nuclear war.
Howard	Some people , there will be some people that will survive. See in a land mass like Russia; like that, you will get some out-laying parts where there would be cover. I think in the future they could work it out that there will be a way that some will survive and I think you will get a government that is prepared to take the sort of risks involved.

The boffin boys' seminar form is a discursive site for the display of their underlying pedagogic competence. Initially, the talk is ritualised and jocular but it soon changes to a discussion on the different issues of nuclear war. Firstly, I shall identify the number and complexity of the assertions and counter-assertions, and secondly, I will make an interpretation of their seminar form. The number of assertions raised were:

1. Gary asserts that the sixth form are pedagogically conceited, James agrees and Howard argues they are inordinately vain in their assessment of other people's opinions.
2. Gary raises the political point of CND, Howard adds a historical reference and he goes on to differentiate between peace in terms of theory and practice.
3. Howard increases the complexity of the argument by speaking about moral issues and Gary notes the apparent logic of the escalation of nuclear weapons.
4. Howard widens the discussion to types of government and technological factors involved.
5. James introduces the idea of communism, but it is Howard who elaborates the difference between the theory and the practice of communism: the two boys disagree.
6. James and Howard also disagree on the value of disarmament. James suggests the basis of communism is false, and Howard asserts the positive nature of the development of CND and the problems of security for the human race.
7. Howard notes the difference between major wars (with nuclear bombs) and minor wars which continue indefinitely, in relation to the suffering they cause.
8. James adds to the discussion the issue of nuclear power, referring to different types of reactors and their potential for disaster.
9. Gary brings the discussion back to use the of nuclear weapons. James agrees with Gary that weapons won't be used, arguing that they function as a deterrent because all sides possess them.
10. I ask them what they thought of Britain's nuclear policy. First; James asserts his support for Britain's nuclear policy. Secondly, Gary argues that Britain does not have a policy but is in line with America.
11. James argues against CND with a hypothetical example where the world disarms and a country retains one bomb. Gary disagrees with this model but is interrupted by James who asserts that it is states that cause war not people.

12. Finally, Howard evaluates the potential for a limited nuclear war, he argues that scientific estimates will be available in the future and depending on the type of government, this will determine whether a limited nuclear conflict could be of value.

In the interpretation of the boffin boys' educational practice as a seminar form, we can identify how the boys develop an aggressive male academic style of debate and practice their secondary habitus (Bourdieu and Passeron 1977). The seminar form operates as a site where the boys display competence through articulation of different and contending arguments. The contribution by any boy occurs in a competitive environment, in accordance with rules and standards which apply to statements and conduct. The seminar form shows the ordered approach that the boys use to achieve success in school. In an all boffin boy situation the seminar form presents a site of available strategies and resources: here they can cooperate, and evaluate themselves in an exclusive context (Ball 1981). The competitive rule-bound environment allows individuals to monitor their own and others' progress, to develop confidence and to check the unity of the group. Thus, the seminar form can operate as a site for the boys to inspect, practice and monitor pedagogic practices necessary to fulfil their social class aspirations.

    In conclusion, there was a similarity between boffin boys and girls with respect to their sharing of a "seminar" form of communication and interaction based upon official pedagogic practice. Presumably, this seminar form had similar functions for both groups. However, the boys seminar form was not only a site for rehearsing and developing their pedagogic competence but was also a site for rehearsing, monitoring and developing conduct appropriate to their class aspirations. This function arose out of the mixed social class membership of the boffin boys and was not found in the boffin girl group, as the girls all shared an established middle class background.

Social class vulnerabilities

In a discussion about daily newspapers, Gary's social class vulnerabilities become an apparent problem for the boffin group.

Howard   The Sun!
James   What do you have?

Gary	No we don't, we (parents: SJB) have the Daily Express. We have the Express.
Howard	Just because you have a couple of big tits on the second or third page.
Gary	No , we don't have The Sun anymore . On Tuesday I get The Sun.
Howard	I know , you sit there with the old paper (Suggestive looks to Gary: SJB).

It is established that Gary's parents used to purchase 'The Sun' also that he still buys the paper himself. The other boffin boys regard this particular daily paper as inferior and as not consistent with their pedagogic endeavours in school. But Gary has another argument, he asserts that he buys the paper for entertainment.

Gary	That is all I want to read . I don't want to read about politics all day. Oh, the government have just put out a new proposal to raise interest two percent. I don't want to know that crap, I want to know who's got beaten up.

Unfortunately, Gary's line of thinking goes against the pedagogic practice and aspirations of the boffin boys. His argument reflects a preference for the expressive, it is too close to working class culture and associated with types from which the boffins are attempting to distance themselves. To prefer entertainment to education is not acceptable to the boffin boys. Gary's assertion has revealed his class vulnerabilities at a deep level and tension and emotion begin to create cracks in the seminar form.

Gary	You are going on about your paper . But because you get a better paper , that means you are higher class.
Howard	No.
Gary	That is when you kept taking the mickey out of me because we used to get The Sun. WHAT IS THE BIG DEAL ABOUT THE SUN?
Howard	You read The Sun. Now this is a true statement. If you read The Sun, it is you know, the writing in it.
Gary	It's one of the most common papers, isn't it.
Howard	But it is not a very good paper , it is easy to read , okay.
Gary	That is why it is for the majority . I only get it for the sport.

Howard	If you read, sort of, a normal paper.
Davey	Yeah, but you don't get it. It's up to your Dad.
James	Mail or Express.
Howard	A moderate one like the Daily Express or Mail . So you get used to a certain type of writing . I think the Mail.
Gary	You cannot take the piss out of me just because I get a paper.
James	I am not taking the piss out of you.
Howard	It is a figure of speech. Sorry.
James	In other words, he's calling him a dimbell (stupid: SJB).
Gary	Because I get The Sun.
Howard	Do you read The Sun?
Gary	No. We used to.
Howard	Do you read The Sun? Do you read The Sun?
Gary	I just look through , if there is anything I want to read I'll look at it.
Howard	Then it doesn't matter . It doesn't affect you does it.
Gary	You get The Sun! You are taking the mickey out of me again.

The boffin boys' pedagogic unity shows signs of being fragmented under the threat of Gary's class vulnerability. These social class vulnerabilities show how far Howard and James direct the group towards their goal of social mobility, to the extent of possible friendship sacrifice. Through Gary's position in the boffin group the remaining members (core and marginal) have a yardstick to measure and maintain their future project. Throughout the fieldwork they were relentless in highlighting social class threats to their academic achievement. The successful elimination of what were assessed as working class cultural traits further reinforced the boffins' argument that they were not an expressive group, that is, their behaviour did not attract unfavourable attention.

This example of the discussion on the popular press has demonstrated the disintegration of the boffin boys' seminar form and pedagogic unity in the face of an inappropriate social class practice. The priority became the eradication of any improper class attitude and pedagogic practice, rather than the development of solidarity. Thus individuals within the groups could be left brutally exposed because as a group, the boffins' social solidarity was not collective but was instrumental and individually based upon pedagogic competence and class aspiration. The principles of the boffin boys' friendship group were organised through rules, regulations, progressions and sequences. They knew how to operate the rules of the school and could in fact work these regulations to support their status position within the school (Bernstein 1990). It could be argued that the boffin boys possessed few insulation devices within their group to protect individuals from structural relations, such as social class, which created oppositions and contradictions in their group identity and project. An insulation device can be defined as a strategy to prevent external structural factors from creating tension within an informal group.

On one occasion I was with them when their behaviour during break time became oppositional and the Head teacher caught them and cautioned the three major members not only for misbehaviour but also for their incorrect school uniform. When the Head teacher delivered his warning, in front of other pupils, the boys were somewhat ill at ease. Furthermore, Howard, James and Gary were told to go to the Head's office later in the day.

In boffin circles such a public reprimand was not only unknown but raised the boys' status to that of the "rebel" boffins. In contrast the other major pupil groups considered this issue of boffin deviance a non-exciting event. The Head's warning to the boffin boys was a significant problem for them, causing momentary damage to their pedagogic goal and to their public identity in school as the conforming pupils. However, from the boffin boys' perspective, because it affected the core group rather than highlighting an individual's class impropriety, they were able to redefine their vulnerability as representing the group's success in negotiating with the Head.

Sexual vulnerabilities

This section examines some of the problems the boffin boys describe as they attempt to move from the security of an all-male group to establish female intimacy. The issues of which the boys speak derive from events leading to, during and after a boffin boy and girl party on a Saturday evening. I arrived at the venue with three of the boffin girls, helped to set things up with them and was one of the last to leave. Here I will be concerned with, firstly: male sexual vulnerability, secondly; violation, dance and vulnerability, thirdly; interpersonal relations; fourthly: public and private bodily contact; and finally: scapegoating: an insulation device.

In order to understand how the boys conduct their relations with girls it is necessary to construct a more precise terms, I shall do this through the elaboration of three different forms of contact: social relations, sexual relations and love relations; together these are to be understood as sources of vulnerabilities for the boffin boys. I shall make the following distinctions:

Social relations: this refers to how the boffin boys address girls in public, this includes inter boffin group relations, ritual and personal insults, forms of address and intellectual discussion through the "seminar form" in the classroom.

Sexual relations: this refers to heterosexual relations with girls. The boffin boys divide this into *public* bodily contact for example dancing, kissing and holding hands, and *private* bodily contact , i.e. 'more intimate sexual contact'.

Interpersonal/love relations: this refers to the boffin boys' everyday relations with the boffin girls, which can be divided into friendship relations, which includes informal talk on school work, leisure issues and common pursuits; and love relations which includes idealisation, romantic advances and caring.

Each of these relations with girls have rules regulating the appropriate sequence of behaviour for proper conduct. These rules allow us to identify and understand how vulnerabilities arise, and to identify instances of violation with respect to sequence, form and contact.

Violation, dance and vulnerability

Pupils who begin a heterosexual relationship gain considerable formal and informal status, both inside and outside school. Within the pupil community establishing a relationship confers a degree of maturity on the partners, and functions to curtail the use of certain abusive sexual stereotypes which flourish in school (Stanworth 1981, Blackman 1987). In a discussion, Gary is singled out by the others for his inappropriate mode of address to one of the boffin girls at the party.

Davey	Yeah. I talked to Sarah about you, she goes you always go up there and take the mickey or something.
Gary	Yeah?

James	She said you are always saying nasty things. Yeah. She goes Howard was all right because he comes up and asked me to dance.
Gary	I went up to her and called her nasty things ? (Denial: SJB).
James	YEAH.
Davey	No. That you always ...
James	No . She said when ever Gary sees me , he is always saying nasty things about ...
Gary	BULLSHIT I don't ever talk to her.
Davey	Bullshit!
Gary	I don't even talk to her. Honestly, all I said was ...
Davey	No. It weren't just, wasn't just on Saturday night. She meant all the time.
Gary	I'm never nasty to her.
James	You are.
Gary	The last time - I do not hardly talk to her. When you started talking about, you remember. I do not talk to her now unless she talks to you.
James	It is probably because you were doing this (Body movement of sexual intercourse: SJB) when we were dancing.
Gary	Well that is not taking the piss is it really , that is not being nasty to her.
Howard	You should have seen him on the way home , right , because these two (Gary and James: SJB) were having a go at each other.

I shall infer here a boffin boy rule that in establishing the first stage of bodily contact, the dance is a recognition of public bodily contact. Not every dance will lead from public to private bodily contact but the possibility may be present. James explains that Howard obeyed the accepted rules of approach in his social contact, thus when he asked Sarah for a dance she accepted.

The assertion is that Gary's desire to dance, that is for public bodily contact, became too dominant. Sarah disliked Gary's approach, she refuses him and he acts badly towards her. The inference is that Gary's behaviour is also similar with regard to other girls, and it threatens the boffin boys' attempts to move from successful social contact to establish public bodily contact. They conclude that because Gary does not follow the rules of address in his social contact with girls, he will always be refused, which will exacerbate his abuse of girls.

They now go on to argue that Gary's behaviour at the party was damaging to boffin boys. James claims that when he was dancing with Sarah, they both saw Gary make gestures of sexual intercourse. Here, Gary has not violated a rule of sequence himself, but through a fantasy display of private bodily contact his behaviour is inappropriate to James and Sarah who are engaging only in public bodily contact.

The boys focus the discussion upon the reason why there was so little bodily contact at the party. James suggests that this was because so few couples were dancing together.

James	Too much drink and not enough people dancing, because there was drink there.
Howard	I think the drink was all right , you need some drink .
James	But not so ...
Gary	If it had been dry it would have been pathetic , would have been boring, everyone would have just sat around.
James	Too many people were drinking not enough dancing , that's the problem.
Gary	Get sweaty and that, and start smelling.
James	Oh! Oh!
Gary	You do. You get all sweaty don't you.
SJB	You had a deodorant on didn't you?
Gary	Yeah. But you still get sweaty.

The inference is that if a girl is dancing or standing by the dance floor it is easy to ask her for a dance rather than make oneself vulnerable by going directly to where the girls are sitting and drinking. For a boffin boy to enter the territorial space of an all-girl group could produce further vulnerabilities. In fact no boffin boy during the party did venture over to the all-girl corner to ask a girl to dance and only a few boys would risk taking over a message from another boy. At the party the boffin boys tended to favour the security of drinking within an all-male group. I observed that the boys would dance in an all-male group for short periods of time, then return to drinking to summon enough courage to face asking a girl to dance or to be prepared for rejection.

James spells out his interpretation of the relation between dance, drink and bodily contact.

James   There was so much drink , right , when a dance came up. Oh, I have started this can (of beer: SJB) I will have to finish it. I am not going to leave that or somebody will pinch it .... I didn't dance with Monica at the party, she didn't dance with me. So nothing.

At the party, the three core boffin boys were gathered in one corner and were surrounded by other members of the group; Davey, Russ, Will, Nick and Paul. The male grouping possessed a supply of full beer cans, but when a boy danced with a girl, two of the more immature boffin boys would drink the beer left behind. This activity continued throughout the evening and James' remarks clearly show that it annoyed him.

The relation between drinking alcohol (beer) and masculinity is well documented (Plant and Plant 1992). Here, James specifies the problem of combining alcohol consumption with a willingness to dance. Clearly, in the all-male drinking group there is security but if a boy dances he does not drink (image of masculinity) but if he drinks he will lose out on dancing (with a girl) if he becomes drunk.

Inter-personal relations

I shall now focus upon the boffin boys' interpersonal contact with girls. Primarily, I will deal with their relation to the love object, Monica, in an attempt to see how interpersonal contact is understood by the boys, and how it affects their internal group relations, pedagogic practice and social mobility project.

James is the only boffin boy to have successfully sustained a relationship with a girl (for over eight months). He is seen as being able to provide support and elaborate rules of how to engage, establish and maintain a steady relation with a girl. However, this is at the cost of introducing further sexual vulnerabilities into the boy group. They discuss which girls they consider most attractive.

Gary   I don't like many of the girls there (at the party: SJB) anyway.
James   I like Madeleine , and I like Sarah and I like Mandy.
Gary   Huh! Huh!
Howard   Some of them really get stroppy.

In general, the boffin boys consider that James is too soft and too susceptible to romantic sway, as they think he wants to fall in love. James is prepared for a relationship with a range of girls; and Gary regards James' many love aspirations as inappropriate to the boffin boys' concept of a single relation. He is not directing his love, this means he is not in full control of his behaviour. The easy access James enjoys in social contact with girls could endanger the boffin boys' pedagogic unity and project. They question James to assess his reliability.

Howard	Do you still fancy her James?
James	No.
Gary	You DON'T? (Denial: SJB).
James	No .
Howard	YOU DO.

Howard and Gary refuse to accept James' word, and affirm that he is not telling the truth. James has introduced further tension into the male group because they are uncertain whether they can trust him. At the party James failed in his attempt to re-establish his love relation with Monica. His confidence in social contact with girls and experience of bodily contact were of no value. The group begin an 'inquest' to understand why James was unsuccessful.

Howard	I think that she is in just the same situation as you though, because you didn't really know if you were going out with her, right, she thought that you weren't.
Gary	She thought that you didn't want to and you thought she didn't want to.
James	Yeah . All right . So I tried to make up to her at the party , right , I goes come on then let's have a dance. I said can I have the next one.
Howard	Yeah. You asked me first, if I thought ...
James	Can I have the next one ? She goes I do not feel like dancing. Sat down. Davey came up, asked her and she got up, so I mean what am I supposed to gather from that?

From the boys' perspective the correct approach and rules of address were employed but the girl's actions seem incomprehensible. Their unsuccessful social contact with girls is becoming exposed within the group. To combat their partially acknowledged rejection, the boys try again to resolve their apparent failure.

James   No , I had every intention of trying her at the party but when she turned me down, and danced with Davey or you (the researcher: SJB)...

Howard   I think you left it too late in the evening because she was almost gone, you weren't sure because you said to me, was it you?

James   I couldn't be bothered to though then...

Howard   Do you think she would have danced with me?

James   Monica was partially, partially was, she was only drunk when she was dancing. Monica was only drunk when she was dancing with me.

All boys   Laughter.

James   Everybody else she was serious with.

In the above quotation they discuss their failure with girls at the party, and weigh up the factors for or against Monica accepting the invitation to dance. The boffin boys' acceptance of 'rational' rules of social contact is disturbed by Monica's behaviour which they understand as irrational. James accuses Monica of operating a dual attitude to dance through drink. James offers to dance with Monica, she pretends to be drunk and he is refused. Another person offers to dance with her, James asserts that she shows she is in fact sober as the invitation is accepted.

In the conversation James lets slip that he did dance with Monica. He argues that when she did dance with him she acted as if she was drunk, therefore, he could not propose further bodily contact because this would not have been honourable. He stands by the rules of social conduct and does not attempt to take advantage of her by suggesting bodily contact. Meanwhile, both Howard and Gary attempt to repair the uncertainties caused by Monica's action by considering possible excuses which weigh in their favour for example, "She was almost gone". The boys are beginning to close ranks in the group, James expresses a ritual insult to Monica, and the boys conclude with laughter to emphasize that he took the right approach and that her behaviour was absurd.

Inside the group there is a growing acknowledgement of their failure to establish public bodily contact with girls, and even to achieve adequate social contact. The boys return to the discussion to seek a rational explanation for their failure.

James   She kind of , right, ignored me all week. Don' take any notice of this lot right. (Giggling, funny noises, laughter and "wacky" expressions from other boffin boys: SJB) I went round (to her house: SJB), she says I have got too much homework tonight, so I went home. And I thought if she has got too much homework tonight, you know, she might have it tomorrow night. So I'm not going round.
Davey   Might have what tomorrow night?
James   OH , SHUT YOUR MOUTH , RIGHT. And so, ur, ur, you Yeah. Because she didn't want to see me for the rest of the week. Well, I went round on Wednesday and she said, oh, she has got too much homework. I mean Wednesday night. You can always leave it till next week, the homework, you know. If she is that enthusiastic she might as well stay in for the night.

To retain dignity James admits publicly that he has been rejected and he invokes a rational pedagogic argument to minimise vulnerability; competition of homework for Monica's time. The boys accept the priority of homework over social and personal relationships. The boffin boys' vulnerability is reduced and the assertion of pedagogic unity prevails over the establishment of a relationship with a girl.

At the same time, some of the boys deride James because even though he has greater social contact with girls, he was unable to be more successful. Davey makes a ritual insult to James, which implies James' inability to move from a public to a private bodily contact. James interprets Davey's "sound" as a personal insult and makes a verbal attack. This conflict and tension forces James to elucidate further and this time he reveals the danger which the boffin boys thought may possibly exist. Namely, that establishing and maintaining a relationship might prove harmful to their pedagogical practices. James is caught by this emotional statement. He is not consistent with their rules when he argues that Monica should push her homework to one side rather than refuse him, as he would do the same for her. By openly stating that homework should be ignored or delayed James is in direct opposition to the practices of the boffin boys.

Public and private bodily contact

Here I want to show that the boys have an ambiguous relation to sexual reality and fantasy. I have argued that Monica is considered a love object by the boffin boys. This causes tension in their management of interpersonal contact with her (or another love object) in terms of either love or friendship. After many conversations with the boys I understood Monica to represent a contradiction to these boys between their present education and sexual state, and their future occupational and sexual state. Their problem was that she seemed to be their ideal partner now, in the present: this gave rise to difficulties in how they could resolve their ambiguities about her.

However, at the party Monica played a highly complex and subtle role as a rejector, which had begun before the specific event. She used strategies which lessened the boffin boys' chance of establishing public bodily contact; firstly, talking and drinking within an all-girl context and space, and secondly, reducing her dance floor availability by dancing in an all-girl group, or dancing only with those boffin boys who would not propose private bodily contact. I shall now deal with the boys' understanding of another boffin girl, Rose, who is considered a sexual object by the group. Here, in conversation, the boys introduce fantasy about Rose to displace their failure in reality with Monica.

James   Anyone dance with Rose?

Paul   There is only one person I know who danced with Rose.

James   I danced with Rose. Did you dance with Rose?

Howard   Yeah. Holding her up.

James   Right. You've got to dance with this bird, and you get pulled along, arm out of its socket, you know. Okay then, did you kiss her?

Here, again it is James who makes explicit the sequencing rule of sexual intimacy, that is, public bodily contact - the dance, can lead to the next stage - the kiss. The fantasy is that the boys are being sexually dominated by the demands of a girl who initiates a dance.

James   Rose was getting off with everybody.

Howard   I think she loves you (To James: SJB).

SJB   Did anybody kiss Rose?

Gary	Oh I don't think so. Huh, I was not that far gone.

Here we see how they position Rose in both reality and fantasy to suit their purpose of minimising their vulnerabilities with girls. Some of the boys begin to admit to dancing with her, they maintain that she is sexually assertive but it is the boffin boys who are in control. Three points can be made: firstly, the boffin boys fantasise that Rose is a sexual object, she is out of control and available for bodily contact, unlike Monica; secondly, the boys are unable to deal with this fantasy as a reality, as they cannot deal with the threat of a girl's overt sexuality; and thirdly, by fantasising Rose as a 'slut' they can reject her and explain their relation to her in the reality of the party. For the boffin boys Rose takes on an active role in their fantasy of formulating sexual relations.

Howard	I was just saying she is really nice , and we all quite like her SOMETIMES!
James	No we don't . I hate her guts . BLOODY putting on being drunk. What did she think, she was stimulating, you know, we are all going to be sexually madly in love with her, because she drinks.
Howard	Well, not exactly. I think she ...
Gary	I don't like her alot.
Howard	I think that she needs to go out with someone myself.
Davey	Oh - Oh , well . Who is going to be the brave fellow ?
Howard	She has been out with Francis.
SJB	Do you think that's what she needs?
James	She said she didn't fancy him but she went out with him.
Howard	Because I reckon that she would go out with anyone who asked her out.
James	She is desperate.

The boys' understanding of Rose's behaviour shows that there is an ambiguous relation between sexual reality and their fantasy about it: in reality Rose has not been out with a boy but in their fantasy she is pictured as a "slag". It is only through fantasy that the boys can ground this view of female promiscuity because in reality she has not begun to be sexually active.

James' claim that Rose anticipates that they will be "sexually madly in love" with her, heightens the ambiguity within the group, because he conflates sex (private bodily contact), and love

169

(interpersonal contact) a division which the boys created in order to reduce their vulnerability with girls. James goes on to suggest that Rose was using drink to establish public bodily contact, not only was her behaviour false i.e. pretending to be drunk when she was sober, but in reality the boys recognise that she threatens to break their sequencing rules. In fantasy the boys are seduced by their interpretation of her behaviour and this leads them on to fantasise how best they can service Rose's sexual demands.

Scapegoating: an insulation device

For the boffin boys, girls are limited to two positions; that of love object and sex object. The fundamental problem for the boffin boys is their perceived failure with respect to both of these two positions, which raises questions for how they relate to and understand girls. What follows is an analysis of how the boffin boys try to escape the problem of their vulnerabilities by positioning a scapegoat to deal with what they were denied (Monica) and what they could not accept (Rose).

The boffin boy group's scapegoat is Paul, a boy in the upper ability band who appears to them as being small, rather weak and childlike. Paul is a square boffin but he also maintains a marginal relation to the boffin boy group. He continually aspires to be one of the group but is largely unsuccessful because they take it in turns to ridicule and denigrate him. To a limited extent, I thought Paul realised the function he served for the group, and thereby could regard himself as partially accepted within this status group at Marshlands. In the discussion below the boys highlight the fact that Paul danced with the love object (Monica) more than any other boffin boy.

Howard	Monica didn't dance with me.
James	Especially Paul, she danced five times with Paul.
Gary	SIX. It was seven yesterday though.
Davey	Randy little sod!
James	Twice.
Howard	Imagination works wonders doesn't it.
Gary	He is telling us seven dances.
All boys	Laughter (except Paul).
James	She had half a dozen with you (Davey: SJB) and half a dozen with Cyril.
Davey	Six, you know, counting eh.

Paul   So it was seven. It was six definitely.

Paul perceived that at the party there was an opportunity for him to gain acceptance within the boffin boy group by dancing with the love object Monica. Later, he also attempts to reinforce this by exaggerating the times he did dance with her.

The boys are negative to Paul, as it appears from his account of the party that he has been successful in establishing public bodily contact. In order to restore their esteem they humiliate Paul. He is insulted with sexual innuendo and then the boys laugh at his impotence and marginality, because he did not follow their sequencing rules to gain private bodily contact. After seven dances he gained not one kiss. Here we can infer that Paul regarded success in terms of the times he danced with Monica, not as a step in the boffin boys' sequencing rules to establish intimacy with a female. As a result of Monica spending most of the evening dancing with square boffins, the boffin boys are able to argue that Monica was unavailable for intimacy and therefore they can solve the problem of their rejection.

The boys appear to have successfully transferred their fear of rejection by the love object onto Paul when they use him as a sexually impotent scapegoat, that is, they imply that he can not achieve intimacy. However, the problem still remains of how they can resolve their vulnerability with respect to their interpretation of Rose's behaviour as promiscuous:

Howard   (To Paul: SJB) I think she is in love with you.
James   She is really desperate.
Gary   Like Paul. I think she fancies Paul.
Davey   Yeah. I do, she kept looking at you.

The boys displace their earlier vulnerability in not being able to accept what they interpreted as Rose's availability, by the offer to set-up Paul, not in reality but in fantasy. The boys do not break their sequencing rules in establishing bodily contact because they select a non-member of the group. During the informal moments of the school day I observed how they would frequently subject Paul to various insults to belittle his masculinity. The boys placed him outside their status group and defined him as sexually uninitiated. This is one instance of how the boys exploit Paul so as to transfer their own failure to initiate bodily contact through fantasising Paul

171

as an acknowledged virgin to meet their fantasy of Rose as sexual wanton.

What effect did the boffin boys' ambiguous sexual reality and fantasy have upon Paul and Rose? In discussion Paul said he considered this as yet another form of "mickey taking" he had to endure, but it also meant he was almost inside the group as a centre piece of conversation. However, he did believe the boys' assessment of Rose's behaviour to be correct. Thus, through this fantasy he was able to join the group and resolve their collective group problem of sexual vulnerability. Rose was aware of the boffin boys' plans and understood their behaviour as rather offensive. The boffin girls assessed the boys' behaviour, in general, as immature, although the girls were unaware of the extent of the boffin boys' sexual fantasy.

The significance of this discussion is that it was an everyday feature of the boys' method of controlling relations inside and outside their group. Superficially, Rose identified the boys' plan for her and Paul to go out as a bad joke, but as I have proposed, this plan was an expression of the boffin boys' sexual vulnerabilities.

Conclusions

The chapter attempts an initial exploration of the boffin boys' class and sexual vulnerabilities and its relation to their pedagogic practice. Wood (1984) notes that there have been few ethnographic studies on conformist male pupils in school, more particularly, there has been no exploration of the effects of the masculine identity of pro-school boy groups upon their school work and upon their relation to girl groups.

The boffin boys' unity is embodied and celebrated in their pedagogic instrumental solidarity. This allows these boys to enforce the correct type of approach to learning based upon a regulative framework, where rules are applied to indicate improper or inconsistent social class practices on the part of any boy. The boffin boy must respect the pedagogic project and its future objective if he wishes to retain the status of belonging to the group.

The boffin boys' movement away from working class images of masculinity, towards a more middle class masculine identity, based upon responsibility and individualism, supports the group's perspective on social mobility. The social dominance of school work serves to make the boffin boys' masculine identity more uneasy because of the importance they (and other male groups) attach to intimacy with females which their studies preclude. Their middle class practice of deferred gratification supports their middle class form of masculinity which leads away from spending time or forming relations with girls. The conflict generated by giving future career priority over present pleasure is resolved by insisting that girls are secondary, but it is a resolution fraught with tension and contradiction.

8   Masculinities and school identity

Introduction

This chapter compares and contrasts the cultural practices and relations of the boffin boys and the mod boys. The aim of the analysis is to describe the two male groups and to suggest that they can be understood in terms of differences, opposition and acceptances. This detailed focus upon the two groups attempts to enlarge the rather narrow empirical accounts of pupil conformity and resistance. There are three sections to this chapter, firstly, pedagogy and deviance, secondly, issues of the transition from school, and thirdly, adolescent male sexuality.

Pedagogy and deviance : intelligence and status

Success in either pedagogy or deviance provides an individual with one type of status or another. Both the boffin boys and the mod boys, in general, were among the pedagogic elite of the school taking formal examinations. The two male groups accepted the high status which derived from the school's evaluation of their intelligence. In contrast, for the criminal boys there was little available status based upon examination success. Both the mod and the boffin boys judge the criminal boys in terms of their perceived lack of intelligence.

Keef   Because they (criminal boys: SJB) are wankers , they
            haven't got the intelligence to realise not to do it .
Gary   Because their leader, he has got the mentality to crime,

174

	hasn't he.
James	They've got nothing better to do, they can't get enjoyment from things that don't involve risk.

The boffin and the mod boys shared many subjects in the curriculum and were together within the same classroom. However, the mod boys were not dependent on pedagogic status in school, as were the boffin boys, in order to gain esteem. As a pupil friendship formation the boffin boys' group had its meeting place in the secondary school. Although they visited friends' houses and engaged in a variety of peer group activities as a group they did not possess territorial space outside the school. The mod boys' set of territorial practices were played out both inside and outside Marshlands. Their reputation outside the school was based on being tough, smart, outrageous and streetwise. At the beginning of a joint discussion the boffin boys acknowledge the mods' physical strength and joke about their reputation in order to defuse any possible tension.

Gary	As long as you don't hit us... I am not very hard. You just slap us around a bit, that's alright.
Howard	They just like giving everyone the shits. No not really, no, they don't cause aggro in the school or anything.
Gary	They are alright.
James	It's out of school, isn't.
Keef	It is the local pub disco tonight.
Gary	I don't mind, providing they don't pick on me.

The boffin boys show respect for the mod boys, and they go on to state that the mod boys' aggression occurs outside school. This gave the mod boys an advantage. Their territorial dominance inside school was not questioned owing to their record of violent behaviour outside school. The mods needed only to assert rather than practise authority in school to ensure their influence.

As a group the mod boys' coherence and strength lay in the practices of their unifying youth cultural style. They applied their pedagogic status and resources acquired inside school to further their symbolic status as a promenading youth cultural group. The mods were not dependent on their school status or banding but rather they used it to articulate the complexity of their style and solidarity. However, the two male groups differed about the means to achieve success in school.

175

Howard	(To Keef and Hat: SJB) You're not really bright.
Gary	They could be.
Keef	Hat ain't bright! He could do, if he worked.
Hat	So!
Keef	If I worked, if. No point is there.

The two boffin boys are in disagreement about whether the mod boys are intelligent enough to pass examinations, but there is agreement on what the mod boys lack, namely the ability to work hard. In general, the mod boys did homework, and occasionally considerable amounts, but little in comparison to the overall efforts of the boffin boys. The following discussion shows the competition between the boffin and the mod boys over their pedagogic status.

James	I got an A for English Language.
Hat	You got an A for Language. What percentage did you get?
James	Seventy.
Hat	Beat you.
James	What did you get?
Hat	Seventy one.
James	Joint Board?
Hat	Mm - got my results this morning.
Gary	Fifty eight.
James	You didn't.
Hat	I got seventy one , some of the new wave girls got higher, one got seventy nine. There was four people in our class that passed.
James	Was it ? Everyone in our class passed , the lowest pass was fifty two.
Hat	What did you get Howard?
Howard	I didn't do it.
Gary	He has already passed it.

James's celebratory announcement of his high mark provides Hat with an opportunity to demonstrate to the boffin boys that he, a mod, is more intelligent because he achieved a higher mark. Hat goes on to point out that some of the new wave girls got even higher marks. He has emphasized that the two youth cultural groups have the capacity to gain status inside the school through academic work. Hat's argument is presented in terms of the success of the youth cultural group, not the pupils or the class; indeed he

176

goes on to further separate the other pupils in his class by stating that they didn't do as well. In response, James reaffirms the boffins' school based relations by arguing that all the pupils in the class passed (not only types).

James notes the lowest score of the passes in the class , to show that Gary's apparently low grade is inside the pass requirement. Gary's boffin status is recovered and it is he who answers for Howard, that he has already passed the examination, to restore the boffin boys' superior academic position.

Schoolwork and going out

There was an acceptance by both groups concerning the problem of chosing between completing school work or going out in the evening. The boffin boys were prepared to spend more time on homework. Howard stated, "You have to do your homework". When they went out in the evening they met with fellow pupils in the environment of the home rather than on the street.

James   You see we , what we do alot is we go round people's houses for cups of tea and that. We play alot of snooker as well.

The home is an important leisure space which also functions as a site where the boffin boys can discuss school relations and exchange homework. In contrast, for the mod boys, Keef argues that the home is the place to escape from rather than to go for leisure.

Keef   The only time I spend in is Sunday night , that's when I work. That's because you are not allowed to go out on Sunday night because when I go out, I don't come back until you know , late , it is eleven , after twelve.

He explains that for the mod boys going out takes precedence over completion of school work, but he does admit to doing some homework. As a group, the mod boys although they were still 15/16 years old had developed a significant drinking culture in public houses. Throughout the fieldwork I usually saw the mod boys on at least two evenings during the weekend at a pub in one of the villages near the school. The boffin boys did not take part in under age alcoholic drinking in local pubs or at discos.

177

Gary	It's not as though we go up the pub or anything.
James	See we don't go up the pub, we ...
Howard	If you go to someone's house you use their stuff.

This is not to say that the boffin boys did not drink, but rather their alcohol consumption took place sometimes in the home but more often at boffin boy/girl parties. Unlike the mod boys, the boffin boys did not possess extensive territorial relations in the local community. The mod boys had to be seen and known to be on the street because they had a reputation to maintain. Consequently, they had less time to devote to school homework. The time spent "on location" by the mod boys - going out, in the street, to the pub, to discos, or on the sea-front - and the practices they engaged in, promenading, drinking, dancing, fighting and courting, did not accommodate school work or school values (Mclaren 1986). When considering school work they shared a degree of acceptance:

SJB	Do you circulate your homework?
Keef	Copy?
James	Oh no.
Howard	I sometimes do copy.
James	If you're late with your homework or you've given some in late then may be you'd do it.
Gary	Howard , we're going to start doing that in geography aren't we, because we're so many units behind. We're going to kind of give each other units and things.
Howard	Because we've got alot of work in that.
Keef	That's what I do. But , I tell you something. You may think it is doing a trick right, but with Miss Wilde I got the mark book; put all the marks on it and that's all you have to do.
Hat	Pencil them in , she has got the mark book and she is really strict with marks. But when she went out after the marks were written in, we nicked the book and wrote a load of marks down.
Keef	They (boffin boys: SJB) could do that, you know.
SJB	You were taking the mark book ...
Hat	Yeah, like a unit , a unit takes up to two weeks, don't it each one, alot of them. You think we probably put down about seven weeks work that we didn't do.
Howard	You don't have to do the work that's the stupid thing , you get these sheets ...

Keef	And you know it anyway when you do it. You don't have to do the work, just as long as you've got the sheets and when you come to revision, if you want to, you do.

The boffin boys, like the boffin girls, have an extensive operation of school work exchange, based upon the principle that each pupil was required to fill their quota of "good work". For the mod boys, Keef is prepared to state that they do copy homework and also engage in the deviant school practice of falsifying results in the mark book.

The boffin boys' commitment was not to school but to school work: not to school values but to an ideology of individualism upheld in the family and at the school (Hammersley and Turner 1980). An essential part of the boys' identity and behaviour towards other pupils was their apparent detachment and ability to use rules and see through the process of schooling. The boffin boys, like the boffin girls, demanded a set of relations from teachers which have been described as a structured pedagogy. When this pupil requirement was not met the boffin boys' motivation was reduced and this possibly affected their preparation for revision. The boffin boys did not take part in explicitly deviant behaviour against the school rules. They had acquired an ideology of individualism, drawn from the school, supported by the family and developed within the friendship group, and which supported their social class aspirations (Woods 1979).

School rules and resistance

I shall attempt to build on the differences identified initially between the two male groups, and here describe firstly, the boffin boys' individualism and rule bound behaviour, and secondly, the mod boys' collective and resistant attitude. Examination of these differences does not exclude shared acceptance by both groups of the rules of the "intellectual game" of acquiring certificates, nor of the sharing of the informal pupil criteria of fun. The boffin and the mod boys discuss the issue of smoking as an example of resistance to school rules, and as an exemplar of informal pupil status.

Keef	I think the attitude towards people in school is just stupid, like smoking.
James	Smoking over sixteen , when you are sixteen but not

before that.

SJB	Do any of you three smoke? (Boffin boys: SJB)
James	I have , I don't buy - go out and buy them . I get given them alot. But I wouldn't go out and buy them. I wouldn't disrespect the school rules because I would be frightened about what would happen when you get caught.
Howard	I think smoking is alright . But I think in enclosed areas it is not really.
Keef	No (In agreement: SJB)
Howard	Because even then it affects other people , you know , because it does affect your health.
Keef	It's different from taking ...
Howard	You know passive smoking , that is a little bit on the side in the street, that is almost as bad as proper smoking because it causes cancer in certain people.
Keef	In certain people.
Howard	See, but I reckon when you are outside...
James	It doesn't matter
Howard	In the school grounds , I think you can just smoke outside, most of them (mod boys: SJB) get away with it anyway. Teachers are pretty lax.
Keef	I enjoy smoking, it's up to us isn't it.
James	Age limit is a pretty good idea.
Keef	I think over ten years of age (joke. SJB)
SJB	What do you think about the people who do go smoking and some of them get caught?
Howard	When they get caught they don't get punished.
James	See the thing is I only smoke, - I don't see the point in risking getting caught and getting done for something that doesn't give you any stimulation.
Keef	It does give you.
James	Does it?
Howard	I think it's funny though . You see some of them they pile round the back and they see the teachers and they run all about.
Keef	I think it is fun. Classic , third year . I used to go and play football, we used to go and run with us and get caught smoking. It's exhilarating, being, the thought that we can get caught smoking. That's the thrill really in school, thinking, I'm breaking the rules, you BASTARDS won't catch us. You know, just run about

with them (cigarettes: SJB) to the limit.   Everybody
loves it, just creased up.

All boys   Laughter

Schoolboy smoking is understood as one of the major ways to
identify anti-school behaviour (Willis, 1982). Here I shall propose
that smoking is not a distinguishing characteristic of the mod boys
as opposed to the boffin boys.   James admits to smoking and I
witnessed other boffin boys smoking at parties or discos. If there
was a distinguishing feature about smoking between the two boy
groups, it was in terms of rules.

The boffin boys' behaviour was shown in terms of their
acceptance of the legal age for smoking and their unwillingness to
disobey school rules.   When the boffin boys did smoke, it was away
from the school site and the gaze of authority figures. In contrast,
the mod boys peer group spokesperson Keef, delighted in his
narrative of anti-school activities.   To be seen to smoke was
important but getting away with it has priority over getting caught;
it is the excitement of resistance, in thought and in action, which
offers status rather than being identified or caught. It is possible to
argue that the mod boys' reluctance to be caught and their complex
strategies devised to evade capture, were closely related to their
acceptance of the intellectual game, which provided them with
intellectual status. For the mod boys smoking was a high status
deviant act of expressive value, whilst the boffin boys stress that
smoking is an individual act of deviance, which breaks rules and
laws. It could also have caused problems for a boffin boy's position
in the pupil hierarchy; their emphasis was on caution, sequence and
consequences of action.

The mod boys did not spend a great deal of time planning their
next smoke because their pattern was largely fixed.   The first
cigarette was smoked on the train journey to school, the second, in
the town recreation ground before going through the school gates,
the third at breaktime behind the mobile classrooms, the fourth at
lunch time in the town, in a cafe, on the sportsground or at
someone's house, the fifth at breaktime in the afternoon behind the
mobiles, in the sports hall or at the local cafe, and finally they had a
last cigarette during the train journey home. The wide variety of
sites for smoking meant that, at least during the fieldwork, the boys
were caught on relatively few occasions. One afternoon Paul and
Keef explained that they were caught by two prefects and sent to the
Head of Fifth Year. They said that they were let off because the Head

liked them, and they were told that as they were in the upper ability bands, "they would have more brains not to do it in the future". This tends to prove Howard's point concerning the absence of punishment. There are however important factors to consider, such as who the pupil was, his/her reputation, history and ability. To be caught for smoking was a serious offence for pupils who were not in the upper ability band.

For the mod boys Keef enjoys promenading and his delivery of an epic tale to the boffin boys has them in fits of laughter. Keef changes the discussion from a talk about an issue of schooling, to one where he is demonstrating the public face of the youth cultural group. A final but crucial point is that Howard further decreases the distance between supposedly conformist and resistant pupils when he explicitly states to the mod boys that their tactics to elude capture are extremely amusing. The mod boys' activities are "publicly celebrated" within the pupil community, whether or not they are caught by the teaching staff. Howard, the senior friend of the boffin boys, gives status to the mod boys group and provides Keef with the opportunity to start his promenading story.

The boffin boys' senior friend and the mod boys' peer group spokesperson assess how power relations operate in school at the pupil level.

Keef	Okay, you (boffin boys: SJB) are fairly good, bright, quiet people aren't you, and Mr Shaw (teacher: SJB) he don't say nothing to you does he? Treats you nicely. I'm sort of bigger than the rest, you know, but I ain't frightened of Mr Shaw. He shows off all the time did you see him when he hit Rich (mod boy: SJB).
SJB	Do you think teachers know how to keep control ?
Howard	No they like ...
Keef	Good pupils, you know.
Howard	Mm, see I ...
Keef	Like them to be quiet, give them easy lessons.
Howard	Mr Shaw doesn't like it , and Rich (mod boy: SJB) , sometimes would not last (i.e. would be dismissed from class: SJB), and Mr. Shaw just sort of gets really short tempered.
Keef	He does!
Howard	See, if I said the same thing that they did , he wouldn't say anything though, he would just say 'oh!'
Gary	We get away with it, with Miss Wilde. She says it alot

Howard	Because I can just say what I want . But they get it (i.e. are punished.
Keef	That is all we were talking about, I got sent out because we were messing about. She got up, I was just sitting there, she told him (Howard. SJB) off four times for messing about but he didn't get sent out. It's just that Miss Wilde hates me, she told me she never wants to see me again.
Hat	What about that discussion in geography with her , she wants me to take her to the cinema.
All boys	Laughter

The mod boys suffer discrimination as a result of labelling. They are reprimanded for marginal infringements, whilst the boffin boys' deviant behaviour is not punished. Keef speaks in terms of resentment, although he perceptively sees through, firstly, the teachers ideal-type characterisation of teacher/pupil relations and secondly, the boffin boys' pro-school image which in reality is sometimes deviant. The boffin boys do not fit the stereotype of the conformist pupil because they have learnt how to operate the resources of their own power relations.

In general, the mod boys tried to counteract the imposition of the teachers' characterisation of them as deviant by completing homework, dressing smartly, working hard in class, giving correct or interesting responses to questions, doing well in tests/examinations and talking with teachers in a mature manner. However, Hat introduces a problem, by suggesting that a female member of the teaching staff is attracted to him. The sexual proposition from a female teacher to a boy pupil strips the teacher of her official status. The teacher is now placed outside a disciplinary relationship to the mod group. This is a highly charged statement because it is known that the teacher has already sent Hat a birthday card, and the remark results in a ritual celebration of laughter by all the boys.

Transition from school

Here the boffin and mod boys discuss the transition from school and reveal differences in aspirations and occupational routes. Their discussion brings up issues of social class, qualifications, education, wages, masculinity and independence.

James	I don't know if I am leaving , it depends, if I stay and I get my qualification I will go straight into my job. If I don't I'll stay on.
Keef	What are you going to do?
James	I'm going in the merchant navy.
Keef	What, in as an officer?
James	Cadet officer, yes.
Keef	Yeah . It's not bad that , you get all over the world but I just couldn't handle it, because you can't get a bird or nothing , or settled down , really . No it's true though.
James	Yeah, but ...
Keef	Okay you reckon you're going to bunk up everybody, you'll catch everything won't you, there - all this disease, pox ridden.
Howard	You don't want to settle down yet though do you?
James	When I am thirty I'll retire and get a desk job. And then I'll prepare for it.
SJB	What about you Howard , what's the main reason for staying on?
Keef	Parent and teacher pressure
Howard	No , I want to go to university , that's what I want, I've heard it's quite good fun.
Gary	They reckon it is a laugh.
SJB	It's a laugh.
Howard	I reckon so, I can't stick work. I wouldn't mind doing work but I think it's pretty boring at the moment, unless you have got a good job to do. I'm not exactly, I wouldn't be an engineer or something like that because I'm going into computers.
Keef	I would, fuck it, there's money in it.
All boys	Laughter
Gary	Er , I want to stay on because the job you are gonna to get isn't going to be very good , if you have just got O' levels is it. So if you're going to get ...
Keef	It all depends, if you know - I'm going to the Electricity Board with three O' levels and I'll be getting paid for taking my A' levels. But you need to take them to go to university.
Gary	But I know I could get higher than just O' levels or an apprenticeship, couldn't I ?
Keef	So? I'm getting paid while I'm doing it.
James	Yeah so , when you're on about thirteen he's on fifteen

	thousand a year, and you are under.
Keef	Yeah, but I'll have enjoyed myself by working, while you're still at school doing homework.
Howard	Going to university you're not just under pressure in terms of money, you are under pressure, you know, to live because you have to pay for your room.
Hat	But you get a grant though don't you?
Howard	Yeah, but it isn't very much.
James	Parents pay.
Keef	My old man couldn't afford it
Howard	You have the pressures, but at the same time it's an experience isn't it. You think, if you want a good job you have to go to university.

The conversation on transitions reveals further differences between the two male groups. Keef, who is both working class and the mod boys peer group spokesperson, finds himself in disagreement with the boffin boys' career aspirations. Throughout the discussion the classic sociological opposition of working class hedonism and middle class deferred gratification is visible. The boffin boys continually assert the necessity to gain more qualifications. The boffin boys are firmly located in a vocational field moving towards a "career" rather than a "job". Entrance to the Services or university is upheld as an aim which in turn will provide the means for a career structure and middle class status. Their commitment to deferred gratification is revealed in their assessment of the correct stages and financial rewards.

In terms of masculinity Keef identifies sexual status in James's career choice of an officer in the merchant navy. The opportunity exists to gain greater access to more women for sex, although this option prevents stability: double standards are explicit. The boffin boys do not respond to Keef's sexual fantasies. As the strongest boy in the fifth year, if not the school, he also has a public reputation for physical aggression and masculinity to maintain.

In terms of employment Keef's argument refers to the present; he shows that he wants to increase his qualifications, like the boffins, and become socially mobile, but he refuses to accept the career/university route outlined by them. Independence is a key element within this discussion. Keef identifies school and homework with university and homework to ridicule the aims of the boffin boys. Here, Howard interjects with a reasoned argument that promotes both the boffin boys independence and

185

individualism. His argument is that by going to university an individual moves away from home and learns to cope with the world, independent of parental influence. The unity of the boffin boy group stems from their pedagogic practice i.e. completion of school work and their aspirations to social mobility. The combination of their present practice and future project sustains friendship within the pupil group.

Adolescent male sexuality

In the present discussion I will concentrate on how the boys in the two groups negotiate elements of male sexual experience. The purpose is to move beyond the simple reading of the boys' statements as expressively sexist, to show how these different boys enter the realm of sexual practices, in order to assess the importance of such relations in the development of adolescent male sexuality. There will be two sections to this discussion, firstly, the boys' discussion of problems concerning parental surveillance of their sexual behaviour, and secondly, their discussion of the condom.

Parental surveillance

Both the boffin boys and the mod boys object to parental attempts to control their sexual development. This can be illustrated by the boys' discussion about going on holiday with the family.

James   I hate going round with them. The holidays they (parents: SJB) like, seeing all those beautiful nice houses, chateau's in the South of France. All I want is to lay on the beach.

Keef   We went up, because my brother went to Bognor Regis last year at Butlins Holiday Camp like, that was a fucking real laugh. I remember the first day. I saw these, you know mods and punks and things, and got off with birds. My mum wanted me to go round with the family, with my sister, fucking good ain't it.

James   That's right. I got off (with a girl: SJB). There are loads of people, in France, in this old holiday camp, you know, we were just talking, walking round the park. Better than going out visiting.

186

Keef	They (family: SJB) were going round , you know , thinking they are fucking enjoying themselves, and sitting there watching shows. I was going out, getting pissed and coming home one o'clock in the morning. She (mother: SJB) is doing her nut. "This is supposed to be a family holiday" and all that, treat you like when you were eight.

The two holiday stories show social class differences; Keef's family have opted for a traditional working class vacation at a Butlin's Holiday Camp, whereas James's family have chosen a middle class holiday in the South of France. Though they may experience different holidays in terms of social class the two boys share a similar experience of resentment towards the family's imposed restrictions on their behaviour. On holiday the boys both identify the opportunity to break away from parental control and establish relations with girls. The boys' grievance against the family is that they are taken round and made to participate in family activities, which do not interest them. Both boys have momentarily stepped outside the family, they analyse its control and relations as being in opposition to them. Here, we can suggest that the family is still a major regulator of boys' sexual development and this results in considerable control problems for the parents.

The boys' problem of parental control on holiday leads the boffin boys to assert their notion of individualism.

SJB	D'you go holiday with your parents?
James	I did last year but I'm not this year , I'm going on my own.
Howard	I'm going on my own as well.
James	Put up camp out in the back garden or something like that!
Gary	Are you going with your brother?
Howard	No . I've been on my own to Germany to stay with friends and I might get some work out there. I don't like going with the family.
Keef	Everybody seems to be in my position with my old girl (mother: SJB) with people on holiday. Everybody just feels the same way, you know, young people.

The boffin boys' basis for a holiday reflects their preoccupations with individualism. Howard and James are strongly against the family holiday, and even consider that the family might be in opposition to the boffin boys' individualism. It appears that the family is seen as infringing on the boffin boys' individualistic principles because they argue that the family tries to dominate them. This illustrates the close relation between independence and individualism.

The boffin and mod boys go on to discuss further issues of parental surveillance of their sexual behaviour, this time in relation to "lovebites" and girlfriends.

Keef	You haven't taken Janet (Hat's girlfriend: SJB) home have you?
Hat	What, yes I have.
Keef	When no one is in.
Hat	I have fucking taken her home , she came in my bedroom.
Keef	Yeah but who was in?
Hat	No one.
James	My mum said , if she (Monica: SJB) comes down our house again, she'll kick her out, Monica.
Keef	Who said that?
James	My mum.
Keef	Don't they like her?
James	No, not now.
Howard	Because she is leading him astray.
Gary	She's ...
James	No . Because it's not that she's leading me astray , just that you know, one minute she is going out with me, the next minute she isn't, she's always having arguments.
Hat	What's she like?
James	What d'you mean?
Keef	Shut up Hat.
Hat	Exciting.
James	She is alright like that.
Hat	She is alright like that.
James	Yeah. But she's not like some.
Gary	I wouldn't talk about it.
Hat	Pardon!
Keef	Another thing , if she (girlfriend: SJB) is covered in lovebites and that ...
James	YEAH, my Dad did his NUT.

188

Hat	What such a - a lovebite looks nice.
Keef	"Oooh, ooh, ooh, slap", anyone'd think they'd never seen it before. It makes you sick.
James	Makes you look, my mum says, don't do that, it makes you look cheap.
Keef	They always say that, you know, who gave you that, and when. What have you got those for? Okay, so they think you are fucking someone because you got a lovebite on your neck, that you can't just be going out with someone.

There are three important elements in this conversation, firstly, Howard's contentious point combining a sexual innuendo with an implied reference to the boffin boys' pedagogic solidarity namely, his remark that James's girlfriend has been leading him astray. Howard's accusation is ambiguous because it can refer to James's sexual relations with his girlfriend which have changed him, or to the fact that because of the relationship he has less time to spend on school work, and this is "leading him astray". Here, James's answer is that his girlfriend has been unreliable, because she continually changes her mind about the relationship. It is Howard's ambiguous question which presents Hat with an opportunity to pose his sexual question to James. Secondly, in the face of Hat's inquiry James protects his (ex) girlfriend's reputation, even though he admits that his parents no longer like her. Hat tries to obtain intimate information from James about his sexual relations with his girlfriend. However, James' reply is subtle and minimal, for he not only defends his girlfriend's sexual reputation "she is not like some", but asserts his own status by suggesting knowledge of her, that "she is alright like that."

Thirdly, Keef introduces the subject of lovebites. In this argument he presents his parents' attitude towards adolescent sexual behaviour as mistaken, for they always assume that bites on the neck mean love making (Lewis 1973). The sign is acceptable to the boys but parents misread the meaning of adolescent sexual behaviour.

As with the boys' discussion about holidays, the subject of lovebites shows that the boys' experience of sexual relations are strongly subject to parental influence and control. Here, the boys discuss intimate sexual matters and questions within an atmosphere of seriousness rather than bravado or exaggeration.

This discussion shows that different types of boys can engage in sex talk without being directly sexist.

Condoms

In the late 1980s condoms became synonymous with protection from AIDS, especially if sexual partners were relative strangers. The use of condoms as a contraceptive device by males has received little empirical investigation in terms of youth experience, which is surprising when we consider the meaning it has for adolescent boys (Spencer 1984, Holland, Ramazanoglu and Sharpe 1993). Condoms are a ritual marker of adult status, an indication to their possessor that he is no longer a child. For male youth the first purchase of a contraceptive device is a major element in the rite of passage (Farrall 1978). Condoms and other means or non-means of birth control, such as withdrawal, are bathed in mythology and are a permanent feature of popular comedy. Here, I shall concentrate on how the boffin and the mod boys attempt to deal with condoms in terms of acquiring and hiding the contraceptives, and various aspects of their use.

SJB	When did you first go out and buy a packet of three then James?
Keef	He didn't buy them.
James	I didn't buy them , I got them off some kid at school.
SJB	How about you Gary?
Gary	I don't buy them.
All boys	Laughter
Keef	It's just embarrassing.
Howard	He's not sixteen yet.
Gary	I'm not really into that.
Keef	I'm shy! (Joke: SJB) I really wouldn't be able to go in a fucking chemist or Boots.
James	I couldn't buy , I couldn't buy one. I got them from a mailing address.
Keef	I had to go to a machine
Hat	Did you use it? (To James: SJB)
James	No, I've got them at home.
Keef	Out the back. (Red Lion public house, gents toilet: SJB) Where you put your money in it goes CLANG!
All boys	Laughter.

Keef   I'm sort of waiting, fucking shit scared if a bloke is going to come in, you know. I'm just saying it shits you up.

The first point is that condoms are still a problem. So why are both groups frightened? The indication is that acquiring condoms brings the boys that much closer to sexual initiation. Keef articulates his embarrassment about obtaining condoms in a story. The communicative form operates at two levels. Firstly, the story transforms the boffin boys into a passive audience witnessing the mods' promenade, and secondly, the story is a means of sidestepping his own vulnerability (Bostock and Leather 1982). It is possible to argue that in acquiring contraceptives, James and Keef present the two different forms of social solidarity in each male group. For the boffin boys, James writes to a mailing address to order his Durex individually, and receives them impersonally in an unmarked envelope through the post; this displays an instrumental detachment. For the mod boys, Keef enters the crowded and enclosed social space of a men's toilet in a public house. Although he chooses a time when no adult is present, this shows the mod boys' territorial and public presence. Interestingly, in his study Schofield (1968) states "No one in the sample got their contraceptive from a slot machine." (p.92).

The boffin boys' approach to contraceptives is based on official rules. Gary states he is not into such an acquisition, while Howard specifies the legal age for sex. They emphasize the regulation of sexual experience and its place in the life sequence.

James   On my sixteenth birthday, she (mother: SJB) said "You know what you are legal to do now, don't you?" And she said, "Take precautions", so if she found them she would know I'd been taking them .

Howard   I don't know , I don't have any serious girlfriends or anything. But I do go out at parties. I don't dash into things.

The boffin boys are concerned with conditions of appropriateness rather than conditions of performance. Their framework for action here is based on official rules with a proper regard for sequence, and is similar to their approach to smoking. The boys indicated that for parents to find condoms would be worse than them finding 'soft' pornography in their rooms.

191

James	I've hidden them , I tell you. They are inside the hi-fi speaker of an old radio.
Keef	Did I tell you she found them?
James	If she found them...
Hat	They'll probably be out of use when you come to use them.
James	Not now, she wouldn't mind, now I'm sixteen.
Hat	What d' you fucking want johnny's for , if you aren't going to use them?
James	It saves me going in the chemist and buying them doesn't it.
Hat	Saving them for two years time.
James	That's right!
Gary	Do you use them then Hat?
Hat	What?
Gary	Do you use them? No? Do you use them?
Hat	I don't usually take a precaution.
Gary	You don't.
Hat	No.
Gary	Have you done it then?
Hat	What?
Gary	You know.
Hat	Have I fucked?
Gary	Yeah?
Hat	YEAH.
Gary	You have. Right.
Howard	Fucking individuals.
Keef	It's something to be pleased about really , isn't it. You've got to do it sometime.
Gary	Yeah.

Here pride and masculinity are at stake, Hat humiliates James for owning and not using condoms, and goes on to answer Gary's primary question of whether he has had a sexual experience. Hat creates ambiguity for the boffin boys because he introduces another sign of sexual experience; sex without using a condom (Thomson and Scott 1991). Here it could be suggested that the mod boys who say they are "early starters" have increased the anxiety of the boffin boys. This is achieved firstly, by an explicit acknowledgement of sexual experience, and secondly, by expression of sexual experience in terms of pleasure, success and satisfaction.

In order to retrieve their masculine status the boffin boys try to assert their reasons for not beginning their sexual career early.

James   Why do it early?
Keef   Why do it early! Fucking hell you'll find out.
Howard   Yeah, if you do it with somebody sort of - this age, usually the person you do it to is a dog (slag: SJB), usually, isn't it.
Keef   What does it matter?
Howard   You just want...
Gary   I want someone to get to know.
Howard   It's alright isn't it!
Hat   It's usually a younger person isn't it, Keef.
Keef   What do you call a dog?
James   Goers and ...
Keef   Because okay, you are saying don't do it but what if you get off with a bird and you really do like her?
Howard   Yeah, then it's different.
Keef   And you ain't got a fucking clue. It's going to make you look a right idiot . You should practice on a dog.
All boys   Laughter

The boffin boys assert the importance of sequence and stages in order to gain an experience of sex. They do not wish to rush into things or just have sex, they are looking for an individual relationship. The mod boys have begun their sexual careers and understand the sexual reluctance of the boffin boys as irrational. In an attempt to defend the boffin boys' position Howard maintains that the girls who are available for sex are of a low moral standard. He protects the masculinity of the group by operating the virgin/whore dualism. To engage in sex with a "dog" would both be beneath them and wrong whereas to engage in sex with someone they really liked would suit their status and be alright. Keef is dissatisfied with the boffin boys' position, firstly, he questions the boffin boys' definition of a "dog", and secondly, he elaborates a hypothetical situation to demonstrate that the boffin boys' sexual strategy of waiting is flawed. The conversation is intense as the two male groups explore further their different understandings of sexual practice.

Keef   Are you going to answer it, Shane?
James   No, just stay with it.

193

SJB	I remember I had a girlfriend in the fifth year.
Hat	Here in this village you just sort of wait for the holiday makers don't you?
Howard	You do?
James	There's that second year, you reckon she's is a real goer.
Keef	No, she looked...
Howard	He likes really well proportioned young girls (gesture miming large breasts : SJB)
Keef	And she was about knickerless , a bit smaller than that, lovely tits.
Gary	You know the trouble , you can get, get away with that, but where we look in fact (the beach and amusement arcades: SJB), you know they're disgusting, kind of thing. I wouldn't touch it with a BARGE POLE.
Howard	It's just that most of the girls we know...
Hat	I know, but what do you define as a dog?
Keef	Someone who's got a black moustache!
James	Screwing around.
SJB	You said most of the girls you know , Howard, are like what?
Howard	Well, you know them Shane (meaning the boffin girls: SJB).
Gary	They are out and out (implying chaste and therefore unavailable: SJB), you know them.
Hat	They wouldn't.
Keef	I don't think they know what one (penis: SJB) looks like.
Gary	Probably.

The boffin boys assert that they are not in competition with the mod boys, but they keep getting drawn into the male sexual competition of "boasting". The discussion has moved out from the strategy of counter argument, the boffin boys' seminar form, to become an arena where the mod boys can display and celebrate their public face to an audience. The boffin boys become increasingly inarticulate and agitated.

The boffin boys' senior friend, Howard, attempts to repair their masculine profile by building on Gary's statement, to argue that they do not have access to the range of girls available to the mod boys. Howard tries to place the blame for the boffin boys' lack of sexual experience upon the boffin girls saying that the girls will not go out with them. To support this assertion about the boffin girls'

194

negative attitude to sex, Howard calls on my experience of knowing these girls. They disparage the boffin girls for being unapproachable for a sexual relationship using a classic sexist argument that girls who have sex are "slags" and those who wait are "tight". The two male groups conclude on an acceptance of their sexual superiority over the boffin girls.

Male virginity

Because female virginity has social meaning attached to it stemming from women's position under patriarchy as chattel, virginity itself is largely treated as a female category. In anthropology female virginity has been studied very much in terms of its meaning for the society, tribe, family and more recently, often by feminists, for the young woman herself (Yalman 1963, Ardener 1978, Hewitt 1986a). In sociology and anthropology the subject of male virginity has received much less attention, possibly because men are regarded as being the generalised sex. Hastrup (1978) argues that,

> Male virginity exists in a biological sense, of course and the transition from "virginity" to manhood may be extremely important to the individual man, but as it is not biologically conspicuous it is not used as a social symbol to the same extent as female virginity. (p.64)

Here, it would seem that virginity applied to men derives from the use of the term in relation to women. I am not trying to suggest that the identity of virgin men is tied up with their sexuality to the same extent as it is for women, but male sexual stages do exist and are important at the time of adolescent male sexual initiation.

The boffin boys' and mod boys' discussion of sexuality shows the considerable influence of parents on their early sexual practices. The boys were subject to parental control but they differed in their acceptance of parental authority and parent attitudes towards their sexual behaviour. The subject of "lovebites" is an example of a control problem between son and parents, because a lovebite functions as a sign of sexual experience. The boffin boys identify the reason for their parents' objection as relating to improper conduct. This is a social class conception of appropriate sexual behaviour. As such this would allow the boffin boys to accept their parents' view, as it fits their project of social mobility. In contrast, the mod boys understand the value of this sexual sign of sexual transition as a male peer group status symbol (Oakley 1972).

The issue which underscores the talk between the two boy groups is that of male virginity. This is brought to the surface by Gary's question to Hat, "Have you done it?". As a result of Hat's reply there now exists a division; the boffin boys are male virgins and the mod boys have sexual experience. It is at this point in the talk about sex that the boffin boys introduce a direct sexist sexual practice, through the use of a double standard which claims that girls who have sex early are "slags". It appears that the boffin boys need to protect their masculinity, because their male virginity presents an ambiguous area of classification in relation to how masculine behaviour is understood in society and across different cultural settings. For example Hersham (1977, see pp 273-4) points out that in the Punjab a young man cannot consider himself a man until he has had intercourse with a woman.

The boffin boys suggest that sex with a girl whom they define as a "dog" does not represent a proper sexual initiation, because they stress that sex is only proper in a love relationship. They are attempting to undermine the mod boys' sexual experience and effectively return them to the category of male virgins by saying sex with with such girls does not count. The boffin boys' masculinity is channelled into an aggressive sexist discourse which describes the girls as being of low moral standards and not worth the effort.

This discussion between the boys shows clearly the opposition between male virginity and its legitimation, and male promiscuity and its legitimation. The boffin boys are the first to use sexually abusive language with reference to girls, in an effort to defend their notion of masculinity in the context of the mod boys' sexual success. The introduction of sexist categories by the boffin boys directs the conversation away from their sexual vulnerability, to allow the mod boys an opportunity to display sexist bravado and exaggeration.

Conclusions

This chapter has attempted to show how the two different forms of social solidarity and aspirations of the boffin and the mod boys, affected and influenced their social relations, practices and communication. In terms of the dominant model of pupil relations in school, we could argue that the boffin boys were a conformist pro-school group and the mod boys were a resistant anti-school group. However, such an explanation does not inform, elaborate, or reveal the complexity of relations and practices in each male group.

Part of the two groups' oppositional behaviour derived from their ability to see through the power relations of the school and perceive how such relations affected each group respectively. The skill of the boffin boys in applying rules, meant that they were able to engage in deviant school activities for which other groups or individuals would be reprimanded. They did not fit the stereotype of the conformist pupil (Fuller 1980, Turner 1983, Brown 1987, Mac an Ghaill 1988). Can we understand the boffin boys' relation in school in terms of resistance? As the boffin boys explicitly aspired to be socially mobile, perhaps the concept of resistance is inapplicable. The concept does not help us to understand their behaviour. The term resistance seems to have more relevance when applied to the mod boys who were more working class and who used the collective values of their youth cultural group as a means to support oppositional behaviour. However, although the collective dominates their activities they pursued the emancipatory potential of school, aiming, individually, at some form of social mobility. Is there a theoretical problem within the notion of resistance in that it contains at the empirical level the hidden concept of social mobility?

On the subject of masculinity both the boy groups rejected parental surveillance of their sexual development. It was not until the subject boundary of male virginity was crossed that the boys engaged in a hostile sexist practice and referred to girls as "dogs". Both male groups reveal deeply felt sexist notions of male superiority over women, although the two groups are differently positioned in the power relations of patriarchy. They saw girls as secondary, and defined as disposable. The boffin boys introduced the duality of bad/good girls, as a prop to restore their masculine status, in the face of the mod boys' sexual success which implied that the boffin boys were not "proper men" because of their lack of sexual experience.

9   Parents, pedagogy and resistance

Introduction

This chapter will explore the two girl groups' responses to the family and the school. The aim of the analysis is to compare and contrast both groups' cultural practices and relations, and to suggest that they can be understood in terms of differences, oppositions and acceptances. This chapter is divided into two sections.

Parental regimes: outlines the girls' different experiences of family life and domestic relations and shows how this affects each adolescent female group.

Pedagogy and resistance: discusses examples of the girls' practices within school, in order to see whether the concepts of conformity and resistance are applicable to the data or help to gain a more theoretical understanding of both groups.

The boffin girls and their parents

Parental regimes attempt to control and to regulate the behaviour of girls both inside and outside the home and the school. An analysis of how the girls interpret those moral regimes will enable us to identify some basic differences within and between the two female groups. What type of relations do these girls share with their parents?

The middle class parents of the boffin girls impose quite strict moral rules on the girls about how to conduct themselves in private and in public. During an informal conversation the girls spoke about how little time they have to pursue interests other than school work. Certain boffin girls were allowed more freedom than others but for all girls the major areas of potential disagreement with parents were clothing, going out and relations with boys.

SJB	What about your clothes?
Ellen	I pay for them myself . I can get almost what I want. Not quite.
Monica	I ask.
Rose	My parents. If my mum - some of the things , say I like that one, she goes I'm not buying it for you. But I choose my own clothes. She buys them but she has to - if they are really way out stuff.... but I don't buy that stuff, anyway, she won't buy it for me. She says, if I want to buy it, buy it out of my own money. But she doesn't mind if I buy it out of my money. But most of the clothes I like, she likes anyway so. But she is very strict on the school uniform.
Kerry	My mum knows it . If she gets me some clothes , like school shoes or something and I don't like them I just will not wear them.
Rose	Yeah, mine is like that.
Kerry	It is a waste of money really , so you might as well get something you like and wear them.
Rose	My mum won't go shopping for clothes without me because she knows I will not wear them. It is just a waste of them.
SJB	So you don't reckon your parents can impose things too readily on you?
Rose	It depends, because ...
Kerry	You get yourself put upon.
Ellen	Well , with old fashioned parents like mine you have not got much choice.
Rose	Well my parents are not exactly up to the middle. I mean my parents are old fashioned.
Kerry	Well , my dad and my mum . My dad thinks I should not go up to London to see my boyfriend because it looks like I'm chasing him. I have only been going out with him for over a year I'm and STILL CHASING HIM AM I? (voice very strained: SJB)
Rose	No . But, I wouldn't say my parents are old fashioned.

	But my parents are - pretty strict. I mean I am not allowed... if I go out generally I have to be in by twelve, if it is a party or something like that.
Ellen	Huh. I have to be in by ten ... urh I go to the parties but none of the discos. I have enough trouble getting to a party, with my parents. Then I just usually sit there... just really boring.
SJB	What would happen if any of you stayed out late ?
Ellen	If I stayed out late I would get told off. I know that. I do not know what they would say because I have never done it, so I do not know. Usually if we (boffin girls: SJB) go places, see everyone comes home later, so my dad fetches me in. So I cannot be late.
Kerry	You see , you say those things, my parents would not let me do that, but you don't know till you ask.
All girls	Laughter
Rose	I mean , I'm sixteen now. I mean , I don't see why I shouldn't be allowed, if I buy my own clothes, I'm allowed to choose them myself, I don't have to have my mum with me. I choose them - but I have to be in bed on school nights by ten. But if I watch something till ten, mum says go to bed after that.

In general, the boffin girls have stable relations with their parents but as the conversation develops we can see that the two topics of clothes and parties bring out the girls' feelings of resentment. The relationship between them and their parents might be understood in terms of negotiating on independence.

They see their parents' attitude on clothes as "old fashioned" because they deny them choice and select fashions as though they were children. Clothes display an individual's taste, style and sexuality. The parents of the boffin girls were quite strict about the type and range of clothes the girls could wear during leisure time. In fact, there was comparatively little difference between their dress inside or outside school. The boffin girls never wore trousers to school but during leisure time these were permitted, together with more colourful blouses and skirts; their outfits could be regarded as realising a stereotype of femininity and prettiness (Hudson 1984).

The subject of shopping with parents for clothes was controversial and the girls claimed it was fraught with tension. Further evidence of this came when I arrived at a boffin girl's house on a Saturday afternoon. The girl's brother let me into the house and explained that his sister had gone shopping, " with the parents". After I had waited three quarters of an hour the family returned, the girl was disappointed, the parents were pleased. The parents described how they managed to dissuade their daughter from buying two items of clothing - a pair of small soft boots and a large sweater dress. The parents were delighted with her eventual choice and her acceptance of a traditional skirt (Margrain 1983).

Disagreement with their parents surfaced at times of ritual - parties, discos, shopping - showing the struggle that the girls faced in order to gain independence. The girls continually had to negotiate existing and further possible freedoms, as though there was an eventual point where total freedom would be reached. A determining factor in the parent/daughter relation was the parents' encouragement and support for the girls' pedagogic aims. This relation made them dependent on the parents in terms of finance and "favours"; the girls would accept their parents' demands for school success, which meant their staying in to complete homework. However, success at school gave them a powerful sense of autonomy, which created a demand for further independence. Within the school community the girls had to deal carefully with their problem of parental restriction because, as the school's top examinees, their status and autonomy could be severely threatened if it became known generally that they were treated as children by their parents.

Overall, the girls would work within the boundaries of parental restrictions, although this did not prevent them from collectively challenging their parents' moral regimes, for example, by getting drunk at a party (see chapter 10). Within the group the girls' official pedagogic practice, that is, their seminar form, allowed them to rationalise their parents' demands and their own resentment. This approach allowed the girls to express opposition in theory without having to rebel in practice.

The new wave girls and their parents

As with the parents of the boffin girls, the parents of the new wave girls were quite strict about behaviour, although the new wave girls as a group had considerably more freedom of action. Here, I shall attempt to identify why these parents gave the new wave girls more independence and what consequences this had for each girl, and their group as a whole. In an informal conversation the girls explain how their particular experience of family life affects them.

Clare	I think they really get on well together , Debbie and her mum.
Steff	That's because they are close , because she is the only female.
Collen	Yeah . I think it is really good to get on well with your mum.
Sioux	Yeah. I get on well with my mum.
Clare	I get on well with my dad.
Steff	Yeah , that's right ... I think it's because I don't see my mum because I live with my dad. He sees that I am growing up. But with my mum she still treats me as if I'm not.
Cat	Because I think your parents don't want you to grow up anyway.
Sioux	My mum doesn't like to see me grown up. But when I go up to stay with my dad he just doesn't mind at all. But the only thing that keeps me from going up to live with my dad is my mum. I am so close to my mum but not the stepfather. The only reason why I think he is staying at our house is because of the money. That's the only reason he's got to be there. But it's not right for me to ruin my mum's happiness is it?
Collen	I live with my mum and her husband , my dad lives away. But my mum - I've got a younger sister a year younger than me, and I think she gets away with a lot because I could do it. But my mum sort of treats me like a sister really, she doesn't try and tell me what to do. But she only allows me out two nights in mid week - seems like that's boring, but apart from that ...
Sioux	That's why we go and stay at other people's houses.
Collen	My dad sort of treats me like a little kid still. We go and visit his friends when I go out with him and it's all the "You have grown up, you was small last time I saw you." It just shows how it is.
Sioux	Yeah, it really pisses me off.
SJB	How do you feel? ...
Sioux	"Haven't you grown since the last time I saw you" (joke voice: SJB)
Steff	It is as though they think beforehand that a midget is

	going to come along and say hello ...
Sioux	I go into the front room and my stepfather either rips holes in me ...
Cathy	What , you mean about your speech , fucking hell. We were sitting there, and she drops one letter and he goes off about her speech.
Sioux	I said bot-um.
Cathy	Well , that one sentence you said to me . You were talking to ME. And he said it all properly and your mum said " I didn't notice". And your stepfather looked at your mum as though she was defending you. I didn't even pick it up (the dropped letter sound: SJB)
Sioux	I know. He just goes on and on and on . The horrible thing is when he's nice, he is really nice. But when he is horrible he's such a wanker. Well - he is honestly that's the only way I can describe him. When he's horrible, he's horrible (chicken noises: SJB)
All girls	(Chicken noises: SJB)

Unlike the boffin girls, the majority of the new wave girls have not experienced entirely stable family relations. Out of a group of ten, six of the girls have experience of living in a one parent family. Over half of the girl group know the feeling of marital break up, divorce, the death or a change of parent. What was the new wave girls' assessment of their family relations? They maintain that positive relations with their parents are important. Collen states that her relation with her mother is "sisterly", this is demonstrated further below:

Steff	I think it's better because your mum is a lot younger. They are young. They're not old fashioned, they try to keep in. Your mum wears all your clothes doesn't she.
Lynne	She's always wearing my leopard skin.

Not all the girls' mothers were young, in the sense that they could participate in sisterly relations such as the exchange of clothes. The girls whose mothers were older would share other relations such as news and support. For example, Debbie stated "She sees my point of view and she wants to know all the gossip". Cathy said "We share all the goings on, so she accepts what I say and helps me out".

In general, the girls felt strong dislike towards their step-parents and saw separated parents as wishing to impose restrictions on their behaviour. This was probably a result of the infrequent contact between daughter and separated parent, who failed to notice subtle personal changes. The new wave girls' dislike of step and separated parents (except for Sioux) was of a similar nature to the boffin girls' resentment towards parents: they felt they were treated as children rather than as young women. It could be argued that by being in a one parent family, the girls had to get used to a variety of household and living arrangements. In most cases they had to share the burden of domestic labour and of domestic responsibility. Under such circumstances, there developed a close relation between daughter and remaining parent as they attempted to retain a sense of pride. This could account in some ways for the girls' resentment towards the step parent who could be seen as an intruder trying to split the daughter-parent relation.

During observation of the girls in the home I saw that domestic duties were accepted by them in order to support the running of the household. Crucially, the girls took an active part in the management of the home. In the exercise of these duties the girls showed their competence inside the home, and used it as a means to support and secure independence outside the home. This represented a domestic exchange; the parents gave the girls space and this allowed the girls as a group an opportunity to meet.

The new wave girls' space and practices were sanctioned by their biological parents. Sioux states that the girls go round and stay at each other's houses during the weekend. I accompanied the girls on a number of those occasions, sometimes their boyfriends were present, at other times they were not. An all girl meeting was called a "gathering", on these occasions the girls would sleep together in one room, smoke cigarettes, drink alcohol and talk intensively. These meetings were a central part of the girls' relations and practices where they could share intimacy. Within the group context each individual girl could do things not likely to be permitted in her own home. Thus, the girl group and its occupancy of different girls' houses became a cumulative means to gain independence and celebrate group activities. However, it would be incorrect to suggest that the girls could ignore the control of step or separated parents, or even do anything they pleased simply because their parents gave support to the group.

Pedagogy and resistance

The first priority of this section is to examine the relationship between academic ability and resistant behaviour, through an investigation of the relations and practices of the boffin and new wave girls. I look firstly at the girls' classroom interaction and school relations, before considering the boffin girls' critical response to education, and examining their instrumental practices in school. Finally, I detail examples of the new wave girls' resistant practices both inside and outside school.

Female classroom interaction and school relations

The boffin girls and the new wave girls were part of the pedagogic elite in the fifth year at Marshlands. The boffin girls were high achievers, regarded by some teachers as "gifted" in academic terms. Although the new wave girls had not taken examinations early like the boffin girls, they were expected to do well. Being in the upper ability band the two girl groups shared many subjects, although not all, because the boffin girls had already passed certain O' levels.

A generalisation which applies to each girl group is that their superior position in school gave them confidence within the pupil community, and made them assertive in class and sure of their own ability to complete school work and to understand issues. Recognition of their pedagogic competence by teachers and (some) fellow pupils meant that strategies to undermine the girls by different boys were less effective.

Earlier we saw how the boffin girls were proficient in arts and science subjects, and also were able to experience examinations as "ordinary" rather than special. This ability could be observed in the boffin girls' conduct of their classroom relations. The boffin girls sat together (always near the new wave girls) and used the power base of the group to neutralise any hostility, and also to promote themselves as identifiable, not just as a "bunch of girls" (Weiner 1985). During lessons the level of pupil participation by the boffin girls would be high. In terms of pupil initiated questions, answers to teachers' questions and quantity of teacher attention, the boffin girls would dominate the boffin boys. However, the boffin girls' classroom participation differed when the new wave girls and mod boys were present. When members of the two youth cultural groups and the two pupils groups were in the same classroom,

205

pupil participation during the lesson was intensive and highly competitive. The battle for classroom domination and reward would be fought out between the new wave girls and the mod boys, but this was not at the expense of either boffin group who would demand substantial teacher attention.

There was little explicit pupil deviance during the majority of lessons and therefore only a limited number of opportunities for boys to use sexist strategies to abuse girls. The boffin girls were never threatened by the new wave girls in class; indeed, the strength of the two girl groups could dominate any combination of boys in the classroom. For both girl groups, in particular the boffin girls, the real threat of humiliation came from the mod boys. Having said this I should add that these were top ability classes and there was no major problem of classroom control. In lessons without the mod boys, the two girl groups would be fiercely competitive, for example during a German lesson, two new wave girls, Sioux and Sally asked the most questions and attracted most teacher time. At one point, when a boffin girl was reading from the text, Sioux interrupted her to state that she had read it incorrectly and questioned the teacher as to whether this was the right thing to be doing. Sioux said she did not understand the connection between the teacher's initial question, nor what the boffin girl was reading. After a short silence, the boffin girl who was reading asked the teacher, "What are we doing, I don't understand what I'm reading." Incidents like this were common. They show how the new wave girls demand teacher attention, and critically question the teachers and other pupils; sometimes this would encourage the boffin girls to do the same.

Within the classroom the boffin girls often whispered and spoke to each other in a secretive manner, usually evading the teacher's attention. The new wave girls also did this, with the addition of regular note passing. Writing and passing on communications was a general feature of the girls behaviour; it was not confined to the classroom and took the form of letters, notes, poems, drawings and paintings. In the classroom I observed how note passing could create problems for teacher control. On occasions where a new wave girl was at the centre of a disturbance another girl would intervene, asking the teacher an important question in order to divert the teacher's attention. If one question did not succeed, a series of questions were put forward. The girls would attempt to rescue each other from classroom conflict through strategies of pedagogic questioning. Obviously, this did not work every time and sometimes a new wave girl was sent out of the classroom. On one occasion, in an English literature lesson, Sally's behaviour was becoming too disruptive and Mrs Holland demanded that she leave the classroom and work in her office next door. As she left the room, Sally stated, "I prefer to work in a small room because otherwise I won't get any work finished. I'll do some Jane Eyre. And anyway when you're on your own people can't see you masturbating". The teacher did not hear her last comment, as she shut the door. However, the pupils did; the boys had blank but amused smiles, the remaining new wave girls were laughing and the boffin girls either blushed or were open-mouthed.

For the new wave girls assertiveness in the classroom was not a problem. A teacher remarked that, "Those girls are very good, they don't appear to be put off by the boys showing off, unlike most other girls. They are ready to speak out." This was evident when I observed a special history lecture on the Polish free trade union, Solidarity. In this lesson three upper band classes were brought together, making a total of approximately fifty pupils. The number of pupil initiated questions or answers were as follows: one by a boffin boy, two by a mod boy, and four by a new wave girl. This was an important lesson given by the Head of Humanities. He was quick to praise the girl for her valuable contribution and interpretation. Additionally, during the lesson two of the boffin girls were told off, one girl twice. Here the boffin girls experienced some sexism and ridicule from boys which made them feel unable to participate in the class: two important factors contributing to this were the size and composition of the class.

The boffin girls could never be described as "quiet girls", in fact, they could show strength and occasionally be aggressive to boys inside and outside the classroom. The girls had a number of phrases which referred to their higher intelligence and "mature" attitude. They did not swear or use metaphors of a sexual nature to insult boys. If the girls were in a conflict situation, rather than use profane language to reinforce their point, they would belittle a boy's intellectual capacity, from a position of strength, as the top examinees.

Inside the classroom the two girls' groups did not operate a manifest strategy to defeat male aggression although there was a latent strategy whereby females would cooperate and provide mutual support. The classroom and the fifth year area were the only spaces shared by the two girl groups. Outside the school there was absolutely no contact between them; they occupied different social worlds and engaged in fundamentally different practices and relations. They had friendly relations within the classroom and weak relations in informal school spaces. The lack of unity, contact and common ground between the two dominant female groups in the fifth year meant that each had to defend itself and to develop their own strategies to deal with male violence. Although there was no overt hostility between the two female groups, there was intense competition for educational success. The only time that the new wave girls subjected the boffin girls to a ritual humiliation was the "famous Durex incident". At the beginning of an afternoon break, I was sitting in the fifth year area when three new wave girls informed me that they had just placed a condom inside the coat pocket of a boffin girl. Later, two boffin girls told me that when the condom was discovered there was uproar. Some girls felt intense embarrassment and horror at finding "this thing". One of them said "God, what is it, oh, it's - it's disgusting", while other boffin girls thought "it was really funny, but where did they get it from?"

For the new wave girls, the condom incident shows that they could successfully play with a 'masculine' instrument of contraception. Possession of, and access to, the condom reveals that the girls have confidence in themselves and solidarity within this group is strong. The condom remains primarily linked to male sexual behaviour and intention. However, the new wave girls use it as a provocateur, their purpose is to cause amusement "a good laugh". The new wave girls' use of the condom as a tool for ritual humiliation also emphasizes wider sexual contradictions within and between the different female pupils at Marshlands Comprehensive (Turner 1967).

In the fifth year area the two groups' territorial spaces remained relatively unchanged. The girls stood or sat reasonably close to each other and there was some talk between them, mainly on school subjects, work and examinations. The boffin girls did not stray from the fifth year area, except to stand just outside the building, in contrast to the new wave girls who would go for walks during break, both in winter and summer. The girls would walk as a group with arms linked making a close unit. They would usually sing songs, for example punk or new wave songs, and sometimes ballads sung in absurd tones or occasionally rude rhymes and limericks. The close style of walking both inside and outside the school was an expression of close physical bonds (Lambart 1976). However, walking with the girls could have its surprises. For example, on one occasion I was strolling around a council housing estate at dinner time with five of the girls. I was behind the main group talking to Sally about why she had a badge, a safety pin and a hole in the back of her large white jumper. In front of us were Lynne, Christina (marginal member), Cat and Collen. Suddenly, completely out of the blue, Collen moved out a little, moved back and pushed extremely hard against Cat, who fell straight on to Christina who in turn hit Lynne, who immediately disappeared from sight. Lynne went flying into the air and fell completely over a garden hedge. Unfortunately, she was wearing a skirt and the force of her unexpected flight ruined her tights and stained her clothes with patches of green and brown from the turf. Surprisingly, Lynne was not agitated by this "unfeminine" display but regarded the event as befitting the values and life style of the group. Everybody considered it a hilarious moment, arising spontaneously, an everyday feature of the girls' walk.

The promenade of walking together marked the girls from all other pupils, they were recognisable, and on such journeys interesting things were discovered or information gained. Their physical unity became a powerful resource for engaging or resisting aggression by boys: indeed, boys saw the grouping as a threat, not as typically feminine (Mclaren 1982, Davies 1984).

Critical conformity ? the boffin girls' instrumental approach

During the last two periods on Thursday mornings I would usually sit in the Humanities Block with the boffin girls who had "free time", when they would sometimes work but generally talk. One particular morning the girls abandoned school work in favour of a discussion of the purpose of examinations. The debate was fierce, with voices raised and everyone making a contribution. On the far side of the Humanities block a classroom door opened and a teacher came towards the girls. She stood over them and shouted that they were misbehaving, abusing the trust placed in them to work alone. The teacher commented further that their work was "not up to standard" and their "behaviour was nothing short of childish". The boffin girls made a couple of "cheeky" comments concerning the pressure they were under to complete work for numerous O' level courses while the teacher returned to the classroom. They called her an "old cow" and agreed to disregard her opinion; they assessed her as, firstly, having low formal status and secondly, making remarks that were irrelevant to their educational aims. One boffin girl said

209

"I only need 35% for an A grade at O' level". Other girls said that they needed less to gain that grade because their assessment work had been so good.

Here the boffin girls display a local form of dissent towards a teacher, what Aggleton and Whitty (1985) describe as an act of contestation. The girls are not directly hostile to the teacher, although, once she is out of sight, they did challenge her authority. These comments within the group context were acts of internal resistance, they were private to the girl group (Anyon 1983). In discussion the boffin girls talk about their "free periods"

Mary	In statistics we were not taught properly, so we...
Rose	Though that's not his fault though, is it?
Kerry	No. But I mean ...
Mary	Because we did Maths early (In the fourth year: SJB) So Mr. Simon had about ten of us then to teach and he said 'you have a choice of two subjects'.
Rose	Which we could do, one or two...
Kerry	Yeah.
Rose	And...
Kerry	Because he can do , he can only teach one subject at a time. So when he is teaching say additional maths, for the people who don't do it, they go and sit in the fifth year area or humanities block and get on with their own work, which is meant to be one of the maths that they do. But it never is.
Ellen	We all just do any homework.
Rose	We talk most of the time, don't we.
Kerry	We have some good discussions, actually.
Rose	We don't do statistics anymore because we finished the course.
Kerry	Oh, we finished the course in six months.

These acts of internal resistance within the boffin girl group, are unknown to many teachers or other pupils. Not doing work or the correct work is a challenge to the teachers' control and power relations in school. The boffin girls use their superior pupil position to support their educational aspirations in ways which operate against local principles of control. Willis (1977) describes this as the way pupils construct their own timetable. At other times the boffin girls' behaviour became more explicitly deviant.

Kerry   In our music lesson with Mr Ridgewell we've got three kids in our class, none of us like him. He can't teach we don't think. He is not that much older than us, he is twenty three, I think. And he's got no sort of authority over us. He had a tantrum the other day and he, it was all our fault, we were provoking him because we don't like him. Everyone started to get him angry, so he had a tantrum and then afterwards he slung a chair across the room and then he came up and apologised and said "I am sorry, I shouldn't have done it". But if he had said "You stupid kids, you kids made me angry on purpose. I am going to punish you for that", then that would have been - he should have done that, so we would have respected him in the future and got things across. But he apologised to us because he sort of let off steam, and we'd been annoying him on purpose, and that's the sort of thing a teacher should do.

Rose   I feel that school teachers aren't strict enough because we get - I mean, my parents said to me, you get away with a heck of alot more than we done at school. They said if we'd done that we would have been caned straight away. Half the stuff I've said is, well... and I'm not exactly the worst person in the class.

These accounts of classroom deviance reveal behaviour not normally associated with the school's top examinees. Statements such as "We were provoking him", "We get him angry" or "We annoy him on purpose" do not square with the boffin girls' public image, as the pro-school pupils. What underlies the boffin girls' non-conformity? The nature of their actions is closely related to their school aim of examination success. Earlier I identified the girls' demand for an adult and structured pedagogic setting for learning, with explicit rules for transmitters and receivers of knowledge. Where reciprocal relations in classroom teaching are not forthcoming, the girls are deviant. The basis of their deviance in the classroom is the desire to restore an optimum learning environment.

Turner (1983) notes "Conformity to rules per se is not in the interest of those who want to pass exams" (p. 104). The boffin girls use strategies of classroom deviance in order to support their academic aspirations. Teachers who fail to observe the boffin girls' structural learning requirements are put to the test. The problem for teachers is that their expectation of these pupils does not fit their actual behaviour. If the teachers admit to professional colleagues that they are unable to teach the school's acknowledged top pupils, their future employment and career may be open to question. The teachers' and pupils' expectations clash in a hostile demand and denial situation.

Female resistance ? : the new wave girls

Resistance as a theoretical concept has as its major weakness a thin foundation in empirical work, upon which grand theoretical constructions have been erected (Giroux 1992). Here, I shall look at some of the new wave girls' practices and relations, in order to present the making of a female youth cultural practice.

Initiation rite

Sioux	What about when we went to Denise's the other night.
Debbie	Opening the gate. We didn't open the gate, we lifted it off its hinges.
Cathy	Denise's mum said she was going to sue us for damages.
Debbie	Because it's broken.
Sioux	Oh is it!
All girls	Laughter.
SJB	Who is Denise?
Sioux	She is the new girl with blonde hair. She has got really thick blonde hair, she is quite tall, she goes round with us, well - ...
Cathy	I haven't noticed.

To damage private property is a criminal act but it cannot automatically be taken as an act of resistance. A new girl arrives at school, she is accepted and taken into the new wave girl group. Here, they describe her initiation rite (Campbell 1984). It is symbolic that the girls should break the gate leading to the house. They are possibly demonstrating to Denise that there is no need to be uncertain about their friendship because of the support the girls can provide. It is significant that Denise lived with one parent, her mother; this fits the dominant pattern of the familial relations of the new wave girls as a whole. Sioux praises the new girl for her "really thick blonde hair". This means she has something of value that makes her acceptable to this youth cultural group. However, Cathy concludes with a note of uncertainty concerning the new girl's acceptance, when she remarks that contrary to Sioux's assertion, she has not noticed the new girl "going round with us".

I began this section with the girls' story of an initiation rite because it brings together a number of separate themes, firstly, the girls' delinquent behaviour outside school, secondly, the girls' relations of openness in sharing their vulnerability within the group and thirdly the group basis and context of ritual outside the home.

Drinking alcohol

At the ages of fifteen or sixteen the new wave girls who consumed alcohol were breaking the law. The places where the girls would regularly drink were public houses, wine bars, parties, gatherings in a girl's house, and at a disco or gig. Additionally three of the girls had jobs in local public houses. The new wave girls identify the pub as a positive place and this was demonstrated throughout the fieldwork by many visits to pubs or wine bars. For the girls under age drinking and the telling of drinking stories were crucial aspects of their promenade as a youth cultural group. This shows their territorial movement and place in the community; as with the mod boys, the new wave girls were recognised. Occasionally, the girls would go to The Bear during lunch time at school, though this was not a regular activity, as the majority of their "heavier" drinking sessions took place at parties or all-girl gatherings.

Debbie	Do you realise that time we got drunk , we didn't cry?
Cathy	I BLOODY DID. Well, we didn't together, I cried after I had been sick on the dog.
Sioux	Well hold on , at that (party: SJB) Lynne was sitting there, she was rocking in the rocking chair and crying "I want Julian", like this and I was so pissed off. I will never forgive myself. I sat there and burst out laughing. I goes, 'you can't fucking have him because he's not fucking here ,' and then I burst out laughing.
Cathy	When you're drunk , you say some really evil things you do. At Clare's party when I was crying, you goes "Oh for fuck's sake SHUT UP".

All Girls	Laughter
Sioux	All right. Cathy and Debbie had being crying and Cathy came out and she was sitting on the stairs, and my mother had had a go at me, and I was depressed. So I said what's the matter Cathy, I put my arm round her and she told me why and then I thought she would stop crying, now she's confided with somebody. But she wouldn't stop crying. Anyway, she sat there still crying so I got up and said "For fuck's sake stop bloody crying", and I walked off.
Debbie	All night long, all we did was cry.
Cathy	Oh bloody hell that was terrible!
Sioux	Cathy was going , 'Where are my cocktail cigarettes. I want something very special, I want to give one of these to' - and she was howling at me and she thought I had lost them and they were only on the side.
Debbie	She was really funny when she was pissed. Walking into the kitchen, staggered in, there are all those boys sitting round and she goes "Hello Gaz" and fell over.
All girls	Laughter.
SJB	Classic entry!
Debbie	Then she is - was leaning over talking to him and she just toppled over . It was really funny . Oh sorry.
Sioux	Just like Sally the other night, Sally came in, that night we had all been down to Sally's. (all girl gathering: SJB) And there was this ashtray right by the door. She comes in, she goes huuhh and she stood straight in this ashtray with all dogends in there and it went crack and it fell all over the place.
Cathy	Yeah when I walked out of Sally's place we were walking up the road and it was really dark and we were talking and I goes Sioux I think someone has dumped an ashtray in my pocket.
Cathy	There was about fifty dogends in there. I got home and I was going like that, there was about three handfuls, all these matches. I goes hold on a minute Sioux. I've got the wrong coat on.
All girls	Laughter.
Sioux	So we had to go all the way back.
Clare	Whose coat was it?
Cathy	Sally's with an ashtray in her pocket.

214

Drinking stories were common currency among the new wave girls, probably one of the most amusing stories concerned the night that Sally and Lynne both fell into a ditch through a combination of drink and "larking about". Superficially, it is clear that this behaviour is not consistent with images of passive teenage girls (Sharpe 1976, Wolpe 1988). These stories are re-presentations of the girls' promenading practices as a female youth cultural group. At a deep level we can identify a rule of the girls' internal group relations: do not hold your feelings back, show your real self. The girls displayed honesty by crying and consoling one another and also by being able to laugh at their own vulnerability; this was an essential dynamic feature of this group. Here, crying is not a weakness but a strength. By being open they share and cope with the problems of their vulnerabilities. I never saw these girls cry as a result of bullying or run to the girls' toilet to escape male violence (Llewellyn 1980). For as a youth cultural group, the new wave girls' territorial practices were conducted through the showing of their public face.

Cigarette smoking

Another example of illegality in the girls' behaviour was the smoking of cigarettes before they were sixteen. In general, the girls would smoke while walking to and from school, occasionally during break time, morning/afternoon, always at dinner time "up the street", "in the graveyard" or "round somebody's house". Throughout the fieldwork a few of the girls were reported by prefects to the teaching staff for smoking outside school. However, they only received cautions rather than punishment. During an informal conversation they speak about smoking at school and at home.

Clare	We smoked in the classroom.
Sioux	Yeah English and Maths.
SJB	You smoked in the classroom?
Clare	We used to smoke in the fucking Maths lesson. Do you remember when we used to have, we used to pass it along the thing, everyone used to stick it under the table.
SJB	Do your parents know you smoke? Because Debbie you said your mother didn't know.
All girls	My mum doesn't know.

215

Debbie	My mum , once I was choking on a cup of tea and she said "Oh you should give up smoking" I just went bright red.
Sioux	Wed. Red. My mum, I don't know if she knows but I could swear blind she would be able to smell it.
Debbie	Yeah, that's what I've always thought.
SJB	Do your parents know what you get up to half of the time?
Debbie	No.
Clare	That is the best thing about it. It makes it more , more exciting.
All girls	YEAH.
Clare	You know, like smoking
Sioux	It is like me , I am never at home at the weekends.
Debbie	No I'm not.
Clare	When you're allowed to smoke at home I think more people would give up. Because all the fun has gone out of it. "Quick here she comes" while you're having a fag ....
Sioux	I sit there (at home: SJB) at lunch time thinking, oh - shall I smoke this cigarette now or shall I leave it for later. And it is a good job I do. Most likely the day when I do light up a cigarette at lunch time my stepfather will come in. So I don't. I save it for in bed at night. When everybody has gone to bed. I sit in bed with my wooden ashtray.
Clare	I smoke in the bath.
Debbie	Yeah
SJB	In the bath!
Clare	We have got a bath tray. I sit there with a fag. It's really great. You can't smell it because there is so much steam and I get my dad's Brute and spray it everywhere. He doesn't know.
Sioux	No I only do it in the bedroom because that is the only place my friends smoke anyway. When my parents are out, then in the living room. I did my finger with bleach last night.
Debbie	Mine are still yellow . Looks like I have been eating yellow sherbet.
Sioux	Yeah , that is what I'll tell mum , I think , she'll say Have you!".

216

For under sixteens to smoke cigarettes is against the law, it is also against school regulations and for some of the new wave girls it is against the wishes of their parents. In the fifth year, the girls were more selective in their oppositional practices against school, thus smoking in the classroom was abandoned in favour of the sports field or the street. Smoking is both an individual act and a collective group ritual. To smoke alone the girls' favourite locations were bedroom, bathroom and toilet. To smoke as a group the girls spend weekends away from home at the house of another girl, where in all-girl gatherings, they were able to break parental rules through the solidarity of their group relations. Excitement is mentioned by the girls as a major reason why they smoke. The thrill of illegality or breaking regulations is more important than the act of smoking itself. However, smoking cigarettes was a central part of the girls' relations and practices .

In the first year of fieldwork the girls tried smoking marijuana on a number of occasions but this was not an important element of their cultural practices until the sixth form.

X   We have tried it over at Fred's one time.
Y   Just makes me feel drunk for about ten minutes.

In the fifth year the girls as a group were uncertain about the purpose of smoking cannabis. In earlier years some of the girls had briefly tried glue sniffing but found it unsuitable as a means of getting high. In the second year of fieldwork some girls began to grow their own "dope" plants. I also accompanied them to places they visited regularly, where it was possible to smoke marijuana. The new wave girls did not take so called 'hard' drugs.

Clothes and school uniform

One of the Head teacher's notices to parents on school uniform for pupils reads,

Once again I must thank most parents for sending their children to school so suitably dressed. You will recall that we also ask that school clothes for the summer term should be restricted in range. Boys should continue to wear ties until specifically told they may not. Light weight blouse type jackets may be worn only in school colours. Girls may continue to wear winter uniform but may instead wear dresses in blue or blue and white (not other colours)

217

with modest necklines and at least small sleeves. Cardigans should be dark blue (not white or other colours). Vests, T-shirts and denims are not suitable (even for sixth formers). Shoes and sandals should be safe and comfortable for the many activities of a school day.

The clothes worn to school by the new wave girls were of great variation such as:- black trousers, skirts, usually black, (few girls regularly wore skirts), jumpers without blouses, no bra, large oversize jumpers, male white shirts, black and grey T-shirts, sweat shirts, brown, grey or black cardigans, copper coloured jackets, Doctor Marten boots, black monkey boots and green shoes. This list of some of the girls' clothes for school is not exhaustive but it shows that they rarely wore the correct school uniform.

Other girls in school generally wore clothes that were within the regulations. The new wave girls were the only girls consistently to wear trousers rather than skirts (Margrain 1983). The boffin, square, straight and remedial girls always wore skirts, the last altering their uniform to sexualise their appearance (Hudson 1984). In contrast, the new wave girls did not adapt their school uniform to make themselves appear more feminine, they wore clothes of a non-school uniform type which were sexually attractive without conforming to conventional markers of female prettiness.

In discussion Mrs Arthurs, the Head of Fifth Year Girls, explained that on a number of occasions she had told off some of the girls for not wearing proper school uniform. Here Sioux relates one such incident, "Mrs Arthurs took one of us in 'cause she had a grey sweat shirt on. That's not school uniform. She took her into her office and she told her off because her cords were too tight. She didn't tell her off for her sweat shirt at all". Sioux relates another incident of a new wave girl caught in non-school uniform, this time by Mr Skull, Head of Fifth Year Boys.

Sioux   Like Mr. Skull he saw her in her jeans and he said why
           have you got jeans on and he laughed. And she goes,
           "Oh I got the motor bike thing in General Studies this
           morning". He just didn't say anything at all, he just
           laughed.

If this pupil had been a boy, it is likely that he would have been sent home. Sioux's statement reveals that some of the male teachers were very lenient towards the new wave girls.

In general, accounts of pupils wearing non-school uniform usually focus on the deviant action in terms of opposition to school, sexual expression or display of a youth cultural style. However, on one occasion Clare, the style leader of the new wave girls, and Rich her boyfriend, one of the style leaders of the mod boys, combined flamboyancy with purpose and imagination in their dress for an O' level English Literature examination. Clare was wearing a long dark grey-silver raincoat with turned-up collar, a Victorian style white lace blouse and dark lambswool jumper, a skirt of heavy dark tartan just past the knee, dark socks and a small pair of black leather boots. Her dark hair was elegantly parted so one side appeared longer, obscuring half of her face to reveal no make-up except for one shaded dark purple eyebrow. Rich meanwhile had a long dark overcoat, black jacket with narrow lapels, a white shirt with a small buttoned-down collar contrasting with a small thin black bow tie. Over his jacket collar was a white silk scarf. He wore a pair of black trousers with pleats which were tight at the ankle displaying a pair of polished red shoes.

When questioned as to the reason for their peculiar dress and appearance Clare replied, "We've come dressed for English Literature in a manner suitable for Shakespeare". The teaching staff were amused and did not send the pupils home to change into normal school uniform.

Skiving

Absence, truancy or skiving are terms denoting non-attendance at school for pupils up to the age of sixteen. There is an ambiguity within the meaning of truancy, for to 'play truant' is to stay away from school without leave, but to be a truant also means one who shirks or neglects duty.

I never knew any of the boffin girls to practice skiving. But if any did, it would probably have been as individuals not as members of a group. The most deviant activity for the boffin girls would be to refrain from work during free periods set aside for homework. The remedial girls would frequently be absent from school, which is consistent with Burgess's (1983) study on low status and stigmatised "Newsom" pupils at the bottom of the streaming system.

The new wave girls in the upper ability band did engage in skiving but it was always a highly selective event, for example "We don't want to watch some boring police film about piss artists driving over people, do we", or "We've completed this section of the course, so we might as well do something more constructive". I attended a number of skiving sessions at the home of new wave girls who lived near the school. Sometimes I would set off with the girls when they made a decision to play truant, at other times I would receive a message through the "grapevine", and make my own way to the house. During these times of absence I usually found the girls helping each other to solve problems in maths, completing history, geography or English literature homework, revising for examinations or filling in forms. Obviously, sometimes they did no work, and just drank coffee, chatted or listened to music, but even these conversations were no idle waste of time.

They generally skived in one another's houses, and utilised the time in a manner not consistent with the term truancy. Their type of skiving is best described as creating an alternative frame of reference to that officially designated by the school. The new wave girls developed a strategy for skiving which was based on manipulating the organisational structure of the school, to support the educational aims they had in common with the school.

However, not all the occasions of the girls' skiving were happy. On one occasion they were almost caught. On Wednesday morning a group of them were gathered at Clare's house. There was a bang on the door, the loud voice of Mrs Arthurs rang out, she was with the Truancy Officer. Inside, the girls hid in silence. The banging continued for some time before the girls could get away through the back garden. Within the girl group this incident caused some initial ill feeling towards those who were not in the house. However, later in the day and again early next morning, two of the girls who were in the house repeated that they were frightened and would think hard about when and where to skive next. Afterwards, the event became a tale of excitement to enhance the girls' deviant promenade. No other pupils had been able to deceive both a Head of Fifth Year and the Truancy Officer.

Girls together: 'lesbian' displays and physicality.

One of the boys in the school described the new wave girls:

Kevin   You lot of girls are fucking weird . You're always holding arms, anywhere, every time. When you say goodbye even for different lessons you kiss each other and touch one another. It's fucking crap. I'll tell you something, me and the rest of us think it's fucking funny and stupid, the way you lot act. Who do you reckon you are?

This aggressive and defensive statement by one of the "hard nut" boys, enables us to see what boys in general disliked about the new wave girls' behaviour. Earlier I mentioned that the girls would link arms when walking at school, they would also kiss goodbye, sometimes when changing classes and always at the end of the school day. This public bodily contact continued during leisure hours outside school.

Cathy	It's lovely and warm in here isn't it.
Debbie	Right, last night in London, it was. This is me and this is Cathy. (Practical demonstration: SJB) All of a sudden she just decided that she wanted to lie over me. Because my - because it was nice and warm on my side of the bed, and then I went like that over her. And then in the end I was over here curled up in the eiderdown, no pillows, just one blanket. She's got about six billion pillows and all the blankets, and the electric fire was over your side.
Sioux	It's like at Sally's party . We all sort of staggered in like this and we were lying there. We had the two air beds on the floor and somebody was on the sofa. Lynne and I were mucking around, pulling around, sitting around and she was thinking about spilling her coffee and she just sat there and she spilt it all down her and she goes isn't it funny how, when you think about spilling you coffee you do it. And then we all got into bed. There was Sally and Pat opposite us, like, because we had them head to head you see. Anyway, Steff was talking in her sleep oh, oh Gaz - patting the sofa. And next morning Sally woke up and she goes where's Pat like this. And apparently Sally had kept rolling nearer and nearer to Pat in the night, so that Pat had got out of bed and got in the other side!
All girls	Laughter
Sioux	You can imagine, so funny

These are a couple of the girls' stories of being together, they represent happy times, cuddling up away from men. At these

221

gatherings the girls would sleep together, smoke cigarettes, drink alcohol (cider, wine, martini) and engage in long conversations. When I stayed overnight at some of the girls' houses it was possible to observe this. It is a distinguishing characteristic that the girls would regularly sleep together in the same room. Sometimes they would tape record their conversations on a cassette before going to bed.

The new wave girls' level of intimacy was intense, their collective rituals and basis of group behaviour supported and strengthened solidarity. By revealing, sharing and accepting their bodily vulnerability and pleasures the girls acquired information about their own sexual responses. In this respect they are unlike the girls in the two feminist studies by Jackson (1980) and Lees (1986). Physical closeness was part of their internal group relations, it was also used as a promenade to promote particular messages.

SJB	There'll be some life in the sixth form with you lot there.
Sioux	Yeah.
Cathy	Yeah, us two lesbians.
Sioux	Me and Sally all over the floor together. My hip hurts, right there. Is that your hip?
Clare	Yeah.
Cathy	Did you hear what Gaz (boyfriend: SJB) said?
Sioux	What did he say?
Cathy	He goes , oh I have been hearing strange things about you and I goes what? (expression of leading him on: SJB) He goes, oh it is going round the sixth form that you two are becoming lesbians, and he said, no, really, he goes I don't believe it but you know that the "stiff's" (straight people: SJB) do.

Here they discuss how their close physical relations have been understood as lesbianism. I have decided to call the girls' open promotion of lesbian behaviour "lesbian displays". What is crucial is the reason for these 'lesbian' displays.

In the girl group there were two apparent lesbian pairings, Sioux and Sally, and Cathy and Debbie. I knew the four boyfriends of each of these girls who thus could not have been only lesbians. I consider that the aim of these 'lesbian displays' was not to define personal lesbian relations but rather to exclude others, promote group unity and to strengthen close relations between pairs of girls.

222

We saw that boys in the fifth year felt threatened when observing the girls' physicality. 'Lesbian' displays frighten the boys because they render their masculine sexual display pointless (Nava 1982).

The new wave girls did not see menstruation as a taboo. Inside the group a girl would say she had started her period; outside the group some of the girls would occasionally tease or try to humiliate a boy by stating "Do you know I'm on". A number of the girls realised the potential use of the subject of menstruation because boys feared it (Lees 1986, Prendergast 1989). Therefore to mention their period provoked images of defilement and consequently disrupted a boy's pattern of sexist abuse. However, they were not immune to intimidation by boys, but sexual abuse was less of a problem for them than other girls.

The girls' lesbian displays and close physical contact was an everyday feature of their relations and bodily stories were normal events.

Debbie	Right , Friday night . When I'm riding by bike , we didn't have any shampoo, so I washed my hair with soap. We didn't have any fucking toothpaste so I had to wash my teeth with salt.
Cathy	Is that it, is that what we are waiting for?
Debbie	No. I didn't have any bog paper either.
Sioux	Drip dry ! I remember I used blotting paper once in the lower school.
Clare	My mum told me to use my middle finger.
Cathy	Remember the time when I knocked the thing down the loo. I told her I couldn't get it out. I said "This is your toilet roll Clare. I have just dropped it in the toilet."
Clare	She was holding it and I said did you flush the loo and she said no.
All girls	Laughter.

The girls possessed an ability to "shock" both boys and other girls by their forthright discussions, stories and jokes about female (and male) bodily functions normally understood as taboo.

Conclusions

One important issue brought out in this chapter is how the girls understand their parents' interpretations of female friendship and the degree to which parents sanction the behaviour of the respective groups. The new wave girls' shared experience of family break up and changes in household arrangements made a strong impact upon the girl group as a whole. Where the step or separated parent did not recognise the daughter's new role in the home or failed to acknowledge the value of the girl group there were degrees of tension and conflict. Parents gave support to the group by allowing greater freedom of action. In exchange for independence the girls would accept domestic responsibility. Changes to the family form brought changes to the conventional relations between daughter and parent (mother or father); because the girls' help was needed in order to manage the household, the girls became partners and were treated more like equals. The parents of the new wave girls allow them independence because they shared responsibility in the household; this exchange relation was a recognition of the strength of the girl group as a whole. However, it also implicitly carried parental expectations that the girls in the group were able to regulate their own behaviour.

The parents of the boffin girls were, in general, more strict about their daughters' behaviour, especially with regard to questions of school and access to boys. The boffin girls also had an exchange relation with their parents to gain independence, although on a different basis from the new wave girls. The academic success of the boffin girls was rewarded by parents holding a celebration party. Although the girls remained within the restrictive boundaries drawn by their parents, they were not denied access to pleasure. Through gaining qualifications the girls gained parental support and resources to hold a party. On these ritual occasions the girls were free to challenge the moral regimes of their middle class parents by "getting drunk" or kissing "unsuitable" boys. In other words, the parents gave limited independence to their daughters.

Essentially it is the middle class boffin girls who more readily accepted school values and norms. However, they were supportive of the school's definition of the pupil role only insofar as it corresponded to their own educational aspirations. Could it be argued that their behaviour was resistant? It was suggested that the girls' behaviour might be understood as occasionally giving rise to acts of contestation. They challenged principles of control by disagreeing with a teacher's opinion or by showing limited disrespect. In private the girls held resistant attitudes towards teachers and schooling; these active responses might possibly be described as internal resistance. In general, the concepts of "contestation" and "internal resistance" are too insensitive and vague as explanations of behaviour. The concepts clarify some moments of the boffin girls' engagement in school processes but they are unable to reveal their subtle internal/external group relations and practices.

The new wave girls conform to school in terms of valuing qualifications and completing work, accepting the instrumentality of school - the means and ends of school - learning but not its moral order. I identified a range of resistance practices of the new wave girls which are oppositional to school and also generally associated with masculine anti-school groups (Lacey 1970, Willis 1977). This raises the question of whether these activities reinforce the girls' subordination by contributing to the reproduction of sexist attitudes (Aggleton 1987). The girls' resistant behaviour of drinking, lesbian displays, cigarette and cannabis smoking and truancy are examples of acts of challenge against power relations across four sites; sexuality, family, school and society. However, forms of oppositional behaviour do not in themselves demonstrate resistance (Giroux 1983) but taken together these examples can be described as aspects of the new wave girls' anti-patriarchal practice. It would be an over-interpretation to argue that their truancy, drinking or wearing non-regulation school uniform indicate this, although these aspects of behaviour show defiance, independence, assertiveness and creativity, not always associated with teenage girls (Walkerdine 1984). However, the girls' cultural practice did encourage critical thinking, and was feminist in the sense of prompting them to question male dominance. Thus it is possible to conclude that the concept of resistance is potentially useful to explain and interpret the new wave girls' actions because the underlying principle of their anti-patriarchal practice is emancipatory.

225

10   Patriarchy and romance

Introduction

On the basis of the analysis in the previous chapter I shall now compare and contrast the two girl groups' relationships to patriarchy and romance. The chapter will be divided into two sections. In the first section I investigate gender groupings and sexism, in order to identify the girls' experience of differing social and sexual relations with boys. Here I shall be concerned with the identification of modes of sexist attack from boys, strategies used by the boffin girls in their relations with the boffin boys and the new wave girls' relationships to boys and boyfriends. In the second section I present an ethnography of two adolescent girls' parties.

Sexism and modes of male aggression

The boffin and new wave girls dealt with a variety of different sexist practices from boys in school. Girls encountered sexism from individual male pupils and groups of boys throughout the school. However, sexual discrimination was not practised by every male pupil, nor were those boys who were abusive to girls consistently sexist in the same manner (Mahony 1985).

The boffin girls were most frequently in contact with the boffin boys (their pedagogic reference group); they spent little time with either square boffin or mod boys. In the following conversation the girls talk about some of the square boffin boys, the boffin boys in general and an incident with a mod boy. The discussion begins with the girls' assessment of the square boffin boys.

Kerry	Because they respect us more.
Monica	I don't know.
Rose	No.
Mary	Chris does I think - but Chris is just shy, um.
Monica	To put it mildly.
Rose	A pain in the neck.
Kerry	I don't go any stronger than that.
Rose	I think they are worth five pains in the neck. He (Chris: SJB) is worse than Joe and that's saying something.
Kerry	A pain in the arm.
SJB	I don't think that Chris and that lot really know so much about the female body.
Rose	No.
Mary	I don't know , I don't know . I think they might do but they're just slow in talking about it.
Ellen	It's awful isn't it, ur
SJB	Why do you think the school separates the girls from boys to give these sex talks?
Mary	I think they probably consider it is nothing to do with boys.
Rose	You have got to admit in the first and second year the boys (boffin boys: SJB) were pretty kiddish and they just laughed about it.
Mary	Yeah true . But they wouldn't if they hadn't been kept separate. Then they wouldn't laugh about it.
Rose	And they did in the third year . It's all right in the fourth year and the fifth year. I think they would have done.
Mary	They might have laughed about it . But then they would have got used to it and they would...
Rose	They are used to it. They are used to it.
Kerry	But how much do they know (boffin boys: SJB) and how much is just what they call and play about it.
Rose	Yeah, but I mean they ...
Rose	They do not just sort of make a laugh about it like they used to in the first and second year.
Kerry	They do. I think they do.

227

Rose	They don't, not in the fifth year.
Mary	Not in the same way.
Kerry	But they still laugh.
Rose	So do the girls.
Kerry	I mean I was standing out there (fifth year area: SJB) the other day reading a notice and Rod (mod boy: SJB) threw a tampon under my feet and said, "Oh is that yours Kerry" I said "No thanks, Rod", and kicked it back. NOW IF YOU DO THAT SORT OF THING, YOU'RE KIDDING ABOUT. (voice loud and strained: SJB).
Rose	I know.
Mary	Yeah but there was a time when they wouldn't have been able to do that.
Rose	They wouldn't have done it.
Mary/Rose	Because they would have been too embarrassed.

The boffin girls understand the square boffin boys as essentially childish. Through observations of these boys, it was apparent that they would tease the girls by pointing out the differences between women and men. According to the boys, girls' bodies have "funny bits" which are assessed as, "stupid" and "weak" because they are not like, or as strong as boys. For the boffin girls this level of sexist attack was least troublesome and could be dealt with by a statement about the girls' academic ability. The girls refrain from returning the boys' aggression because they see them as children and feel secure in their own more responsible and mature attitude. They see these boys as practically asexual. However, the boys' childlike actions are based upon powerful sexist assumptions which insult girls (Spender and Sarah 1980).

Essentially, when these girls speak about boys, they refer to the boffin boys. They see the boffin boys' behaviour towards them as "kiddish", although they disagree about the degree of sexist practice shown by the boffin boys. They consider that their hostile attitude comes from being "kept separate" during talks about sex which breeds resentment and ignorance about the functioning of the female body. But the girls are optimistic and assert that the boys behaviour would change if they were given more information about female sexuality. However, the girls reassess the boys behaviour asserting that they are ignorant and still laugh about the reproductive and excremental aspects of the female body. The problem identified by the girls is that boys' sexist abuse changes, it is "not the same". The story of the tampon incident reinforces the girls' interpretation of male behaviour as negative. In conclusion, the boffin girls were confronted with a variety of modes of male aggression in changing ways from the first to the fifth year.

Understanding boys

It is worthwhile examining in detail some of the girls' responses to the boffin boys' actions.

Rose	No . The trouble with Howard and Gary is they think they are too good for us, don't they? They think they are too good for everybody.
SJB	Have the boffin boys been out with any girls in the lower years?
Rose	Gary did.
Monica	For about a week.
Mary	They (the younger girl: SJB) always chuck them.
Rose	For a week he was - Gary was - so upset when she chucked him. Not because he was upset that he was not going out with her. But because she chucked him.
Mary	He was crying.
Rose	Because me and Paul were up in the computer room and Gary was up there. And you should have heard him, "oh she chucked me". And he was worried that she chucked him, that he didn't chucked her.
Mary	SERVES HIM RIGHT.
Rose	He was so worried about that.
Monica	Damage of ego.
Rose	Yeah, I mean we had fits (laughter: SJB) we just sort of, corr, you know. He was just so worried about what everybody would think.
Kerry	A lot of boys are just one big ego . Mainly that lot . (boffin boys: SJB)
All girls	Laughter
Mary	Because if they go out with any of us ...
Kerry	You, ol, ...
SJB	Go on Mary.
Mary	Because if they go out with anyone , they take the mickey with their friends. They all sort of,...
Monica	Tease each other.
Mary	That is the biggest reason why they don't go out with

anyone in our year because they, everyone, they all know each other. And they all know - because they think they're above us. Then if any of them went out with any of us, then they'd tease each other so much.

Two strategies used by the girls to distance themselves from the boys are rejection and teasing. The girls observe a boffin boy's behaviour after rejection from a younger girl; they are not sympathetic. The boy's reaction to being "chucked" brings out the girls' dislike, even resentment of him. To be the "chucker" carries status and determines the validity of "your account", whereas to be "chucked" is to be in a weak position. This adolescent notion is fundamentally related to the structure of sexual relations, to the concept of reputation and the vocabulary of abuse. The girls turn their initial rejection by these boys, into a celebration of laughter. Their joy focuses upon the boffin boy's vulnerability. Although this enables the girls to tease the boy it also brings out the dilemma of the status of obtaining a boyfriend, and the fear of rejection. The dramatic concept of "being chucked" is crucial in shaping the aftermath of rumour and reputation at the close of the relationship. For the boffin girls the fear of rejection, even before entering a relationship, is also one of the main reasons why no relationships exist. Fear is supported by the notion of familiarity in that the girls use friendship as a basis to maintain distance.

Mary	We are just all sort of friends with them aren't we.
Kerry	We know them too well to go out with them.
SJB	Do you think so?
Kerry	Rose has known James since the juniors. I have known Gary all through the juniors, and Paul.
Rose	Most of them think they are too good for us.
Mary	Yeah.
SJB	Do you think that?
Mary	They do.
Rose	They do.
Mary	I mean Howard has actually said it.
Kerry	Gary.
SJB	Has he?
Rose	Howard does, doesn't he.
Kerry	Yeah. "Oh Howard's too good for us" (joke voice. SJB)
Rose	Yeah.
Mary	They do, they think, ...

230

Rose	Right . They were taking the mickey out of me , right, Gary, Howard and - they said that Paul fancied me, right. And I was saying "Oh God", well not exactly that. But Gary goes "Why don't you go out with him?" They said "you (meaning Rose: SJB) couldn't get anybody better".
Mary	That's exactly what he said to me.
Rose	Yeah. That's what he said to me . IT IS ABOUT YOUR LEVEL, isn't it. HIM or something like that, something that meant THAT. (loud raised voice: SJB)
Mary	The thing is that too many people fancy them, alot of people in the third and fourth year.
Kerry	Yeah , but look, they are all, they don't really, third and fourth year, a lot of them are still immature.
Rose	A lot of them. ALL OF THEM.
Kerry	Well they are if they fancy that lot.
Mary	No the thing is they have got so many people that want to go out with them that they think , you know.
Ellen	Everybody wants (them: SJB)
Mary	That they can get anyone that they wanted.
Rose	They are so big headed.
Mary	They only want PRETTY PEOPLE.
Kerry	They think that your life revolves around them . If one of you, if someone is upset, say Mary was upset the other day (the boffin boys say: SJB) "Oh what have we done, what have we done, we must have made her upset" (joke voice: SJB)
Rose	And they are pleased about it.
Mary	Yeah.
Kerry	They weren't then , because they were being nasty .
Mary	And then they do really childish little things , like last Monday, um - Gary and Howard and that lot were having a competition to see who could be the nastiest to the girls.
Rose	Oh yeah.
SJB	Yeah, were they really?
Mary	It's stupid.
Rose	I reckon Howard is the worst one.
Mary	Yeah, Gary is getting like that.
Ellen	They are getting absolutely terrible at saying you fancy so and so, or so and so fancies you. It just gets round the school doesn't it.

The sexist assumptions of the boys result not in the girls going out with them but in increasing the distance between them and their potential partners. From the viewpoint of the boffin girls the interest shown by younger girls in the boffin boys has the effect of making the boys 'bigheaded' and thus more unapproachable. This is presented as another reason supporting the girls' reluctance to attempt to go out with them. The boys are assessed as playing uncaring games and being 'horrible'. The experience the girls are discussing is part of their everyday life. As the boffin girls refuse to go out with the boffin boys they then try to humiliate the girls. The ironic contradiction that the girls face is that these are the only boys they come into contact with. If the boffin girls want a relationship to prove to their parents that they are mature and require more freedom, they must select a boffin boy since their parents would not approve of any other boys, but for the girls this amounts to an impossible choice.

The new wave girls' understanding of the sexism of boys at school is somewhat different from that of the boffin girls.

SJB	What about boys?
Sioux	They don't mature as quickly.
Collen	It is not as though we can compare different parts of the body, like boys do about girls.
Steff	It is through socialisation that we are different.
Sioux	They can't back anything up , they don't really know what they are arguing about, do they. So their solution is to hit. I am equal now as I want to be, but it depends for all - what you mean by equal.
Clare	They are brought up to be sexist by their parents.
Collen	They just want someone to play around with, because if you are sort of big around the breast. They only care about the body, you know, "look at her". But for the girls it is not as though we can compare different parts of the body, and say like boys say about parts of the bodies of girls. We cannot compare different parts of the boys' body, even when you talk about boys willies. It's stupid, it is just not possible for girls.

Fifth year boys at Marshlands did not regularly speak with the new wave girls; the only male group which had frequent contact with the girls was the mod boys. However, it would be incorrect to assume that they did not experience other modes of male aggression, similar to that experienced by the boffin girls. The new wave girls saw sexism as being a result of socialisation and the family as a crucial site for the reproduction of gender discrimination. Two key issues raised by the girls are, firstly, male violence, and secondly, the ideology of male sexual needs (McIntosh 1978).

Male violence: Sioux, argues that she is "equal now". It is possible to suggest that her claim of equality derives from the strength and solidarity within the female youth cultural group: such an assertion might not be possible for an individual girl or girls within a weaker group. Sioux maintains that a boy's last resort to prove his dominance is physical violence, "to hit". Male violence towards girls is seen as not acceptable, it is irrational: "they do not really know what they are arguing about".

Ideology of male sexual needs: Collen's assessment of male abuse is explicitly sexual; she expresses the view that boys reduce the value of a girl to parts of her body, for example a big breast: a girl has assets which are her "component parts" (Wood 1984). Collen is critical of the male attitude towards girls, especially when boys are together, she argues they compare different parts of a girls body, in isolation from her feelings or mind. The suggestion is that a boy's physical appearance doesn't show externally i.e. willies are hidden, but even if girls could comment on boys' bodies it would not have the same effect because the power relationship is different. Colleen emphasises that boys' sexist practice shows that they look down upon girls as exploitable objects to provide them with pleasure.

New wave girls: an anti-patriarchal practice.

This section will present essentially ethnographic data of the new wave girls in a variety of different contexts. Here I shall be concerned with how the girls confront and control their relations with boys and boyfriends.

Dance

The new wave girls would attend discos and sometimes went to see local bands play in public houses. Early in the fieldwork I went to a gig at the school youth wing; the band, called Alternative Signs, consisted of Marshlands pupils. I arrived at the youth wing slightly late owing to the haphazard bus service, but before the band had started. Inside the building I was instructed to go to the back room and see the teacher leader who had a message. Mr. Prett greeted me in an enthusiastic mood and asked whether I would write a review of the band for the local Argus. I agreed, thanked him and went into the main hall where I joined the new wave girls. I bought them some lemonade drinks (only soft drinks were permitted on school premises), while they asked "What were you seeing him for?"

There were many pupils and ex-pupils dressed in a variety of youth cultural styles. The band began the first number and I started to write a few notes. The new wave girls preferred to stay at the back of the hall where there was more light than near the stage. I went for a walk round the venue, stood by the stage watching everything to sense the atmosphere of the evening and then returned to remain with the girls. The youths at the front were engaged in a variety of dances, from a rocker stamp to punk pogo.

Gradually, the new wave girls began to dance. Sioux and Sally were moving slowly, stretching out their legs and collapsing on everybody, Lynne and Steff wheeled round the side close to the floor while Debbie and Cathy were leaping about, crashing into the girl group. The dance was not strictly in time with the music, fast or slow, but the movements had the effect of making the boys move out, to leave the girls space to dance in this complex and subtle manner. The girls were laughing, playing, hopping and dancing in this particular ritual for about an hour. I asked Sally and Debbie what they were doing and whether their dance had a name. Sioux jumped straight over and said it was an adaptation of something that they used to do in P.E. lessons in the lower school called "exercising the vaginal muscle".

Cigars"

There were minor squabbles between the new wave girls and the mod boys concerning territory in the informal school spaces, but no physical violation. However, interaction and exchange between the two groups could be highly charged with ritual insults at the level of action and sound. Members of each group would parry these verbal and symbolic assaults with an array of words, poses, objects or gestures. In general, the girls thought that the mod boys were "okay" and "friendly" although this was qualified by their knowledge that they could be offensively sexist. They made contact in the first year, but by the fifth year Debbie considered that "they did not stay together very much".

Throughout the fieldwork I observed only one major incident of conflict between the two youth cultural groups. I was standing in the corner of the fifth year area talking with a couple of boffin boys. It was half way through afternoon breaktime and the pupils were milling round, as they usually do. Five of the mod boys and some of the "criminal boys" rushed into the area through the main doors, after secretly smoking a cigarette and began to pester other pupils and "have a laugh". The "criminal boys" went back outside again, while the mod boys stood in front of the girls. The boys started to show off, trying to intimidate the girls by shouting and touching them. To counter the abusive insults a couple of the new wave girls placed tampons in their mouths and moved rapidly towards the boys, thrusting out the tampon between their lips asking the boys for a light to their "cigars". The boys began walking backwards, stumbling and waving their hands in disturbed motions attempting to knock the tampon away from their faces. There was an uproar in the fifth year area, girls laughing, boys shocked and pupils attempting to get out of the way. Two days later I interviewed girls from a remedial class in the fifth year area and they described what the tampon incident meant to them. They did not censure the new wave girls as "slags" for putting tampons in their mouths (Shacklady 1978, Lees 1986, Prendergast 1989,). They considered that for these boys it was "up theirs" and "really amusing". The girls in the remedial class "hated" these boys and others, as they were on the receiving end of much sexist terrorism. Interestingly, they reflected "we couldn't have done it". One girl concluded that the new wave girls were "leaders in style, the only real girls, group of girls, in the school".

Valentines cards

One afternoon at the beginning of breaktime Sally and Sioux passed a message to me, to go round and see Cathy at her house. It was bright sunshine and the walk to her mother's house took ten minutes, by the short-cut. I was let in by Debbie; the two girls were apparently doing some school work (Maths). Cathy made Debbie and I a cup of tea, we sat on the floor and began to talk. It was a few days before Valentine's Day. Cathy explained that she had composed a number of short poems, both describing and evaluating the state of the relationship between each new wave girl and her steady boyfriend. To accompany the valentine verse she had sketched a number of pencil drawings to show each boyfriend's penis and testicles, plus what she called "one good looking male bottom".

After a second cup of tea the two girls decided to have a valentine quiz. Cathy would read out her verse to Debbie and I was also invited to guess for which partner, either boyfriend or girlfriend, she had fictitiously composed the lyric. When reading out the verse, she would mime a caricature of the person we were supposed to be guessing. The test caused immense hilarity and laughter when our replies did not coincide or were incorrect. The content of the valentine poems varied according to how Cathy viewed the individual partners and their relationship. Overall, there was a concern with how boys treat girls simply as sexual machines without individual feelings, needs and ideas. Her descriptions were serious, absurd, ridiculous and sensitive to the weakness, strength and vulnerability of each girl.

Poetry

Below is a poem composed by the new wave girls concerning all their boyfriends.

Toss chops united

If we could show how much we want to hate
We'd make you live in hell
But you're just so fucking boring
We're just too scared to tell.

Your psychedelic talks on music
You really think you know
You worship all these poxy groups
And go to every show

At parties you smoke pot
That's the "Hip" thing to do
Tiring quickly of your old friends
Searching for someone new.

But let's just get this straight.
You're the ones "who're" stupid
We never even tried to act
Or think like poxy Cupid.

"copyrite" Sioux and Debbie

On the page with each stanza the two girls had drawn large heart shape bubbles, within which were written together two boyfriends' names, such as Slim and Peter or Stephen and Gaz, with a comment alongside stating "true love forever", "4 ever and ever" and "true love". These phrases, taken from teenage girl magazines, suggest that their boyfriends are in love with each other.

The poem and love bubbles are an active response by the new wave girls, heavy with irony, wit and contradiction. The title is a play on words which ridicules male sexuality - toss - to masturbate, and male leisure - united - is a football team eg West Ham United. Put together the negative assertion is a doubly weighted reference that defines the boyfriends as collective masturbators or "Toss chops united". The first verse establishes the girls' intention, they have minds of their own, refuse to be taken for granted and find boys tedious and boring. The second verse focuses upon how their boyfriends uncritically accept things, blindly assert that they know everything about today's music and discount any girls' contribution. The third verse is critical of the boys' self centred behaviour and fantasies induced by smoking cannabis which interfere with social relations. It makes them selfish and fickle in their friendships: reinforcing the meaning of the title, in that it implies the boys use their relationships only as a means of self gratification. The final stanza also suggests the girls' autonomy in that it redefines the relationship they had with the boys, thus countering and asserting as false the boys' assumptions that they were 'in love' with them. Thus it rejects traditional notions of romantic love. It explicitly reverses the patriarchal opposition of male = knowledge, female = emotion thus countering the male symbolic order upheld by the boys (Cixous and Clement 1991).

The poem and their celebration of it reclaim the right to speak ("copyrite") and make definitions denied them by masculinist society. This is also affirmed as the aim of the poem in the first stanza which asserts the way in which the girls cannot show their real feelings or 'tell' what they think i.e. it emphasizes the

237

restrictions placed on them. The boys exercise a right to speak "Your...talks", which is denied the girls (Shiach 1991).

Boyfriends

I had regular contact with the new wave girls' boyfriends in the upper sixth form. The boys did not treat me in an aggressive manner nor were they defensive because I spent time with their girlfriends. Three months into the fieldwork I brought four boyfriends together for a discussion, the purpose of which was to ascertain how much influence they had upon the girls. Almost immediately the talk began, the boyfriends discussed their feelings against the girl group. A central accusation was that "you can't do anything on your own" (meaning as a couple) without all the girls finding out. They stressed that the group structure was an obstacle encountered when a boyfriend made any type of suggestion. The boys maintained that the girl group had been strong in the lower years and even though there had been some internal group struggles, by the fifth year the group was still impenetrable. The boyfriends were "amazed" at my acceptance amongst them as a group, in pairs or individually. In general, they thought I could do something about their problem and change the girls' behaviour to something more to their liking.

After one of the new wave girls' all night parties at a boyfriend's house one of the girls asked whether I would walk her home. It was eight o'clock in the morning with the frost crisp on the grass. She gave me a note as we ambled along. The message, which had been cut from a magazine, read "The beauty and love of sleeping next to a woman without making love with her". The girl said her boyfriend had given her this piece of paper that morning, after they had gone to sleep together. In addition, she spoke of her virginity as a problem, stating; "I feel it is important who you give it to, whether they respect you. Perhaps in a few years' time, I might think I was really silly and stupid but at the moment it feels important". She began to smile and said further "I would have let him do it last night but the stupid sod did not have one (condom: SJB) did he". She concluded that this message was "really nice".

238

Two adolescent girl parties: an ethnography

I was fortunate to be invited to a party arranged by the boffin girls and one arranged by the new wave girls. I shall first compare differences in the setting of the two parties and then describe activities at each party.

Setting: the boffin girls' party

The boffin girls' party took place at the village 'New Hall'. I arrived at the hall in Monica's parents' car with Monica, Rose and Claire. The car was parked, and Mary emerged from the back of the building clutching the keys to the hall. It was just before seven o'clock and quite dark although the warm breeze was refreshing. The hall doors were opened and I helped Rose and Monica bring in the sound system, which was a hi-fi, while Mary brought in different people's record collections. Inside this dusty building both parents did the heavy work of unfolding tables, preparing a space for food and drink (wine, beer, cider, lemonade and orange juice) and making sure the record player was secure and working.

Gradually, more boffin girls began to arrive in pairs and small groups; a festive atmosphere was developing and everyone began to get excited. The girls took on roles of responsibility by organising tasks for different girls. The kitchen was allocated to a couple of girls. The toilets were working and sufficiently stocked with paper, others moved chairs into neat lines. The sound system was working, the food and drink were in a proper place, so "nobody would fall over anything". Brooms and bin liners were ready if somebody was sick or knocked glasses over. The girls were preparing everything in fine detail, sorting out problems, assessing possibilities and assuming an air of responsibility: the parents' help was quickly made unnecessary by the girls' efficiency. Everything was double checked, so that whatever might happen they had something prepared to deal with it in the kitchen or in the first aid box. During the preparation stage no boy arrived, but by half past eight everybody who was coming to the party was present.

Setting: the new wave girls' party

The new wave girls' party took place at Cathy's mother's house. I received a lift to the new wave girls' party as a pillion passenger on a scooter belonging to Paul, a mod boy, who had a blue Vespa 50. I arrived at Cathy's house at about half past eight. When the engine was switched off music could be heard outside the house. Debbie opened the door and we were met by Cathy, Sally and Sioux. I gave Cathy a small badge for her party celebration. A few minutes later Clare and boyfriend Rich (mod boy) followed. I was given a drink and sat in the lounge with the five girls who spoke eagerly about the clothes they were wearing, whether the party was going to be as good as or better than previous ones and when the boyfriends would arrive. Cathy explained how she had arranged that her mother would be away that evening and night. In fact, her mother arrived about half past seven the following morning.

The girls moved the television out of the main room and shifted the breakable objects to cupboards. In the large room on the right towards the middle was a sturdy table on which were placed the record and cassette players, with a collection of LPs, singles (7" and 12") CDs and cassettes, pre-recorded and home taped. Just before nine o'clock Collen, Steff, Lynne, Cat and Denise arrived, followed by some boyfriends, boys and marginal members of the girl group. The party was beginning to get going by half past nine with people rushing about, playing records, performing brief strange dances and sorting out drinks. By ten o'clock all guests had arrived and the party was in full swing.

The parties

Here I shall provide a chronological description of events, firstly, at the boffin girls' party and secondly, the new wave girls' party.

Boffin girl party

Monica's parents were the disc jockeys, they could be described as true amateurs, playing records at the wrong speed, or selecting incorrect LP tracks, and B sides rather than A sides were occasionally heard. The parents stood in front of the two speakers and each time I talked with them they said that they thought that the music was too loud.

The mod boys were the first to dance but immediately the parents played a joke on them, by increasing the speed of the record. The parents and boffins laughed, as they returned to sit down. It was almost twenty minutes before the mods took to the dance floor again; after two records some of the boffin girls also began to dance

240

in groups. The amusing intervention by the parents h a d unfortunately delayed dance floor activities and opportunities for public bodily contact between the girls and boys. Even though the majority of girls were dancing by nine o'clock the boffin boys still stood against the wall or leaned on the back of chairs drinking cans of beer. It took some time for the party goers, especially the boffin boys, to ease out of their "stiffness". Part of the problem for all participants was the continued presence of the boffin girls' parents, who also held the powerful position of playing the music.

It was not until a certain amount of alcohol had been drunk that the atmosphere became more relaxed. It did not take much alcohol to make the boffins merry and soon the boffin boys were dancing behind the mods. After half an hour of dance floor competence and display the slow records were selected and pairs danced. When dancing with the boffin girls the boffin boys would stroke their partners' bottoms. While on the dance floor I could observe that this display of caressing operated at a number of levels. Firstly, boys looked at other boys, dancing or standing nearby and made suggestive facial signs; secondly, square boffin boys who danced with boffin girls did not engage in such behaviour, thirdly, boys spoke to other boys, some made hand signals about their partner while others made explicitly rude propositions, and finally after a dance or number of dances with the same girl, the couple might go to one of the darkened "kissing corners" for a short time.

The mod boys did not dance with the boffin girls, they watched the boffin boys' activities and drank more. After a dance the boffin girls usually returned to the girls' space and there they began to talk about their immediate male partner, his behaviour, who they had or had not danced with, and who they would like a dance with. By half past ten some of the boffin girls were behaving as if they were slightly drunk, collapsing into chairs, clinging together, laughing out loud, bumping and falling around. Two of the square boffin boys were quite drunk and appeared to be dancing or doing staggering dance steps by themselves in a semi-coma. The boffin boys were still in pursuit of the boffin girls although by half past ten some of the girls had gone home, other boffin boys were swaying rather than dancing and two boys claimed they had been sick outside the hall.

The party came to an end at precisely eleven o'clock. The cleaning and clearing operation was accomplished by five boffin girls, with an "annoying" couple of boffin boys hampering their

241

efficiency. I thanked the parents, said good night to the girls who remained and left with two mod boys.

New wave girl party

In contrast, the new wave girls' party got into full swing at about the same time as the boffin girls' party finished. Here there were no parents present. By half past ten a fairly large amount of alcohol had been consumed by certain people. One boy, Phil, was the first person to be sick in the kitchen while another male accidentally banged his head and another pulled a curtain down. These were relatively minor incidents which made little impression on the general hubbub. The music was blasting out very loudly from the sound system in the large room. The main activity was movement between the two bedrooms and the lounge. The porch and toilet were places for a temporary stop, before returning to the central area of movement.

There were various types of dancing by the girls in manners which bore very little similarity to the movements of participants at the boffin girls' party. Clare and Rich were manically waltzing throughout the house, carefully avoiding objects, bodies and doors. Their gliding movements were ridiculous and funny. They continued for about an hour, until they fell down in the porch quite drunk and stayed down. In fact Clare sported a black eye for the next couple of days.

Everyone mingled in the lounge changing LPs by The Cure, Siouxsie and the Banshees, Talking Heads and Teardrop Explodes and then some cassettes, one of reggae, until one o'clock in the morning. Phil was sick again in the kitchen, appeared to lose all his clothes and stamped about naked in the pale reddish light until he disappeared. During the next hour sleeping positions were being sorted out to decide who would be in which bedroom or the main room. The girls changed their clothes and were walking round wearing longish night gowns or men's shirts. Often somebody, male or female, who was wearing only underwear (who was standing about) had their underwear pulled down and possibly thrown out of the window.

The party resembled a "Carry On" film, laughter, running about and messing around. Although collective undress was general, this was no sex orgy but perhaps a homage to hilarity. A boyfriend left one of the bedrooms to get some condoms. When he returned and handed out the condoms Sally said "We took them, blew them up and played balloons until they burst. It was a great laugh". At around three o'clock the record player in the lounge stopped but a cassette player was still playing loud music in one of the bedrooms. Suddenly some of the girls and other guests decided to go for a walk. It was quite cold as seven people hurried a quarter of a mile to the breezy beach. Everyone huddled together for warmth as some had little clothing on apart from coats. The group swayed drunkenly on and off the pavement on the way to the seafront. By the shoreline everyone threw stones into the sea, pushed each other over and had piggy-back rides. When this group returned from the beach the music was still playing in one bedroom and a few bodies were asleep in the main room. At around half past four another walk was suggested.

Between six and seven some people were beginning to emerge and scramble about, moving a few things. One bedroom was cleared and the lounge looked almost as it did before the party. The participants sat in the comfortable chairs looking likely to fall asleep. Bits and pieces were finally cleared, "dead bodies brought back to life" and a semblance of order was restored by seven, with all party goers gathered in the lounge. Tea and coffee were served and outrageous incidents and events discussed. The first time the music stopped was during the discussion before and after Cathy's mother arrived at half past seven. She was pleased everybody had had a good time, and that nobody was injured or the house damaged. At quarter to nine I left with Paul on his Vespa scooter.

Music and romance

Here I shall make a contrast between the purpose, site, organisation and interaction of the two parties; this interpretation will refer to the differing controls on intimacy. The most basic and obvious difference between the two parties was the venues, since both the hall and the house imposed restrictions on people's behaviour and offered an environment where different things were possible. At the boffin girls' party the boys were male friends and pedagogic colleagues, not boyfriends. At the new wave girls' party the boys were boyfriends and some male friends. This fact underlies the different types of behaviour and bodily contact by girls and boys at the different parties.

The boffins girls engaged in a complex relation of refusal and acceptance through the medium of dancing i.e. public bodily contact, and private bodily contact in the kissing corners. To obtain a boyfriend or girlfriend for bodily contact was not the sole object of the party, although both girls and boys were very determined to dance with the opposite sex. The girls were talking and laughing about their dancing partners, how they danced, and who they wanted a dance with. The boys were bragging amongst themselves, especially through their displays when dancing, to show that a girl had accepted private bodily contact. The boys' caressing of the girls' bottoms and thighs were displays to other boys standing around to show further status. The boffin girls' response to the boys' actions were described as "removing their wandering hands", or in some cases a visit to a kissing corner.

The new wave girls' party at Cathy's mother's house offered a possible space for private bodily contact between "steady partners". The fact that there were no parents present, plus the familiarity and comfort of the house made sexual contact less difficult. At the outset the party had been planned to go on all night and in the available, if somewhat cramped, space couples had an opportunity to sleep together, albeit en masse. On the one hand the girls had to gain acceptance from parents for such an occasion, and on the other hand, Cathy's mother conferred collective responsibility on the girls by leaving them in charge of a party to be held at her house.

Each party had a different type of musical setting. At the boffin girls' party both fast and slow music was provided by singles and LPs by different artists. The dancers did not know what the next record would be. This was important for couples dancing because it determined whether they remained on the dance floor or separated. Also it was Monica's parents who were the disc jockeys operating this controlling music which may or may not have brought girls and boys together to dance.

The music at the new wave girls' party was usually chosen by the girls, and comprised a few "singles" but mostly LPs and later cassettes, which replaced the playing of individual songs which at the boffin girls' party had cut dance floor activity into segments and created uncertainty about the next record. In contrast, an LP, CD or cassette would determine the musical setting for a longer time than a series of singles. The girls knew the music and those dancing were not subject to a succession of discontinuities with different artists creating different contexts. The musical setting for the new wave girls' party related to the whole concept of the party and the girls could anticipate responses the music would produce.

Each party had a specialised type of musical setting which demonstrates how different musical forms regulate and influence the flow of communication by party participants. Music can provide one set of rules for circulation amongst girls and boys. The musical form was one aspect of the boffin girls' party which the girls did not control.

Party post mortems: celebration and rumour

The boffin girls' party took place on a Saturday evening, and the following Monday morning at school they were ready with stories and rumours which were talked about during registration, breaktime, lunchtime and for the rest of the week. The girls were publicly celebrating the success and the fun of their party. Incidents were dramatically acted out, causing some considerable commotion in the fifth year area. The girls were boasting and teasing each other about who went off for long kissing sessions with boys. I questioned the girls informally about their interpretation of the boffin boys' antics.

SJB	Do you think the boffin boys normally dance like that or just because they had alot of beer?
Mary	No. They did it before.
Rose	They did it before.
Mary	They show off. You get Gary and Nick and that lot ...
SJB	Someone told me that there was some competition amongst the boys about who could dance with who ...
Rose	The least. They had that I think. Gary was going to see if he could dance with - um, the least, with somebody, I think he said.
Kerry	Well he danced with me . So he did not not have a dance.
Mary	He danced with me once because I made ...
Monica	He doesn't normally
Kerry	I reminded him of the time before when I asked him to dance and he was drunk and he stormed out of the room.
Mary	He always says like , oh my leg hurts or groin strain.
All girls	Laughter
SJB	How much of the boys' behaviour at the party was sort of display ?

Mary	Most of it.
Rose	I don't think it was , actually , because some of them just didn't realise what they were doing....
Kerry	You should drink to enjoy yourself and you know if it's going to make you feel bad, you shouldn't do it. It is pigheadedness.
Rose	That's what I mean . Gary said to me on Sunday , he said alot of people drank but Tosh wasn't sick. He's really stupid. He knows he couldn't drink that much, he was just doing it to show off.
Mary/Kerry	Mm.
Rose	I mean he could have gone , he could have spewed up all over the floor and then that would've taken ages to clear up.
Mary	Yeah. And we would've had to do it.

The girls seem to oscillate between passive and assertive roles in their relations with the boffin boys. The girls take part in sexist games which subordinate them but also they are clear sighted and critical and laugh at the boys' pretensions, such as "he had groin strain!" In public the girls assessed their behaviour at the party as being "slightly drunken" but more importantly, they had partially disobeyed powerful parental codes. In the fifth year area the girls spoke about the party, emphasizing their parents' disapproving reactions "Well, didn't anybody stop them", "Weren't there any parents there?", or "getting drunk at this age, terrible." The girls celebrated the success of their party and made fun of their parents. Collectively, through their depiction of parental disapproval the boffin girl group had broken their pro-school image to become 'rebel boffins'. This is in contrast to the way the girls adopted their parents' moral code in private to criticise one girl's behaviour.

Rose	I was only drunk for the last ...
Mary	Four hours.
Ellen	Ooooohhhh. You were drunk as soon as we got there, practically.
Rose	I was not, Ellen
Kerry	You were happy when I got there and I got there at quarter to eight.
Rose	I hadn't had anything to drink at quarter to eight , when you got there.
Mary	At about ten past eight you told me not to let you drink

	anymore.
Monica	Yeah. She said that, didn't she.
Rose	At quarter to eight when you got there.
Ellen	At half past eight, you were drunk.
Rose	At half past eight, I was not.
Monica	You were.
Mary	At about half past eight you were on the way , but you weren't ...
Rose	I had two drinks . After I'd told you not to let me drink anything. I didn't have anything else to drink, until after quarter to nine ...
SJB	Well, what about everyone getting ...
Rose	Drunk.
Mary	Yeah . That's alright , if they wanted to. Nobody acted really stupid.
SJB	How did you feel on Saturday (addressed to Rose: SJB)
Rose	I wasn't too bad. I mean my stomach felt really rotten, really sick, just sort of mentioning the word made me turn over. Towards the end (of the next day: SJB), four o'clock or five o'clock, I was alright. I was going to go out. But I just couldn't eat anything.
Mary	Such a martyr.
All girls	Laughter.

In private the girls are critical of how easily Rose let go of herself but in public this behaviour was celebrated. From my observation at the party, Rose was probably the most drunk of the girls, although there were at least five others who were almost equally drunk. By arguing that the only cause for group vulnerability was the behaviour of one girl, the boffin girls can celebrate their party and disperse their collective vulnerability. If the girls had admitted as a group to being drunk, this would have created more problems than they actually experienced or confronted. Crucially, the girls make a symbolic heroine of Rose by jokingly calling her a "martyr" in the cause of their celebration. In general, the girl group's public celebration of their party and private castigation of Rose's behaviour offer protection, group unity and strength, while also demonstrating that boffins deviate from conformist norms.

The new wave girls thought that the boffin girls' revelry and high spirits were superficial. They were not attempting to disparage the boffin girls' party but indicated they were particularly not interested. The new wave girls' party was on Friday night and

247

throughout the weekend the girls visited each other as usual. The following Monday morning at school there were no demonstrations of vitality in the fifth year area to match the boffin girls' sparkle and *joie de vivre*. What emerged more gradually was a sense of profound intrigue and curiosity among all groups of pupils in the fifth year. Rumours were abundant. "Did the girls sleep with their boyfriends?", "Was everyone naked?" or "Who was there?"

The central question which I heard from other pupils was "What went on?" During the days after the party I did not see or hear any boffin girl question a new wave girl about the party. I was asked about it by some boffin girls as they heard that I was present. My reply was vague, never specific. It is difficult to express the extent of rumour circulating as it became so considerable. The desire of some pupils to be shocked may itself play a part in eliciting more outrageous rumours, eg. "It was a sex orgy". Within the school pupil community (fifth and sixth year) the resonance produced by the new wave girls' parties affected pupils because of the myths to which they gave rise.

Both parties are clearly public spectacles but subject to different principles of control of physical intimacy. The boffin girls' party contained an official 'private space' referred to as "the kissing corners". However, couples using it were always noticed either on their way or through their absence. This was in every sense an official private space as it was sanctioned by the parents. In the case of the new wave girl party there were no private spaces. Indeed all practices were public and sheer numbers made any privacy difficult. Thus the fact that the space was public itself acted as a control to limit physical intimacy.

Conclusions

This chapter has attempted to show the different relationships to patriarchy within and between the boffin girl and the new wave girl groups. In school all girls experience sexism and sexual aggression. However, the form that this discrimination takes is not homogeneous but heterogeneous. Different boy groups employ varying modes of sexist aggression both inside and outside the classroom, from the mild body references of the square boffin boys, to the explicit pornographic comments of the 'criminal' and mod boys.

248

The boffin girls developed a series of strategies to overcome each level of sexual abuse; their strategies were most successful with the boffin boys. Claims by these boys that the girls had traded knowledge for "femininity" (Jones 1985) were ignored by the girls, who knew that their own chief goal, that of academic superiority, was unrivalled in the school. However, because the boys' displays exhibit an apparently more advanced level of sexual knowledge, the girls are drawn into the boys' sexual mythology of misinformation. The girls are forced to deal with the boys' insults using the same terms of reference introduced by the boys. In this way the boffin boys exercise some power over the boffin girls' understanding and expression of their own sexuality, and the girls are therefore less adept at parrying insults (Black and Coward 1981).

Education was understood by the boffin girls as a source of valuable qualifications, which would lead to economic independence, and a gratification of personal, as well as social needs. In terms of social class analysis such an outcome corresponds to previous research findings (Fuller 1980, Griffin 1985). But what is of interest here are the contradictions experienced and played out by the boffin girls in the process of achieving this end result. Such contradictions occur because the education of girls is given conflicting meaning under patriarchy; their understanding of the potential of education is at odds with the social imperative of marriage and family responsibilities which deems girls' education to be secondary and social rather than personal.

The new wave girls did not experience the same degree and variety of sexist discrimination as the boffin girls because the male pupilswere more reluctant to interact with them. Within the pupil community at Marshlands the new wave girls' sexual identity was powerfully controversial, owing firstly to rumours of unorthodox sexual/social behaviour arising during their parties, and also from their displays of 'lesbian' or homo-erotic behaviour. The parents of the new wave girls did not prohibit relationships with boyfriends. The new wave girls entered into heterosexual relationships with boys without necessarily desiring marriage and motherhood. This is possibly an effect of their shared experience of family break-up, and of their household responsibilities which may have given these girls a more critical understanding of marital relations, and dispelled notions of romantic love. It might also be suggested that the break up of the family which according to feminist analysis is the first site of woman's oppression, had a positive result for the new wave girls, by giving them a sense of independence and autonomy from the traditional domestic pattern (Barratt and McIntosh 1982). The new wave girls' group was strongly cohesive and developed its own autonomous cultural identity of female sexuality. The intensity of their relations can be illustrated by their close physical contact. The girls' reputation for lesbianism amongst boys in the fifth and sixth year gave them protection from heterosexual aggression and sexist harassment. In this sense the girls' ritual play undermined the boys' masculinity by posing a specific threat to patriarchal social relations. These young women demonstrated a clear ability to enjoy themselves and develop cultural practices in the absence of men.

11   Conclusion: positions and oppositions among youth

Throughout this study the analysis has been at two levels. On one hand I have been concerned with an interpretation of the specific group practices, meanings, rituals, relations and communication as they are lived by the groups. This we could call the local ethnography. On the other hand, within the same descriptions we have been concerned with wider references and understandings of culture, relations and structure. This we could call the 'general ethnography'.

In the introduction I discussed variations between competing definitions of subculture. The concept was considered inappropriate for purposes of analysis because it was inadequate to describe youth cultural groups in action. Similarly other organisational descriptions such as the differentiation and polarisation thesis uncritically rely on the terms 'gang' and 'subculture' which contain unexplained and ambiguous theoretical connotations (Sugarman 1967, Redhead 1990).

In order to account for the specific practices of, and relationships between, youth cultural groups it was necessary to create a new theoretical language. The models, interactional practices and structures which the fieldwork analysis revealed were found to be inapplicable to the boffin groups. This limitation of the theoretical description had two effects. The restriction of the theory to the youth cultural groups threw into greater contrast the relationships between youth cultural and boffin groups. Further, it became necessary to develop a theoretical description specific to the boffin groups. The theoretical description of the youth cultural forms explores and develops the possibilities of the sets of relations existing in the youth cultural field. The model I hypothesise could be applied to any group which is an exemplar of a youth cultural style. This is a matter for future research.

The modelling of the specialised positions provides an understanding of the complex rules and forms of communication, both within, and outside, the groups. It allows the possibility of charting the relations of conflict, challenge and celebration, and it also offers a perspective on the inner and outer worlds of exclusive groups. The specialised positions found within the youth cultural group worked to strengthen and elaborate their social and symbolic relations. The distinction between the social and symbolic forms made it possible to trace the lines of potential tension and cooperation and to note the distribution of responsibilities for the social and aesthetic features of the various groups.

It was found that the style leader and peer group spokesperson engaged in ritual celebration and exaggeration of the group's promenade, whilst the peer group consolidator and cultural ransacker are concerned more with maintaining the reality principle in the group, so that exaggeration does not threaten group unity. The four specialised positions have particular functions to perform. The duties are not always in play but remain possibilities when the moment is relevant.

The social relations of the face describes the different types of interaction within and between groups. The concept of the social relations of the face provides a more explicit, detailed and less metaphorical understanding of youth groups in private and public practice. This reading of the groups' actions enables us to grasp the variation and significance of ritual practices. At the micro level the data indicated that there is often movement from the private to the public face, when an audience becomes available for the promenade. This transformation of faces can be identified by the different forms of exchange between the specialised positions.

The analysis of the specialised semiotic revealed the internal practices of the youth cultural group, the rules which create and relay a style with coherence, order, meaning and possibilities. The semiotic is an expression of agency, where the cultural style of communications is a creative practice of the group. The ethnographic data allowed the following conceptual distinctions: *choreography* which refers to dress and appearance, techniques of the body including posture, gesture and facets of mobility;

narrative, which includes music, literature, drugs and argot; *circulation* which refers to social sites and territorial movement.

Analytically it was useful to employ an integrating concept at a higher level of abstraction than the concepts which form the description of the groups in order to grasp the coherence of youth style. The concept of "signature" integrates specialised positions, social relations of the face, and the specialised semiotic and points to the unity, recognition and legitimacy of the youth cultural forms. The book questions the validity of present theories and concepts of youth culture. The research provides the basis for a new theory of youth cultural forms, these concepts bring coherence and understanding to the wide ranging data, which integrates structural, communicative and semiotic practices. This theory goes beyond the purely abstract literary or cultural forms of analysis to provide an alternative social understanding of young peoples' actions (McRobbie 1994).

The book has explored social relationships within and between four pupil groups all of whom are regarded by the school as belonging to the academic elite. A significant finding was that the data made it possible to distinguish a series of complex status positions within each of the groups, including the demonstration of academic abilities, displays of youth cultural style, use of feminism, belief in choice and individualism, promotion of sexual confidence and use of aggressive violence. In each group any one status position may be dominant depending upon the context of interaction. There was more homogeneity in the boffins' status and this made it easier to identify social class relations in action, whereas there was a greater variety in the status positions available to the youth cultural groups, which made social class analysis more complex. However, a major finding of the study was that the distinguishing marker of all the groups studied, irrespective of their differences, was the common celebration of their pedagogic status and the privileges to which this status gave access. The evidence strongly suggests that status rather than class can be perhaps the more crucial agent in the generation of different forms of behaviour that might be described as showing degrees of resistance and conformity.

Both boffin groups had an approach to schooling based upon a regulative framework of action, operating in a Weberian sense in terms of an instrumental means end chain. Location in the upper ability band conferred status and the classroom was a site to display competence and confidence: the boffins made a large investment in the opportunities provided by school. Intellectual achievement was displayed and facilitated by what I called their "seminar form" of communication and interaction. This display was termed a "pedagogic promenade". The only significant social class difference between the two boffin groups was that, whilst both groups used the seminar form as a site for displays of pedagogic competence, only the boys' group used it for rehearsal, development and monitoring of conduct appropriate to their social class aspirations. Promotion of a middle class pro-school image ensured that other pupils unquestioningly saw the boffins as fully supportive of the school order: however, they were far from completely conformist. Sometimes the boffins explicitly challenged local principles of control through a limited disrespect of teachers. These actions can be understood as acts of "contestation". However, their school deviance was always significantly limited by their instrumental acceptance of the school. A significant social difference between the boffin groups was that the boys were more expressive in their actions and this has its origins in the competitive masculine promenades of male groups. A recurring issue was the difficulty in balancing their status as the school's top male pupils with the accusation that devotion to homework and consequent lack of sexual experience undermined their masculinity (Mac an Ghaill 1994).

A difficulty in assessing the mod boys' social class position arose out of their violent masculinity. The mods' promenade of male solidarity was more significantly related to territorial responses as a youth cultural style than an expression of social class resistance. Their 'tough behaviour' did not in any sense become an anti-intellectualism: the mod boys pursued fighting and gaining qualifications with equal rigour. In school it was their potential for violence rather than the reality which formed the basis of their authority: this represents an apparent contradictory dualism unremarked in the literature. The only real challenge to the mod boys' patriarchal power came from the new wave girls. Most importantly, the girls showed that they could see through the mod boys' public face rituals of exaggeration. As a promenading youth cultural group, the new wave girls were able to read the subtext of the boys' public face behaviour. They were the only group of pupils who successfully opposed and countered the ritualistic patriarchal behaviour of the mods.

A major finding of the study is that the play of gender relations was crucial for almost every type of interaction, both within and between groups. A fundamental tension existed between the two boffin groups over their sexual vulnerabilities. The pursuit of excellence in school work is played out against the backdrop of love aspirations. Educational ambitions dominate the boffins' life, including much of their leisure time, creating an opposition between pleasure and pedagogy. Here, we can see at work the classic sociological opposition between deferred gratification and hedonism, and this accounts for the relation within and between the boffin groups.

In contrast, the new wave girls can be understood as becoming feminist. Their capacity to exploit and use different forms of sexual expression derived from their celebration of their sexuality as 'natural'. Female bodily experience became the communal responsibility of the group. This behaviour was presented as part of their rituals of integrity: close and intense group relations created a powerful social base for opposing and challenging the patriarchal stance of both the school hierarchy and male pupils. Sexuality is an area where male control over women is strongest and is exercised at the level of language: in naming, defining and denying speech to women/girls. The new wave girls' discourse is about the right to speak and to define, and about identifying and challenging male control of language. They identify the power differential in language, between female and male use of meaning. The new wave girls, through their spoken interactions and written communications, reverse the symbolic order of language; they demonstrate the denial of speech and then set about reclaiming the right to speak, define and know.

In conclusion, this book on youth cultures demonstrates the sociological importance of ethnographic research techniques, for the construction and articulation of micro concepts and macro understandings. The fieldwork methodology created the opportunity for the generation of new theoretical descriptions which document achievement and dissent inside and outside a secondary school by female and male pupils who are academically successful. This analysis has a range of implications for the development and implementation of social and educational policies which affect young people because of the way in which it shows their experience both of structural relations of the school and the pressures which affect their learning. It is this aspect of ethnography which would appear as its key strength in its ability to allow the subjects of research to voice their own experience within the context of their own cultural setting and meanings.

255

Bibliography

Aggleton, P. (1987) *Rebels Without a Cause*, Falmer, Lewes.

Aggleton, P. and Whitty, G. (1985) 'Rebels Without a Cause? Socialisation and Subcultural Style Amongst the Children of the New Middle Classes', *Sociology of Education*, Vol.58, No.1, pp.60-72.

Allen, H. (1982) 'Political Lesbianism and Feminism - Space for a Sexual Politics?', *M/F*, No.7, pp. 15-34.

Amos, V. and Parmer, P. (1981) 'Resistances and Responses: the Experience of Black Girls in Britain', in McRobbie, A. and McCabe, T. (eds.) *Feminism for Girls: An Adventure Story*, Routledge and Kegan Paul, London pp.96-108.

Anyon, J. (1983) 'Intersections of Gender and Class: Accommodation and Resistance by Working Class Girls to Contradictory Sex-role Ideologies' in Walker, S. and Barton, L. (eds.) *Gender, Class and Education*, Falmer Press, Lewes pp.19-37.

Ardener, S. (1978) (ed.) *Defining Females*, Croom Helm, London.

Askew, S. and Ross, C. (1988) *Boys Don't Cry: Boys and Sexism in Education*, Open University Press, Milton Keynes.

Back, L. (1995) *New Ethnicities Multiple Racisms: race and nation in the lives of young people*, UCL Press, London.

Ball, S. J. (1981) *Beachside Comprehensive*, Cambridge University Press, Cambridge.

Barnes, R. (1979) *Mods*, Eel Pie, London.

Barratt, M. (1980) *Women's Oppression Today: Problems in Marxist*

Feminist Analysis , Verso Editions and New Left Review, London.

Barratt, M. and McIntosh, M. (1982) *The Anti-Social Family* , Verso, London.

Barthes, R. (1977) *Image-Music-Text*, Fontana/Collins, Glasgow.

Becker, H. S. (1951) 'The Professional Dance Musician and his Audience ', *American Journal of Sociology*, LVII, pp.136-144.

Benjamin, W. (1970) *Illuminations*, Jonathan Cape, London.

Bernstein, B. (1959) ' A Public Language : Some Sociological Implications of a Linguistic Form', *British Journal of Sociology*, X, pp.311-326.

Bernstein, B. (1990) *The Structuring of Pedagogic Discourse* , Routledge, London.

Birdwhistle, R. L. (1970)*Kinesis and Context: Essays in Body-`motion Communication*, Penguin Press, London.

Black, M. and Coward , R. (1981) ' Linguistic , Social and Sexual Relations', *Screen Education*, 39, pp.69-85.

Blackman, S. J. (1983) 'Fear and Loathing on the Isle of Wight Run', *Undecided's Scooter Club Magazine*, Issue 3, Autumn, pp.1-10.

Blackman, S. J. (1987) ' The Labour Market in School : New Vocationalism and Socially Ascribed Discrimination', in Brown, P. and Ashton, D. (eds.) *Education Unemployment and Labour Markets*, Falmer Press, Lewes, pp.27-56.

Blackman, S. J. (1992) 'Pro-School Pupils', *Journal of Youth and Policy*, No. 38, pp. 1-9.

Bostock, Y. and Leathar, D.S. (1982) 'The Role of the Mass Media Advertising Campaigns in Influencing Attitudes Toward Contraception Among 16-20 Year Olds' , *British Journal of Family Planning*, 8, pp.59-63.

Boston, V. (1978) *Punk Rock*, Penguin, London.

Bourdieu, P. (1984) *Distinction*, Routledge and Kegan Paul, London.

Bourdieu, P. and Passeron, J. C. (1977) *Reproduction in Education, Society and Culture*, Sage, London.

Bowlby, J. (1946) *Forty Four Juvenile Thieves* , Tindall and Cox, London.

Bowlby, J. (1953) *Childcare and the Growth of Love*, Penguin, London.

Brake, M. (1980) *The Sociology of Youth Culture and Youth Sub-culture*, Routledge and Kegan Paul, London.

Brown, P. (1987) *Schooling Ordinary Kids*, Tavistock, London.

Brown, P. and Ashton, D. (eds.) (1987) *Education, Unemployment and Labour Markets*, Falmer Press, Lewes.

Bulmer, M. (1984) *The Chicago School of Sociology*, University of Chicago Press, Chicago and London.

Burgess, R. G. (1983) *Experiencing Comprehensive Education : A Study of Bishop McGregor School*, Methuen, London.

Campbell, A. (1984) *The Girls in the Gang*, Basil Blackwell, Oxford.

Chambers, I. (1981) 'Pop Music : A Teaching Perspective', *Screen Education*, 39, Summer, pp.35-46.

Chambers, I. (1985) *Urban Rhythm*, Macmillan, London.

Cixous, H. and Clement, C. (1991) 'The Newly Born Woman', in Eagleton, M. (ed) *Feminist Litrary Criticism*, Longman, London.

Clarke, G. (1982) 'Defending Ski-Jumpers: A Critique of Theories of Youth Subcultures', Stencilled Paper, Centre for Contemporary Cultural Studies, University of Birmingham.

Clarke, J., Hall, S., Jefferson, T., Roberts, B. (1975) ' Subcultures, Cultures and Class: a Theoretical Overview', in Hall, S. and Jefferson, T. (eds.) *Resistance Through Ritual*, Working Papers in Cultural Studies, No.7/8, University of Birmingham, Centre for Contemporary Cultural Studies, pp.9-74.

Coffield, F. and Gofton, L. (1994) *Drugs and Young People*, Institute for Public Policy Research, London.

Coggans, N. and Mckellars, S. (1994) 'Drug use amongst peers: peer pressure or peer preference', *Drugs: education, prevention and policy*, Vol. 1, No.1. pp.15-26.

Cohen, A. K. (1955) *Delinquent Boys - The Subculture of the Gang*, Collier-Macmillan, London.

Cohen, P. (1972) 'Subcultural Conflict and Working Class Community', in *Working Papers in Cultural Studies 2*, Centre for Contemporary Cultural Studies, University of Birmingham, Spring, pp. 5-51.

Cohen, S. (1980) *Moral Panics a nd Folk Devils*, Martin Robertson, Oxford.

Corrigan, P. (1973) 'Secondary School and Juvenile Delinquency'. Unpublished Ph.D. thesis, University of Durham.

Daly, M. (1978) *Gyn-Ecology: The Metaethics of Radical Feminism*, Beacon Press, Boston.

Daniel, S. and McGuire, P. (ed.) (1972) *The Paint House*, Penguin, London.

Davies, L. (1984) *Pupil Power: Deviance and Gender in School* , Falmer Press, Lewes.

Delamont, S. (1973) 'Academic Conformity Observed'. Unpublished Ph.D. thesis, University of Edinburgh.

Delamont, S. (1983) 'The Conservative School? Sex Roles at Home, at Work and at School' in Walker, S. and Barton, L. (eds.) *Gender, Class and Education*, Falmer Press, Lewes. pp.93-105.

Dollard , J., Miller, N., Doob, L., Mowrer, D., Sears, R. (1939) *Frustration and Aggression*, Yale University, New Haven.

Douglas, M. (1968) 'The Social Control of Cognition: Some Factors in Joke Perception', *MAN*, N.S. 33, pp.361-376.

Douglas, M. (1970) *Natural Symbols*, The Crescent Press, Barrie and Rodcliff.

Dove, R. (1983) 'Sex Roles in Conversation'. Unpublished Paper, Birkbeck College, University of London.

Downes, D. (1966) *The Delinquent Solution*, Routledge and Kegan Paul, London.

Downes, D. and Rock, P. (1982) *Understanding Deviance*, Clarendon Press, Oxford.

Dunphy, D.C. (1963) 'The Social Structure of Urban Adolescent Peer Groups', *Sociometry*, 26, pp. 230-246.

Evans-Pritchard, E. E. (1973) 'Some Reminiscenses and Reflections on Fieldwork', *Journal of the Anthropological Society of Oxford*, Vol. IV, No.1, pp. 1-12.

Farrall, C. (1978) *My Mother Said .... the Way Young People Learn About Sex and Birth Control*, Routledge and Kegan Paul, London.

Farrant, M. R. (1965) 'The Nature and Structure of Groups in an Adolescent Society'. Unpublished M.A. thesis, Exeter University.

Filmer, P. (1977) ' Literary Study as Liberal Education and as Sociology in the Work of F.R. Leavis', in Jenks, C. (ed.) *Rationality, Education and the Social Organisation of Knowledge*, Routledge and Kegan Paul, London, pp. 55-85.

Fountain, N. (1987) *Underground: London Alternative Press* , Comedia, London.

Freud, S. (1916) *Wit and its Relation to the Unconscious*, Fisher and Unwin, London.

Friedlander, K. (1947) *The Psycho-analytical Approach to Juvenile Delinquency*, Routledge and Kegan Paul, London.

Frith, S. (1981) 'The Magic That Can Set You Free: The Ideology of Folk and the Myth of the Rock Community', in Middleton, R. and Horn, D. (eds.) *Popular Music 1*, Cambridge University Press, Cambridge, pp.159-168.

Frith, S. (1983) *Sound Effects: Youth, Leisure and the Politics of Rock'n'Roll*, Constable, London.

Frith, S. (1988) *The Pleasure of Music*, Polity Press, Oxford.

Frith, S. and Horne, H. (1987) *Art Into Pop*, Methuen, London.

Fuller, M. (1980) 'Black Girls in a London Comprehensive School', in Deem, R. (ed.) *Schooling for Women's Work*, Routledge and Kegan Paul, London, pp. 52-65.

Geertz, C. (1973) *The Interpretation of Culture*, Basic Books, New York.

Gilroy, P. (1993) *The Black Atlantic*, Verso, London.

Gilroy, P. (1987) *There Ain't No Black in the Union Jack*, Hutchinson, London.

Giroux, H. A. (1983) *Theory and Resistance in Education*, Heinemann Educational Books, London.

Giroux, H. A. (1992) *Border Crossings*, Routledge, London .

Glaser, B. G. amd Strauss, A. L. (1967) *The Discovery of Grounded Theory*, Weidenfeld and Nicolson, London.

Gleeson, D. (1989) *The Paradox of Training*, Open University Press, Milton Keynes.

Goldthrope, J. H., Lockwood, D., Bechofer, F. and Platt, J. (1968) *The Affluent Worker: Political Attitudes and Behaviour*, Cambridge University Press, Cambridge.

Gramsci, A. (1971) *Selections From the Prison Notebooks*, Lawrence and Wishart, London.

Griffin, C. (1985) *Typical Girls?*, Routledge and Kegan Paul, London.

Griffin, C. (1993) *Representations of Youth*, Polity, Oxford.

Grossberg, L. (1986) 'Is there rock after punk?', *Critical Studies in Mass communication*, Vol.3, No. 1. pp. 50-74.

Hall, E. (1959) *Silent Language*, Doubleday, New York.

Hall, S. and Jefferson, T. (eds.) (1975) *Resistance Through Ritual, Working Papers in Cultural Studies, 7/8*, Centre for Contemporary Studies, University of Birmingham.

Hammersley, M. (1985) 'From ethnography to theory; a programme and a paradigm in the sociology of education', in *Sociology*, 19, No. 2, pp. 244-259.

Hammersley, M. (1992) *What's Wrong with Ethnography*, Routledge, London.

Hammersley, M. and Turner, G. (1980) 'Conformist Pupils', in Woods, P. (ed.) *Pupil Strategies*, Croom Helm, London, pp.29-49.

Hammersley, M. and Atkinson, P. (1983) *Ethnography: Principles in Practice*, Tavistock, London.

Hargreaves, D. H. (1967) *Social Relations in a Secondary School*, Routledge and Kegan Paul, London.

Hastrup, K. (1978) 'The Semantics of Biology: Virginity', in Ardener, S. (ed.) *Defining Females*, Croom Helm, London, pp.49-65.

Hebdige, D. (1979) *Subculture: the Meaning of Style*, Methuen, London.

Hebdige, D. (1981) 'Object as Image: The Italian Scooter Cycle', *Block* (5), pp.44-64.

Hebdige, D. (1982) 'Hiding in the Light', *TEN*, 8,pp. 5-19.

Hebdige, D. (1988) *Hiding in the Light*. London, Routledge.

Henderson, S. (1992) 'Luvdup and DeElited', paper given at South Bank Polytechnic.

Hersham, P. (1977) 'Virgin and Mother' in Lewis, I. (ed.) *Symbols and Sentiments: Cross Cultural Studies in Symbolism*, Academic Press, London, pp. 269-292.

Hewitt, R. (1986a) *Structure, Meaning and Ritual in the Narratives of the Southern San*, Helmut Buske Verlag, Hamberg.

Hewitt, R. (1986b) *White Talk Black Talk*, Cambridge University Press, Cambridge.

Hirschon, R. (1978) 'Open Body / Closed Space: The Transformation of Female Sexuality', in Ardener, S. (ed.) *Defining Females*. London, Croom Helm, pp.66-88.

Holland, J. (1985) 'Gender and Class: Adolescent Conceptions of the Division of Labour'. Unpublished Ph.D. thesis, Institute of Education, University of London.

Holland, J. , Ramazanoglu, C. and Sharpe, S. (1993) 'Wimp or Gladitor?: contradictions in acquring masculine sexuality', *WRAP paper*, No. 9, Tufnell Press.

Holly, L. (ed.) (1989) *Girls and Sexuality*, Open Univerisity Press, Milton Keynes.

Hudson, B. (1984) 'Femininity and Adolescence', in McRobbie, A. and Nava, M. (eds.) *Gender and Generation*, Macmillan, London, pp.31-53.

Jackson, S. (1978a) 'On the Social Construction of Female Sexuality', *Explorations in Feminism*, No.4, Women's Research and Resources Centre, London.

Jackson, S. (1978b) 'How to Make Babies: Sexism in Sex Education', *Women's Studies International Quarterly*, Vol.1, pp.341-352.

Jackson, B. and Marsden, D. (1962) *Education and the Working Class*, Routledge and Kegan Paul, London.

Jones, C. (1985) 'Sexual Tyranny: Male Violence in a Mixed Secondary School', in Weiner, G. (ed.) *Just a Bunch of Girls*, Open University Press, Milton Keynes, pp.26-39.

Jones, S. (1988) *Black Culture, White Youth*, Macmillan, London.

Knight, N. (1982) *Skinhead*, Omnibus Press, London.

Kochman, T. (ed.) (1972) *Rappin' and Stylin' out: Communication*

261

in Urban Black America, University of Illinois Press, Urbana.

Kochman, T. (1983) 'The Boundary Between Play and Non-Play in Black Verbal Duelling', *Language on Society*, 12, 3, pp.329-37.

Krige, E. J. (1968) 'Girls Puberty Songs and Their Relation to Fertility, Health, Morals and Religion Among the Zulu', *Africa*, Vol.38, pp.173-98.

Lacey, C. (1970) *Hightown Grammar* , Manchester University Press, Manchester.

Laing, D. (1985) *One Chord Wonders: Power and Meaning in Punk Rock*, Open University Press, Milton Keynes.

Lambart, A. (1970) 'The Sociology of an Unstreamed Urban Grammar School for Girls'. Unpublished Ph.D. thesis, University of Manchester.

Lambart, A. (1976) 'The Sisterhood', in Hammersley, M. and Woods, P. (eds.) *The Process of Schooling*, Routledge and Kegan Paul in association with the Open University Press, London, pp.152-159.

Labov, T. (1982) 'Social Structure and Peer Terminology in a Black Adolescent Gang', *Language and Society*, 11, pp.391-411.

Labov, W. (1972) Language in the Inner City, Pennsylvania University Press, Philadephia.

Lees, S. (1986) *Losing Out*, Hutchinson, London.

Lees, S. (1993) *Sugar and Spice*, Penquin, London .

Leonard, D. (1980) *Sex and Generation: A Study of Courtship and Weddings*, Tavistock, London.

Lewis, R. (1973) 'Parents and Peers : Socialisation Agents in the Coital Behaviour of Young Adults', *Journal of Sex Research*, Vol.9, No.2, pp.156-170.

Lipsitz, G. (1994) ' We know what time it is: race, class and youth culture in the nineties', in Ross, A. and Rose, T. (eds.) *Microphone Fiends: youth music and youth culture*, Routledge, London, pp. 17-28.

Llewellyn, M. (1980) ' Studying Girls at School: The Implications of Confusion', in Deem, R. (ed.) *Schooling for Women's Work*, Routledge and Kegan Paul, London, pp. 42-51.

Mac an Ghaill, M. (1988) *Young Gifted and Black*, Open University Press, Milton Keynes.

Mac an Ghaill, M. (1994) *The Making of Men : masculinities , sexualities and schooling*, Open University Press, Milton Keynes.

Macdonald, M. (1980) 'Socio-cultural Reproduction and Women's Education', in Deem, R. (ed.) *Schooling for Women's Work*, Routledge and Kegan Paul, London, pp.13-25.

Mahoney, P. (1985) *School for the Boys*, Hutchinson in association with Explorations in Feminism Collective, London.

Mannheim, H. (1965) *Comparative Criminology, Volumes 1 and 2*, Routledge and Kegan Paul, London.

Margrain, S. (1983) 'Why Must Girls Wear Skirts', *Education*, 5, August, pp.105-106.

Mauss, M. (1936) 'Les Techniques de Corps', *Journal de la Psychologie*, Vol.32, pp. 271-293.

Mays, J.B. (1954) *Growing Up in the City*, Liverpool University Press, Liverpool.

McIntosh, M. (1978) 'Who Needs Prostitutes? The Ideology of Male Sexual Needs', in Smart, C. and Smart, B. (eds.) *Women, Sexuality and Social Control*, Routledge and Kegan Paul, London pp.53-64.

McLaren, P. (1982) 'Being Tough : Rituals of Resistance in the Culture of Working Class School Girls' *Candian Women Studies*, Vol.4, Part 1, pp.20-24.

McLaren, P. (1986) *Schooling as a Ritual Performance*, Routledge and Kegan Paul, London.

McRobbie, A. (1980) 'Setting Accounts with Subcultures: A Feminist Critique', *Screen Education*, Spring, No.34, pp.37-49.

McRobbie, A. (1984) 'Dance and Social Fantasy', in McRobbie, A. and Nava, M. (eds.) *Gender and Generation*, Macmillan, London, pp.130-161.

McRobbie, A. (1994) *Postmodernism and Popular Culture* , Routledge, London.

McRobbie, A. and Garber, J. (1975) ' Girls and Subculture ' in *Working Papers in Cultural Studies, 7/8*, Centre for Contemporary Studies, University of Birmingham, pp.208-222.

McRobbie, A. and Nava, M. (eds.) (1984) *Gender and Generation*, Macmillan, London.

Measor, L. (1984) 'Gender and the Sciences: Pupils' Gender-based Conceptions of School Subjects', in Broadfoot, P. (ed.) *Selection, Certification and Control*, Falmer Press, Lewes, pp.171-191.

Melly, G. (1972) *Revolt into Style*, Penguin, London.

Merchant, J. and MacDonald, R. (1994) 'Youth and the Rave Culture, Ecstasy and Health', *Youth and Policy*, No 45. pp.16-39.

Merton, R. K. (1938) 'Social Structure and Anomie' , *American Sociological Review*, 3, October, pp.672-682.

Merton, R. K. (1957) *Social Theory and Social Structure*, John Wiley, New York.

Meyenn, R. J. (1980) 'School Girls' Peer Groups', in Woods, P. (ed.) *Pupil Strategies*, Croom Helm, London, pp.108-142.

Middleton, R. (1990) *Understanding Popular Music*, Open University Press, Milton Keynes.

Milne, K. (1988) 'The New Conformism', *Observer*, 15th May.

Mintel, (1988) *Youth Lifestyles*, KAE House, London.

Moore, A. (1993) *Rock: the primary text*, Open University Press, Milton Keynes.

Mungham, G. (1976) 'Youth in Pursuit of Itself', in Mungham, G. and Pearson, G. (eds.) *Working Class Youth Culture*, Routledge and Kegan Paul, London, pp.82-104.

Murdock, G, and Phelps, G. (1972) 'Youth Culture and the School Revisited', *British Journal of Sociology*, Vol.23, No.2, pp.478-482.

Nava, M. (1982) 'Everybody's Views Were Just Broadened: A Girls' Project and Some Responses to Lesbianism', *Feminist Review*, No.10, pp. 37-59.

Negus, K. (1992) *Producing Pop: culture and conflict in the popular music industry*, Edward Arnold, London.

Oakley, A. (1972) *Sex, Gender and Society*, Temple-Smith, London.

Parker, H. (1974) *View From the Boys*, Davis and Charles, London.

Patrick, J. (1973) *A Glasgow Gang Observed*, Eyre Methuen, London.

Perkins, T. E. (1979) 'Rethinking Stereotypes', in Barrett, M., Corrigan, P., Kuhn, A., and Wolf, J. (eds) *Ideology and Cultural Production*, Croom Helm Ltd, London, pp. 135-159.

Plant, M. and Plant, M. (1992) *Risk-takers: alcohol, drugs, sex and youth*, Routledge, London.

Polhemus, T. (1994) *Streetstyle*, Thames and Hudson, London.

Polhemus, T. and Procter, L. (1984) *Pop-Styles*, Vermillon, London.

Poxon, G. (1976) 'Skinheads and the Shop Floor', *A Youth Question Publication*, No.2, September.

Prendercast, S. (1989) 'Girls' Experience of Menstruation in School' in Holly, L. (ed.) *Girls and Sexuality*, Open University Press, Milton Keynes, pp.85-108.

Prett, R. (1984) 'Notes on music', Private communication.

Ramazanoglu, C. (1989) *Feminism and the Contradictions of Oppression*, Routledge, London.

Redhead, S. (1990) *The End of the Century Party: youth and pop towards 2000*, University of Manchester Press, Manchester.

Redhead, S. (1993) *Rave Off: politics and deviance in contemporary youth culture*, Avebury Press, Aldershot.

Rees, H. (1986) *14:24 British Youth Culture*. The Coram Foundation, The Highland Press, London.

Reid, J. (1987) *Up They Rise*, Faber and Faber, London.

Rimmer, D. (1985) *Like Punk Never Happened*, Faber and Faber,

London.

Robbins, D. and Cohen, P. (1978) *Knuckle Sandwich*, Penguin, London.

Rocheron, Y. and Whyld, J. (1983) 'Sex Education' in Whyld, J. (ed.) *Sexism in the Secondary Curriculum*, Harper and Row, London, pp.261-268.

Ross, A. and Rose, T. (Eds) (1994) *Microphone Fiends: youth music and youth culture*, Routledge, London.

Savage, J. (1991) *England's Dreaming*, Faber and Faber, London.

Scales, P. and Kirby, D. (1983) 'Perceived Barriers to Sex Education: A Survey of Professionals', *Journal of Sex Research*, Vol.19, No.4, pp.309-326.

Schofield, M. (1968) *The Sexual Behaviour of Young People*, Penguin Books, London.

Shacklady, L. (1978) 'Sexist Assumptions and Female Delinquency', in Smart, C. and Smart, B. (eds.) *Women, Sexuality and Social Control*, Routledge and Kegan Paul, London, pp.74-88.

Sharpe, S. (1976) *Just Like a Girl: How Girls Learn to Be Women*, Penguin, London.

Shaw, C. and McKay, H. (1927) *Juvenile Delinquency and Urban Areas*, University of Chicago Press, Chicago.

Shepherd, J., Virden, P., Vulliamy, G. and Wishart, T. (1977) *Whose Music? A Sociology of Musical Languages*, Transaction Books, New Brunswick and London.

Shiach, M. (1991) *Helene Cixous: a politics of writing*, Routledge, London.

Shilling, C. (1993) *Social Theory and the Body*, Sage, London.

Spencer, B. (1984) 'Young Men: Their Attitudes Towards Sexuality and Birth Control', *British Journal of Family Planning*, 10, pp. 13-19.

Spender, D. and Sarah, E. (eds.) (1980) *Learning to Lose: Sexism and Education*, The Women's Press, London.

Stanworth, M. (1981) 'Gender and Schooling: A Study of Sexual Divisions in the Classroom', *Explorations in Feminism*, No.7, WRRC, London.

Street, J. (1986) *Rebel Rock: The Politics of Popular Music*, Basil Blackwell, Oxford.

Stuart, S. (1987) *Rockers!*, Plexis, London.

Sugarman, B. (1967) 'Involvement in Youth Culture, Academic Achievement and Conformity in School', *British Journal of Sociology*, June, pp.151-164.

Swanwick, K. (1984) 'Problems of a Sociological Approach to Pop

Music in Schools', *British Journal of Sociology of Education*, Vol.5, No.3, pp.303-307.

Tagg, P. (1982) 'Analysing Popular Music : Theory, Method and Practice', in Middleton, R. and Horn, D. (eds.) *Popular Music*, Cambridge University Press, Cambridge, pp.37-67.

Taylor, I. Walton, P. and Young, J. (1973) *The New Criminology*, Routledge and Kegan Paul, London.

Taylor, L. (1968) *Deviance and Society*, Michael Joseph, London.

Thomas, H. (1993) (ed.) *Dance, Gender and Culture*, Macmillan, London.

Thompson, E. P. (1972) 'Rough Music : Le Charivari Anglais', *Annals*, Vol.22, No.2, pp. 285-312.

Thompson, H. S. (1966) *Hell's Angels*, Random House, California.

Thomson, R. and Scott, S. (1991) 'Learning about sex', *WRAP Paper*, No. 4, Tufnell Press.

Thrasher, F. (1927) *The Gang*, University of Chicago Press, Chicago.

Toop, D. (1984) *The Rap Attack*, Pluto Press, London.

Turner, G. (1983) *The Social World of the Comprehensive School*, Croom Helm, London.

Turner, V. (1967) *The Forest of Symbols: Aspects of Ndembu Ritual*, Cornell University Press, New York.

Vulliamy, G. (1977) 'Music and the Mass Culture Debate', in Shepherd, J., Virden, P., Vulliamy, G. and Wishart, T. *Whose Music? A Sociology of Musical Languages*, Transaction Books, New Brunswick and London, pp.179-206.

Walker, I. (1984) 'The Rockers Reunion', *New Society*, 23 August, pp. 165-167.

Walkerdine, V. (1984) 'Some Day My Prince Will Come', in McRobbie, A. and Nava, M. (eds.) *Gender and Generation*, Macmillan, London, pp.162-184.

Warren, C. (1988) *Gender Issues in Field Research*, Sage University Paper, Qualitative Research Methods Series, No.9, London.

Weiner, G. (ed.) (1985) *Just a Bunch of Girls*, Open University Press, Milton Keynes.

Who, The (1973) *Quadrophenia*, Polydor Records, London.

Whyld, J. (1983) (ed.) *Sexism in the Secondary Curriculum*, Harper and Row, London.

Whyte, W. (1943/55) *Street Corner Society*, University of Chicago Press, Chicago.

Wicke, P. (1982) 'Rock Music: A Musical Aesthetic Study', in Middleton, R. and Horn, D. (eds.) *Popular Music 2*, Cambridge University Press, Cambridge, pp.219-243.

Widgery, D. (1986) *Beating Time*, Chatto, London.

Willis, P. (1972) 'Pop Music and Youth Groups'. Unpublished Ph.D. thesis, Centre for Contemporary Cultural Studies, University of Birmingham.

Willis, P. (1977) *Learning to Labour*, Gower, Farnborough.

Willis, P. (1978) *Profane Culture*, Routledge and Kegan Paul, London.

Willis, P. (1982) ' Male School Counterculture'. V203 *Popular Culture*, Block 7, Unit 30, Open University Press, Milton Keynes, pp.75-103.

Willis, P. (1990) *Common Culture*, Open University Press, Milton Keynes.

Willmott, P. (1985) 'The Institute of Community Studies ' in Bulmer, M. (ed.) *Essays on the History of British Sociological Research*, Cambridge University Press, Cambridge, pp. 137-150.

Wolpe, A. (1988) *Within School Walls*, Routledge and Kegan Paul, London.

Wood, J. (1984) ' Groping Towards Sexism: Boys' Sex Talk', in McRobbie, A. and Nava, M. (eds.) *Gender and Generation*. London, Macmillan, pp.54-84.

Woods, P. (1979) The Divided School, Routledge and Kegan Paul, London.

Yalman, N. (1963) 'On the Purity of Women in the Castes of Ceylon and Malabar', *Journal of the Royal Anthropological Institute*, Vol.93, pp.25-58.

Index